THE LOST PRINCE

a screenplay

Stephen Poliakoff, born in 1952, was appointed writer in residence at the National Theatre for 1976 and the same year won the *Evening Standard*'s Most Promising Playwright award for *Hitting Town* and *City Sugar*. He has also won a BAFTA award for the Best Single Play for *Caught on a Train* in 1980, the *Evening Standard*'s Best British Film award for *Close My Eyes* in 1992, The Critics' Circle Best Play Award for *Blinded by the Sun* in 1996 and the Prix Italia and the Royal Television Society Best Drama award for *Shooting the Past* in 1999. His plays and films include *Clever Soldiers* (1974), *The Carnation Gang* (1974), *Hitting Town* (1975), *City Sugar* (1975), *Heroes* (1975), *Strawberry Fields* (1977), *Stronger than the Sun* (1977), *Shout Across the River* (1978), *American Days* (1979), *The Summer Party* (1980), *Bloody Kids* (1980), *Caught on a Train* (1980), *Favourite Nights* (1981), *Soft Targets* (1982), *Runners* (1983), *Breaking the Silence* (1984), *Coming in to Land* (1987), *Hidden City* (1988), *She's Been Away* (1989), *Playing with Trains* (1989), *Close My Eyes* (1991), *Sienna Red* (1992), *Century* (1994), *Sweet Panic* (1996), *Blinded by the Sun* (1996), *The Tribe* (1997), *Food of Love* (1998), *Talk of the City* (1998), *Remember This* (1999), *Shooting the Past* (1999) and *Perfect Strangers* (2001) for which he won the Dennis Potter Award at the 2002 BAFTAs and Best Writer and Best Drama at the Royal Television Society Awards.

by the same author

STEPHEN POLIAKOFF PLAYS: ONE
Clever Soldiers; Hitting Town; City Sugar; Shout Across the
River; American Days; Strawberry Fields

STEPHEN POLIAKOFF PLAYS: TWO
Breaking the Silence; Playing with Trains; She's Been Away;
Century

STEPHEN POLIAKOFF PLAYS: THREE
Caught on a Train; Coming in to Land; Close My Eyes

Perfect Strangers (screenplay)

Remember This

Shooting the Past (screenplay)

Sienna Red

Sweet Panic/Blinded by the Sun

Talk of the City

THE LOST PRINCE

Stephen Poliakoff

Introduced by the author

Methuen

Published by Methuen 2003

3 5 7 9 10 8 6 4 2

First published in Great Britain in 2003 by
Methuen Publishing Ltd
215 Vauxhall Bridge Road,
London SW1V 1EJ

Photographs cover and inside: Gary Moyes,
Laurie Sparhan and Sarah Ainslie

Methuen Publishing Limited Reg. No. 3543167

A CIP catalogue record for this book is available from the British Library

ISBN 0 413 77307 8

Typeset by SX Composing DTP, Rayleigh, Essex
Printed and bound in Great Britain by
Cox and Wyman Ltd, Reading, Berkshire

Acknowledgement

The permission of Her Majesty Queen Elizabeth II to include material
from the Royal Archives is gratefully acknowledged.

Disclaimer

Caution

The Lost Prince was produced by Talkback Productions Ltd for BBC Television and was first screened in January 2003 by BBC1. The cast was as follows:

Queen Mary	Miranda Richardson
Lalla	Gina McKee
Edward VII	Michael Gambon
Stamfordham	Bill Nighy
George V	Tom Hollander
Queen Alexandra	Bibi Andersson
Asquith	Frank Finlay
Mr Hansell	John Sessions
Fred	David Westhead
Lloyd George	Ron Cook
Tsarina Alexandra	Ingeborga Dapkunaite
Young Johnnie	Daniel Williams
Johnnie	Matthew Thomas
Young Georgie	Brock Everitt-Elwick
Georgie	Rollo Weeks
Kaiser Wilhelm	David Barrass
Tsar Nicholas	Ivan Marevich
Callender	Graham Crowden
Dr Hetherington	Jonathan Coy
Dr Longhurst	John Rowe
Fine Looking Woman	Fritha Goodey
Knutsford	Nicholas Palliser
Olga	Vanessa Ackerman
Maria	Nastya Razduhova
Anastasia	Algina Lipskyte
Tatiana	Holly Boyd
Suffragette	Henrietta Voigts
Young Mary	Mary Nighy

May	Kate Manning
David	Dominic Colenso
Lady In Waiting	Maggie McCourt
Fat Mary	Roz McCutcheon
Russell	Joe Sowerbutts
Doctor	Robert Swann
Violinist	Martin Wimbush
Orderly	Paul Brennen
Admiral	Andrew Hilton
General	Neil Stacy
Lady Warrender	Suzanne Burden

Director Stephen Poliakoff
Producer John Chapman
Music Adrian Johnston
Director of Photography Barry Ackroyd, BSC
Editor Clare Douglas
Production Designer John-Paul Kelly

Foreword

One morning in the spring of 1998, I saw a photograph of an ungainly looking boy staring out of the front page of a national newspaper. He was dressed in the customary sailor suit that most Edwardian upper-class children wore, but there was something about his gaze that was both unsettling and welcoming. This was the first time I had seen what Prince John looked like and I was immediately fascinated. The headlines that accompanied the article screamed that this was the first time a photograph had ever been published of the hidden prince. This, in fact, turned out to be nonsense because several photographs of Johnnie, as he was known to his family, had appeared during his lifetime, quite frequently when he was small and before he was sheltered away from the world.

I had known about the existence of Johnnie for many years ever since I wrote *Clever Soldiers*, a play about the First World War, when I was a student at Cambridge. I had read one sentence about him in a general history book which blandly referred to Johnnie as the brain-damaged youngest child of George V and Queen Mary, and how he had been shut away until he died. The image of a hidden prince had stayed with me, but I had never been drawn to find out any more about Johnnie until I saw him staring out of a photograph on that spring morning.

I quickly discovered that there was practically nothing published about Prince John, most royal biographies confining themselves to a few sentences about the poor epileptic and autistic prince who had to be sheltered away from the rest of his family and the world. But as I gradually pieced together a picture of Johnnie from the few snippets of information that were sprinkled over a wide range of royal histories, I realised that a different boy was emerging. It turned out that Johnnie was very far from being the 'monster child that grew enormous for his age whilst having the mental age of a three-year-old', which is the way, for instance, one article on the Internet described him. Johnnie had learning difficulties and was prone to severe epileptic fits, but he was also capable of interesting and humorous observations about people and situations, and inspired devotion and love from his nurse Lalla, a devotion that lasted nearly half a century after his death.

But for me the truly haunting fact about Johnnie was that his short life spanned one of the most momentous periods in our history. He was born into the extravagant and Ruritanian fantasy world that was the court of Edward VII and Queen Alexandra at the height of British imperial power. But when he died at the age of thirteen and a half on the very day the politicians sat down to negotiate the Treaty of Versailles, the whole of Europe had changed completely. Several monarchies had collapsed, Emperors had fled into exile, there had been the Russian Revolution and the entire adult world had been engulfed by the worst catastrophe of the twentieth century, the First World War.

The longer I thought about the story, the more it revealed the chance to write about these events from a unique angle: the gaze of a child. Johnnie at the beginning of his life was right in the middle of this imperial family, often the centre of attention because of his funny and charming remarks, only to find himself being hidden away at the very moment the adults around him completely lost control of their destiny. At the start of the story his family and relations presided over practically the whole of Europe, nearly all the kings and queens were related, and the Western world seemed stable, prosperous and confident. Within a handful of years, Britain was at war with the King's cousin, the Kaiser, millions of people were dying and the whole interlocking family fabric was being torn apart.

I have always instinctively felt that if one wants to dramatise history and historical figures, like George V and Mary, Lloyd George and Asquith, it is best to do it through a half-open door, as they might appear to a child. For if we were to achieve that perennial fantasy of time travel and propel ourselves backwards into any time but our own, we would almost certainly find ourselves staring at it with the same mixture of cool detachment and deep curiosity that children naturally possess. It was also a chance to celebrate a child with disability not as a victim, but as somebody who progresses through the story and achieves an inner equilibrium. While Johnnie is achieving this journey, the adult world has been overtaken by disaster and had all their confidence and certainty drained out of them. At the end of the story, all the major historical characters have become helpless shadows of their former selves.

In the following pages I trace how I evolved the story from the few fragments that are available about Johnnie's life. I explain why I altered certain things and why I invented certain episodes, but I also demonstrate that a great proportion of *The Lost Prince* is completely true, certainly in the sense of being faithful to the essence of the characters and the real events. All the major public events in the story are true: the suffragette throwing herself at the feet of Queen Mary inside Buckingham Palace, the disastrous Irish conference, the speed with which the royal family changed their German name, and perhaps most intriguingly, George V's involvement with the fate of the Russian royal family. George V's desperate and successful efforts to get the invitation to his Russian cousin to come to England revoked have long been in the public domain, but have never been, to my knowledge, dramatised before. The sequence of events shows that George V was capable of cunning and pragmatism during the darkest days of the war when the royal family was filled with what can only be described as panic about the survival of the monarchy. I also feel the alacrity with which they changed their name will surprise many of the audience, the ancient resonance contained in the name Windsor being completely artificial. People will continually debate the validity of dramatising and therefore fictionalising, history, but in writing this screenplay I was guided by the principle that if I invented something it could only be in the cause of expressing a wider truth.

In one sense, it is easy to relate *The Lost Prince* to my most recent work because it is about a family and history, both subjects I have written about before, not least in *Perfect Strangers*, *Shooting the Past*, and my 1998 stage play *Talk of the City*. But in another sense it is, I feel, a very different kind of subject for me, firstly because it is a true story and I have nearly always avoided dramatising true stories, and secondly because it is about the royal family, a collection of individuals I never dreamed I would ever want to write about. In fact, my reluctance was so great I found it difficult to write the words 'Buckingham Palace' in the screenplay. This reluctance was almost entirely due to the fact that the royal family is such a surreal and unnatural institution it is very difficult to write about them without either parodying the characters or showing contempt for them. For this reason I left the project slowly cooking in my imagination while I made *Perfect Strangers*, and people familiar with that work will recall the photograph of a small boy dressed as a prince staring through the banisters of a grand staircasee at the adult world below that played a vital part in the plot of that drama.

So ultimately I realised *The Lost Prince* was a story I had to attempt not least because as I sat down to write it in the autumn of 2001 the world was once again setting off to war. And as I write these words we are once again hovering on the brink of a war with Iraq. All historical stories will have modern echoes, depending when and how they reach people. The modern parallels for us are clearly: a dysfunctional royal family, the confidence that a short war can remain a short war, even the return to a world power arbitrated by a dynastic family, in this case the Bush family. But for me the most surprising modern echo of *The Lost Prince* is how, nearly a hundred years after the events I describe, we are only fractionally more flexible and wise about how we treat children that are 'different' than the Edwardians were.

Stephen Poliakoff
November 2002

Introduction

Part One

Queen Alexandra's birthday and the concert

The Lost Prince begins with us moving with Johnnie through the opulence and indulgence of Edward VII's court. I chose to use Queen Alexandra's birthday party in 1909 as my starting point because there is a very full account of it in a book by Viscount Knutsford entitled *In Black and White*. He wrote the book for his children and in it he paints a vivid and often slightly comic picture of his stay at Sandringham. The scene he describes is full of evocative and almost hallucinatory details, including the towering birthday cake which is populated by goldfish, the dozens of agate animals made by Fabergé that the Queen adored collecting. They twinkled in a special electrical cabinet that lit up at night, and there was a concert of dramatic balalaika music, which surprised all the guests.

The startling opening image of the butter race, although not witnessed by Knutsford, is mentioned in several royal biographies. Edward VII enjoyed playing with his grand-children, and this extraordinary race of competing butter pats oozing down the creases of his trousers was one of his tricks. It was a mystery to us how he managed it, because it proved an extremely difficult race for the art department on the film to recreate. The modern squares of butter simply refused to run down the creases of Michael Gambon's trousers, however many times they were melted.

> Everybody smoked, the Queen included . . . She lighted her cigarette after luncheon with a very pretty little flint steel contrivance, and when I admired it, said: 'I will give you one . . .'

The Queen likes most agate animals, of which she has a magnificent collection in two large glass cabinets in the drawing-room, which every evening are lit up by electricity . . .

The birthday cake was a huge erection in about six tiers, with bowls of water containing small goldfish between each tier . . . Most of the presents were perfectly lovely . . . There were quite forty different agate animals, monkeys, penguins, dogs, birds, chinchillas, all exquisitely modelled by this Russian, and all made to order . . .

The table was beautifully decorated with autumn-coloured grape leaves. The Queen likes high decorations, so they went half-way up to the ceiling in great arches, with bunches of grapes hanging down...

The Prince of Wales' children were all there, romping about and eating the chocolates . . .

I look forward to tonight's dinner as it will be a grand affair with the Russian band afterwards, about which there is great excitement; it is so wonderfully good . . .

The Russians have no instruments, except a sort of guitar, and an instrument made like a piano, only with wire, which they played with their fingers like a zither. The music was like wind whistling through violin strings, quite lovely, and very exciting.[1]

I have changed the precise date of these events because I wanted the Russian band to come before the entrance of the Tsar in the story rather than after. This is much more dramatically effective, the band as it were heralds the first appearance of the Tsar rather than ploddingly appearing after his arrival. It implies that the story begins in December 1908 rather than when Knutsford described the events, which was 1909.

Nevertheless, what is clear from his account is the fact that the children were around at these events, including the shooting party, which we will come to later, and also the extraordinary mix of formality and informality that I have dramatised in these early scenes. It is also from Knutsford's account that I discovered the clocks were set half an hour fast.

> Colonel Streatfeild (now Colonel Sir Henry Streatfeild), the Equerry, an old friend, came up to me and said I was to shoot tomorrow, 10.15, Sandringham time, which is half an hour in front of Greenwich time.[2]

The image of Lalla being almost tied to Johnnie comes from a different source. A description of her walking up a hill, being literally roped to the child and never letting him out of her sight, an observation which was made by another royal guest. 'Loelia Ponsonby remembered him as "a nice little boy" at Balmoral when she was a child, noticing nothing unusual about him apart from the fact that when they climbed the hills he was roped to his nurse, which the other children thought "sissy".'[3]

The royal children

During the concert in the film, we see all the royal children sitting in a row watching the recital except for Johnnie who has a special seat with Lalla towards the back of the room. At this moment in Johnnie's life nobody thought he had any particular problem, only that he was a little fidgety, a touch delicate. He was the youngest of six children, the eldest was David (who became Edward VIII and then the Duke of Windsor), then came Bertie (the present Queen's father, the future George VI), Mary, who was also known as May, Henry (who became the Duke of Gloucester), Young George (who became the Duke of Kent) and Johnnie.

David, eleven years older than Johnnie, was a very vain and

self-regarding young man, and by all accounts quite stupid. Bertie was a shy and inhibited boy who nevertheless possessed a ferocious temper. Mary was a no-nonsense quite sensible young woman and Henry was a rather dull, stolid boy.

I have not featured any of them in the story because there is something about a gaggle of royal children that is profoundly undramatic. I wanted to see the action through Johnnie's eyes, and later in the story through Young Georgie's eyes too. As soon as the children start to multiply in number, the story becomes, for me at least, markedly less engaging. Also, by excluding the other children from the narrative, I was remaining true to what happened, because Johnnie saw very little of his siblings once his illness was diagnosed.

The Tsar's visit to the Isle of Wight

The Tsar and his family visited the Isle of Wight in the summer of 1909. At Cowes there was an enormous display of ships, not just yachts but also a large section of the British Fleet. During their stay, the Russian royal family had tea with George and Mary at Barton Manor, which is a stocky Victorian house on the Osborne Estate.

Osborne had already been given to the nation by Edward VII; he detested the place, but it was still used for official functions, and the Russian Royal Family paid a visit to wander around. But I have confined the scenes in the Isle of Wight to their tea at Barton because I wanted to show the great contrast between the absolute monarch and the curious, unassuming behaviour of the British heir to the throne. David (the future Duke of Windsor) was very impressed by the security that surrounded the Tsar. The Russian royal family had an immense bodyguard which was very much in evidence during their visit:

Uncle Nicky came for the Regatta with his Empress and their numerous children in the Imperial Russian yacht

Standart. I do not remember him as a man of marked personality; but I do remember being astonished at the elaborate police guard thrown around his every movement when I showed him round Osborne.[4]

There is no account of what transpired between the Russian royal family and George and Mary during their tea, but it is true that George found the Tsarina an extremely difficult character. Since they only met a few times in later life, she must have done something deeply annoying during this visit.

It was during their visit to Barton Manor that the photo of the two cousins, George and Nicholas, the Prince of Wales and the Tsar, standing together, was taken. There are also photographs of the Russian royal family and the English royal family taken together on other occasions during this holiday. I have no direct proof that Johnnie was present during this holiday, but the children were definitely around and, since the royal family had not realised the extent of Johnnie's problems at this stage, there seems no reason why he shouldn't have been there.

The account of Mary walking along the beach picking up shells on the sand with the Russian royal children, comes from her diary for Tuesday, 3 August 1909, where she writes, 'Went with May to Osborne, where I met the charming little Russian children, four girls and a boy. Picked up shells with them on the beach . . .' and from a letter she wrote to her aunt Augusta, where she describes the Russian children as 'the delicious Russian children'.

The image of the Tsar swimming, which plays such a part in the story, may or may not be an invention. Again, I have no proof that he went swimming during his visit, but it is true that the Tsar loved water, and there is a fine photograph of him in a rowing boat during his visit to the Isle of Wight. He *was* a very keen swimmer, and there's a splendid account of his mobilising the Russian Army and then going for a swim in

A. J. P. Taylor's essay 'The First World War' in his collection *British Prime Ministers and Other Essays*.

I was very taken by this image, of the Tsar mobilising the Russian Army, which Taylor claims was one of the major causes of the First World War, and then going for an afternoon swim. The Tsar carefully recorded the fact that he'd gone for a swim in his diary, but makes no mention of his momentous decision to mobilise the Russian Army. Hence, this became one of the major images of the whole story.

Life at York Cottage and Sandringham

York Cottage is a hideous late Victorian villa that sits at the bottom of the garden at Sandringham (it is now the estate office). Both George and Mary loved it passionately – they much preferred being there than anywhere else. It suited both their natures – George because he liked being in small spaces from his time in the Navy (he was extremely happy at sea), and Mary because she was an intensely private person and was not a natural performer on the big stage.

There are endless observations by visitors to York Cottage about what a strange place it was for a king and queen. It seems to have struck nearly everybody that came through the door, how odd it was that the royal family was squashed into a warren of tiny rooms.

One of these tiny rooms was the schoolroom presided over by Mr Hansell. Hansell was an extremely frustrated character. There is a reference to David, aged about thirteen, coming across Hansell standing alone in the garden of Sandringham staring across at the surrounding fields. David asks Hansell what he's thinking about and Hansell replies, 'I don't think you will understand, but for me it is freedom.'[5]

There's also a reference to him commenting on teaching Johnnie, 'Now I can give all my time to Prince George and Prince John – though there is little I can do with the latter, alas!'[6]

Hansell was not alone with the children. There was also a teacher of French, M. Gabriel Hua, but Hansell clearly did feel very isolated, and that is what I have dramatised. In the film the children leave York Cottage with Lalla and walk to the big house through a sunlit garden dotted with policemen and past the royal dogs being fed off silver trays by liveried footmen – there were extra guards deployed round Edward VII towards the end of his reign because of threats against his life from various sources (mostly lunatics rather than revolutionaries). There was a tramp that used to come up to him at the royal station at the bottom of the estate, who particularly worried the security forces at the time.

Policemen and detectives were dotted about the place . . . I met the head detective, Stephens . . . He told me that he was with the King always, and had always to be on the look-out, not against criminals, but against lunatics . . . 'There is an old man at Wolferton station with a box full of letters he insists on showing to the King. They have tried to pacify the old man, but in vain, so he is shadowed always.[7]

Alexandra's dogs were an important feature of life at Sandringham during this period, and she took a great deal of interest in how they were fed. She had a large number of dogs, probably about thirty at the time this scene is set. She had a great preference for borzois which she had imported especially from Russia. Many of these dogs promptly died when they reached Sandringham. Alexandra was undeterred and immediately ordered some more.

There are clear references in the royal biographies to the children of George V having to play between planets rather than nations when they played with toy soldiers. For instance, John Van Der Kiste writes, 'The boys would play battles with lead soldiers. The King took keen interest in these games but made a rule that the armies were not to be from existing countries but that battles had to be between different planets like Earth and Mars'.[8] When he had the time George V would supervise these war games, a stern and serious presence rather than a playful one. And so the image of the two adults kneeling among the toy soldiers seems to me to be accurate – the King and the heir to the throne crawling around a miniature army.

The nature of Johnnie's illness

Johnnie suffered from epilepsy. His fits manifested themselves around the age of five or six, just about the time Edward VII died. The fits became increasingly severe as he grew older, until they caused his death in January 1919. Also, Johnnie had what we would now call learning difficulties. During his lifetime and for a long time afterwards, people believed his brain was increasingly damaged by epilepsy, but there is no documentary evidence to support this. What seems more likely is that Johnnie had some form of language difficulty from birth; a problem with processing information and then articulating it in a conventional way. This was a separate condition from his epilepsy.

As a very small boy, Johnnie expressed himself in a charmingly idiosyncratic way compared to any of the other royal children – 'his funny sayings' as the family called them. As he grew, the strange way he used language remained consistently inconsistent, neither deteriorating nor greatly improving. There are telling clues in his letters when for instance, he sometimes signs his name 'Johnny' and at other times 'Johnnie'.

The word autism is sometimes used in connection with Johnnie but, as we know, autism covers a huge spectrum and Johnnie was definitely not autistic in the way that the term is more frequently used – a child cut off from the world, locked in a private mental space of his own. On the contrary, Johnnie was very engaged with the world and with those around him.

It is clear that the royal family was slow to realise that Johnnie had problems. This is partly because his symptoms were much milder when he was a little boy but also because the peculiar way he expressed himself seemed to fit his personality perfectly.

I have surmised that Lalla must have had a greater knowledge of Johnnie's condition than his parents, just because she was so very close to him. I cannot believe that she had no inkling before the royal family did, and I have chosen to dramatise this in Johnnie's first fit after the scene with the toy soldiers. It may well be that his early fits were mistaken for the convulsions that young children often have (and which can be very alarming).

A century later, the terms we have at our disposal to describe learning difficulties are still painfully inadequate. We lump children with very different problems into a few arbitrary categories. It seems most probable that Johnnie, like almost all children with learning difficulties, did not fit neatly into any one category.

We will never know what the correct modern medical term for his condition should be, but it is clear that though Johnnie had problems expressing himself in conventional language, that did not mean he was less intelligent than other children of his age. He was just different, and saw the world in a different way, as many children with learning difficulties do.

When Lalla returns to York Cottage after Johnnie's first fit, she is interrogated by Mary. This scene allows me to work in a reference to Mary's hearing. She was famous for her keen sense of hearing, being able to pick up remarks made right at the other end of the dinner table.

The shooting party

This sequence is based on several sources, including

Knutsford's account in *In Black and White*, and photographs of Edward VII's shooting parties.

Knutsford describes his experience of shooting in the rain and the mud next to the king – a bleak and tense scene. The shooting sequence also gives me the chance to dramatise the mood swings Edward VII was prone to. He only had a few months to live when this shooting party took place, and yet there are bursts of considerable energy in Knutsford's account of him. Nevertheless, his life of excess was clearly catching up with him very fast at this stage and this is what I have chosen to portray.

Then the rain came in torrents, and the King went off to the luncheon tent while we went to shoot a small covert. Bitterly cold and only a few birds. The head keeper said that he was very disappointed with the weather . . . The Queen and ladies had arrived by the time we got to the tent.[9]

In the scene in the film we see George shooting next to his father. He was an extremely good shot and obsessed with the sport. He slept with a gun by his bed, not because he felt under threat from burglars or Michael Fagins of the period, but because he could practise dummy shots as he got ready for bed. That would have seemed too close to high comedy, however, so I have not dramatised it in the script. But we do see George V's love of shooting in the sequence and his extreme proficiency at it.

Knutsford does describe the children being around the meal in the marquee after the morning shoot, and hence I felt justified in placing Young George and Johnnie there too. Although there is no account of Johnnie holding the marquee spellbound as he does in the screenplay, there is an account of him entertaining Theodore Roosevelt in public with surprising charm and enjoying the attention: 'Lord Esher met him [Johnnie] at Balmoral in 1910 and he amused Theodore Roosevelt at Buckingham Palace in 1911.'[10] I have chosen to transpose that scene to the marquee and show him in conversation with his grandfather. At this stage of his life Johnnie was regarded as a public asset, a charming child who would say unexpected and funny things.

The household watches for Halley's Comet

On 7 May 1910 the parks, the rooftops and the streets of London were full of people trying to see Halley's Comet. It was a very cloudy night in London and people were disappointed that they couldn't see very much.

The Prime Minister, Asquith, recorded: 'On 7 May, 3 am there came the terrible news that shortly before midnight the King had died.' He was on a cruise to Lisbon, when he heard the news: 'I went up on deck and I remember well that the first sight that met my eyes in the twilight before dawn was Halley's comet blazing in the sky.'[11] There's a fine picture in the *Illustrated London News* of people standing around with telescopes trying to see the comet.

Two of the princes learned that their father had become king by parting the curtains of their bedroom at Marlborough House and seeing the flag flying at half-mast. The Duke of Windsor later recorded: 'Next morning I was awakened by a cry from my brother Bertie. From the window of our room he cried, "Look, the Royal Standard is at half-mast!"'[12] For the purposes of storytelling, I have changed these figures to Young George and Johnnie.

There is no reference to the youngest boys being around the funeral, but Johnnie was allowed to watch the Coronation parade from a window in Buckingham Palace. 'Prince John was allowed to watch the processions from a window in the State Apartments of Buckingham Palace'.[13] I took this as a sufficient excuse to allow him to be able to peer down at the funeral procession.

Mary's mother, Mary of Adelaide

Both George V and Mary felt extremely nervous at taking on the roles of king and queen, and I have chosen to dramatise this in a series of short scenes on the eve of the funeral. I show Mary's preparations for the funeral being interrupted by a flashback as she thinks about her mother, Mary of Adelaide. Mary's mother was a woman of enormous proportions and was nicknamed 'Fat Mary' by various members of the family. Queen Victoria herself was extremely shocked by her appearance, and expressed sadness to various members of the family that 'Fat Mary' had allowed her splendid personality to be obscured by her truly gigantic size. She wrote, 'It is a real pleasure to see Mary now – she is so bright and happy and also her fine qualities come out to such advantage now that she is happy. But her *size* is fearful! It is really a misfortune!'

The visit to the dancing class is true, as is the embarrassment that the young Mary felt. 'At Taglioni's dancing classes at her little house in Connaught Square, the other children would giggle when they saw that Princess May's mother needed two gilt chairs, not one, to sit upon.'[14] For all that, Mary of Adelaide seems to have been a rather life-enhancing character; she used to turn her face to the crowd in royal processions when the rest of the family were staring ahead.

Watching Edward VII's funeral and the aftermath of Johnnie's fit

A photograph was taken of the nine kings who were in London for the funeral of Edward VII, and this is one of the chief images of the funeral sequence. The kings were, Haakon VII of Norway, Ferdinand I of Bulgaria, Manuel I of Portugal, Wilhelm II of Germany, Gustav V of Sweden, Albert I of

Belgium, Alphonso XIII of Spain, George V of England and Frederick VIII of Denmark.

Around 1910/11, Johnnie's condition became obvious to the family, and I have chosen to dramatise this by showing Johnnie having a bad fit while he roams around the palace on the morning of the funeral. I also introduce the character of Lord Stamfordham during the funeral preparations. Stamfordham was the king's private secretary and is described in all the royal biographies as loyal and devoted to George V. He was a royal adviser of enormous experience, having worked for the royal family for a number of years as Arthur Bigge, before being created Lord Stamfordham. As we will see later, he kept a full record of the events surrounding the Tsar's proposed exile in England, and the account that he wrote at the time, for his own private use, shows him to be a shrewd and intelligent man with a hint of steel.

His relationship with Young George is speculation on my part. But Young George was an extremely clever and precocious boy and I feel would certainly have peppered him with questions. The scene between Mary and Lalla after the funeral is obviously an invention on my part, since nobody can know what happened when Mary first became aware of Johnnie's condition. I have gleaned Mary and Lalla's relationship from the way Mary recorded events surrounding Johnnie's death in her diary, and I have had to work backwards from that, construing the dynamic between them. As we have seen, there's no doubt that Lalla was fiercely protective of Johnnie throughout his short life.

The anecdote about Johnnie and the leaves is recorded by Charlotte Zeepvat: 'Someone told him that the spirits of dead people leave their bodies to inhabit the wind: on the day of his grandfather's death, the four-year-old Prince made a pile of leaves in the garden. He called this "sweeping up Grandpa's bits".'[15] The doctors' examination of Johnnie is based on the tests they did at the time to gauge intelligence, some of which still remain in place today among certain practitioners.

Johnnie's isolation at York Cottage

After the discovery of the full extent of Johnnie's condition – his epilepsy and learning difficulties – he was isolated at York Cottage and kept away from the rest of the family for most of the time. David Duff writes, 'He was kept apart from his brothers and sister, as was the fashion of the day.'[16] Young George was his companion until he, went away to school. Anne Edwards, in her book *Queen Mary and the House of Windsor*, writes, 'Placed entirely in Lalla Bill's care, he remained in the nursery at York Cottage where his brother, Georgie, treated him in almost parental fashion.'[17] Young George started at St Peter's Court in the summer term of 1912 (at the age of ten) and it was from this period that Johnnie was left alone with Lalla and the servants of York Cottage.

There is a time jump between scenes 40 and 41, from 1910 to 1914: the garden and the scenes in the classroom with Hansell are happening in the spring of 1914, and the visit to the doctors is on 28 June.

Opinions differ about how complete Johnnie's isolation was at this stage of his life. Some of the brief mentions in the royal biographies say that he was categorically not allowed to meet any visitor at all, and others say it depended on who it was. Obviously I have chosen the former course because it works so well dramatically and may also be true. But whether Johnnie was literally kept out of sight or merely lived in seclusion, it is clear that he was increasingly isolated from his siblings and other children as he grew older. One of the very few references that I found by any of the royal family about Johnnie during the First World War said that he longed for a companion of his own age. But, as the war progressed, a few visitors did catch glimpses of Johnnie from a distance.

Johnnie's garden

Johnnie had a garden at York Cottage and took pleasure in gardening. I have obviously embellished the image of Johnnie's garden for dramatic purposes, but it was very central to his world:

> He enjoyed gardening and had his own small area, with a plaque saying 'Prince John's garden', where he dug with a trowel, and the gardeners planted flowers for him.'[18]

His 'escape' from the garden to interrupt the tea party is an invention on my part, based on an incident recounted by Charlotte Zeepvat in Royalty Digest:

> One day, Lalla went out, leaving John in the care of the undernurse. As she cycled home she was horrified to see the little boy waving to her from the roof. 'I thought it would have killed me when I saw him sitting there,' she said.[19]

This incident shows him escaping supervision, just as he does in the film, and managing to climb on to the high roof of York cottage. I did not use this exact episode in the film because visually it was rather reminiscent of *The Turn of the Screw* – a lone figure poised among the chimneys as his nurse returns on her bicycle. Instead, Johnnie's escape into the sunlit garden, his encounter with the Fine-Looking Woman and his interruption of the family tea party allowed me to dramatise the serene, unsuspecting atmosphere just before the outbreak of war.

The glimpses of Asquith in the script are inspired by Lytton Strachey's account of meeting him in 1916 at Garsington. Strachey's view of him almost has the clarity of a child's vision, immensely vivid, and immediately makes you feel you're sitting opposite him:

> I studied the Old Man [Asquith] with extreme vigour, and really he's a corker. He seemed much larger than he did when I last saw him – a fleshy, sanguine, wine-bibbing mediaeval Abbot of a personage – a gluttonous, lecherous, cynical old fellow . . . On the whole, one wants to stick a dagger in his ribs . . . and then, as well, one can't help liking him – I suppose because he *does* enjoy himself so much.[20]

Although Asquith's comments about York Cottage are actually based on remarks made by Harold Nicolson, it was such a generally held view among the ruling class that I felt free to allocate them to Asquith. In fact Stamfordham, Lloyd George and he had made repeated efforts to persuade the King that York Cottage was not a suitable residence for the royal family in the country:

> I spend the morning visiting York Cottage . . . There is nothing to differentiate the cottage from any of the villas at Surbiton . . . The rooms inside, with their fumed oak surrounds, their white overmantels framing oval mirrors, their Doulton tiles and stained glass fanlights, are indistinguishable from those of any Surbiton or Upper Norwood home.[21]

The description of Johnnie appearing out of the bushes is based on various glimpses that visitors caught of him inadvertently. Robert Lacey writes that 'Guests at Balmoral remember him during the Great War, as a distant figure, tall, muscular but always remote, who would be glimpsed from afar in the woods escorted by his own retainers'.[22]

The image of Lloyd George flirting with a pretty woman

clearly needs no specific historical reference, but I also wanted to dramatise the fact that Lloyd George was addicted to cheap novels about the Wild West. And both Lloyd George and Asquith made patronising remarks about the King to various friends and colleagues, although they both later claimed to have grown to respect him over the years they dealt with him. Lloyd George wrote to his wife from Balmoral: 'The King is a very jolly chap, but thank God there's not much in his head. They're simple, very, very ordinary people and perhaps on the whole that's how it should be.' Lloyd George, when he was summoned to Buckingham Palace in January 1915, remarked to his secretary, 'I wonder what my little German friend has got to say to me'.[23]

Lalla and Mary discuss Johnnie's future

In this scene I wanted to express the emotional distance that Mary felt in relation to her own children. Like a lot of the Edwardian upper class, she regarded her children as strange creatures that might be members of another species: 'She remained tragically inhibited with her children. She loved them and was proud of them but . . . they were strangers to her emotionally.' [24]

Johnnie's education

The scenes with Johnnie's tutor, Mr Hansell, in the school-room are based on this description of him:

He was tall and good-looking, a bachelor without much sense of humour . . . His was not a warm personality and he was prone to fall into long periods of abstraction when, pipe in mouth, he would gaze vacantly into space.[25]

Clearly, this was not the sort of personality that would have succeeded in recognising Johnnie's real qualities. I saw him as a tragicomic, Chekovian figure, going quietly mad as he realises he is just as much a prisoner as Johnnie.

Queen Mary and the suffragettes

Mary watched this incident from a window in Buckingham Palace with her daughter May. The queen detested the suffragettes and found their actions completely inexplicable. She felt not a shred of sympathy for their cause and indeed viewed them as a threat to the stability of the country and the established order, the values that her whole life was dedicated to preserving.

Her attitude to the suffragettes is best summed up by a letter to her aunt Augusta in 1913: 'Those horrid suffragettes burnt down the little tea house close to the Pagoda in Kew Gardens yesterday morning at 3 am . . . There seems no end to their iniquities.'[26]

Johnnie's letter and the Irish Conference

Johnnie's letter is one of several scenes in the story that shows his interest in his cousins and his family tree. I have no documentary evidence of this letter, but I know from his letters to his parents in the Royal Archive that he makes several mentions of his various aunts and uncles and other relations which are not immediate family. From my research for another project into children with similar learning difficulties to Johnnie, I came across many instances of these children becoming very interested in their family trees, the visual representation of family relations is something that appealed to them greatly, and which they found particularly fascinating. I thought it was a reasonable assumption to have Johnnie share the same interest.

The Irish Conference actually took place a few weeks later than in the script – the date was 21 July 1914 and I've set the conference in the script about six weeks earlier (before the assassination of the Archduke, which happened on 28 June). I didn't want too many incidents crowding into Buckingham Palace simultaneously at the end of the first part of the story for this would have created a very muddled narrative.

The conference was called by George V at Buckingham Palace on 21 July 1914, with Asquith, Bonar Law, Redmond and Carson, leader of the Ulster loyalists, present. It ended in stalemate. 'At the end,' Asquith noted, 'the King came in, rather émotionné, and said in two sentences, "Farewell, I am sorry. And I thank you."'[27] What is fascinating about the timing of this conference is that it shows the king being far more concerned with the problems in Ireland than with the threat of war in Europe, although the start of the First World War was less than two weeks away.

Johnnie's trip to the doctors in London

There is no record of Johnnie having been examined by doctors in London, but it must have happened at some point, since his fits were of great concern to the family. As in the previous doctors scene, the tests are based on those that were practised at the time.

One of the perennial question that doctors ask a patient to test how effectively the brain is working is 'Who is the Prime Minister of this country?' This has remained astonishingly consistent throughout the last hundred years. My father was asked this question by his doctors in 1996 to see if his life was worth saving by doing an operation on him.

From references, we know that Johnnie was moved from place to place and that he never travelled with the royal family but always followed them with his own escort – usually Lalla and one of the other servants. Hence the car ride to London with him peering through a chink in the blind at the outside world.

Young George and Johnnie and the *Empress of Ireland*

The seating at royal banquets is still carried out in close consultation with the Queen. It seemed a reasonable piece of speculation on my part that Stamfordham would have planned important banquets with George V, since George seemed to consult him on most things.

I have created the relationship with Stamfordham and the Young George to give the audience an insight into the workings of the court and to inform them about the various events that are happening in the outside world, without it seeming imposed on the story. The scene where Young George and Johnnie stare at the pictures of the sinking of the *Empress of Ireland*, is based on an extremely vivid spread of photos and paintings in the Illustrated London News. The sinking of the *Empress of Ireland* was a great disaster that now seems largely forgotten, but played on the imagination of the nation very strongly at the time. It came just two years after the sinking of the *Titanic* and over a thousand people died in the disaster.

Mary and Lalla's discussion of Johnnie's illness is also speculation on my part, since there is no record remaining of whether they did discuss it. However, I'm fairly sure that my portrait of the two women is close to the truth. Lalla was a spirited and plain-speaking woman, and Mary had a poignant combination of considerable intelligence and powers of observation mixed with great emotional inhibition.

Mary and the kneeling suffragette

Young George and Johnnie's desire to watch the banquet is an invention on my part based on two sources. The first is a screen in the ballroom at Buckingham Palace from behind which it is possible to view banquets discreetly. I feel certain that the royal children, at some stage in their lives, would have watched a banquet from this position. The second is Charlotte Zeepvat's account of Johnnie escaping from his bedroom to watch the guests arrive for a great occasion: 'Once, on the occasion of a party at Sandringham, the young Prince went missing from his bed. After a long search he was found behind a large pot of ferns, watching the party guests.'[28]

The scene between Mary and the suffragette is a very well-documented incident which actually took place on 4 June 1914 (not on the 28, which is the date it is set in the script). After the event, Mary told many people the story of how a woman threw herself at her feet begging her to stop torturing all women and how she must put a stop to this persecution at once. The woman had managed to smuggle herself into the palace and blended in with all the other guests as she waited her turn with the Queen. Mary's own account of the incident was confined to two lines in her diary: 'In the evening, a tiresome suffragette fell on her knees before us and held out her arms, "Oh Your Majesty, stop torturing the women."'

Interestingly, in her diary, Mary has carefully cut out and pasted below her own account, a description of the incident published in *The Times*, which includes great praise for her conduct saying that she was 'a masterpiece of dignity and composure'.[29] This is one of the reviews of her conduct that Stamfordham brings to show her in the scene after the banquet. The fact that she needed to paste the cutting into her own diary suggests an intriguing lack of self-confidence on her part.

The banquet

The banquet is just one of many formal occasions that would have been held during those months leading up to the First World War. It is there to show how completely unprepared people were for the disaster that was about to overtake the whole of Europe. Very little real tension was felt at court in the weeks that led to the declaration of war. In fact, as we have seen, the king was more preoccupied with trying to sort out the problems in Ireland than he was concerned about the possibility of war. He had met the Kaiser in Berlin the year before in a great show of royal pomp. The Tsar was also present at this occasion, and George V put on a German helmet to ride in a parade, to show his solidarity with the German royal family.

> The King and Queen . . . were pleased to be invited to the wedding, in May 1913, of the Emperor's only daughter Princess Victoria Louise to their cousin Ernest Augustus. Sir Edward Grey persuaded the King that any Royal visit to Berlin for the Brunswick wedding, which took place in circumstances of imperial pomp on 24 May, must be regarded as a private family affair . . . It was the final appearance of the 'royal mob', the last time that King George and Queen Mary would see the German Emperor and Empress, the Tsar Nicholas and the Tsarina.[30]

The presence of the politicians from rival parties facing one another across the table is an important detail in the sequence. Some historians believe one of the reasons the Liberal government took Britain into the First World War is because they were worried that they would be accused of being soft by the Tory opposition. Johnnie's response to the music at the banquet is based on my research into the fact that children with language problems are often extremely sensitive to music, and Young George was very musical – one of his chief interests in life.

After the banquet and Mary's scene with Johnnie

It is well documented that George V didn't at first realise the full significance of the death of the Archduke Ferdinand, the heir to the Austrian throne. Events moved extremely fast from the death of the Archduke on June 28 to the outbreak of war on August 4, these events make up the opening scenes of Part Two.

The scene between Mary and Johnnie is based on some of Johnnie's letters, in which flowers from his garden or from the surrounding woods near York Cottage and Wood Farm, were one of the chief topics that he wrote to his parents about. The letters often contained pressed flowers he'd either picked from his garden or the surrounding woods.

Dear Papa,
I'm sending a box of snowdrops for you which I have picked . . . these two daisies I have picked out of my garden.[31]

My dear papa,
I'm sending you in a box some lilies out of Wolferton Woods . . . The garden is very nice here . . . I am very busy here.
Best love from your devoted son, Johnnie.[32]

George V and the parrot

One of George V's most passionate hobbies was stamp collecting. He took this enormously seriously and took great pride in acquiring new stamps. He even went so far as extending Buckingham Palace to accommodate a special suite of rooms for his stamp museum. When he was Prince of Wales he gave instructions to his curator of stamps to buy at any price a particular 2½d Bahama stamp in an auction and it realised as much as £1,400.

A week later Sir Arthur Davidson, Equerry to King Edward, had occasion to telephone to the Prince of Wales about something, and having finished, he added: 'I know how interested Your Royal Highness is in stamps. Did you happen to see in the newspapers that some damned fool had given as much as £1,400 for one stamp?' A quiet restrained voice answered: 'I was the damned fool.'[33]

Courtiers were also pressed into service: 'The King is delighted to hear that you are endeavouring to pinch as many stamps for him as you can during your travels,' one wrote to another in 1920.[34]

George V's parrot was called Charlotte, and was allowed to fly freely around rooms in the palace:

His parrot, Charlotte, ruled the table. Sometimes affable, more often bad tempered, she would roam among the plates, picking at a boiled egg or helping herself to marmalade. When she messed, George would slide the mustard pot over it so that his wife should not see.[35]

Breakfast was the only informal meal, made hazardous by the presence of the King's parrot, Charlotte, whom he allowed to roam at will.[36]

The clocks

I have no documentary proof that George V tried to introduce Sandringham time to London. But the strange *Alice in Wonderland* logic of having the clocks half an hour fast in Sandringham is an appealing detail, a way of trying to control the uncontrollable, of keeping ahead of events by living half an hour ahead of the real time. It may also have been introduced to give more daylight time for shooting. I therefore dramatised this idea by having the clocks being adjusted half an hour fast in London as well. Since the story is about the adult world losing control of events, the image of the clocks being put forward and back is something that runs throughout the story.

Mary witnesses Johnnie's big fit

Johnnie's big fit is dramatic speculation on my part. I did not have access of course to records showing exactly when Johnnie had his fits (if such records existed which they almost certainly do not). What we do know is that Johnnie's fits became increasingly more violent as he got older and were probably far more frequent than I've shown in the story. To dramatise these too often would have diminished their impact, so I had to construct one particularly vivid sequence that would demonstrate the real severity of Johnnie's disability. It was very important to me that Johnnie's illness did not become a heavy-handed metaphor: a child growing sicker as the adult world plunges into a bout of collective madness. Instead we see Johnnie's fit coming out of a moment of pure joy as he pursues the parrot through the corridors of the palace.

The images of the cars arriving at Buckingham Palace and the officials gathering are based on the fact that ultimately everything did revolve around Buckingham Palace rather than 10 Downing Street. It was George V himself who sent the ultimatum, on behalf of the government, to the Germans. And it was also at Buckingham Palace, as we shall see, that the first War Council was held. It was around the palace in London that the crowds gathered to see what was happening. This was the last time in our history that a monarch issued a declaration of war.

Part Two

The Tsar swimming and the outbreak of war

The scenes in Russia are based on the image of the Tsar mobilising the Russian Army and then going for a swim, as recounted by A. J. P. Taylor:

The Chief of the General Staff rashly said in the Tsar's presence, 'It is very hard to decide.' The Tsar, who was one of the most weak-willed men there had ever been, was roused by this and said, 'I will decide: general mobilisation.' He then, according to his diary, having made this decision, went out, found a pleasant warm day and went for a bathe in the sea. His diary does not mention mobilisation.[37]

In the film I have changed the location of the swim to a lake because it made it easier too recreate Russia in the heart of the home counties. The scenes where Stamfordham and George V visit the telephone exchange in Buckingham Palace is based on the following passage:

After a Serb fanatic murdered Archduke Ferdinand, heir to the Hapsburg throne, and his wife in Sarajevo on 28 June 1914 the terms of the ultimatum to Serbia were discussed within Austria on the phone. With the 84-year-old Emperor Franz Joseph, who originally had a desk instrument for decoration only, at the end of what was probably a poor line to Bad Ischl, his Alpine summer retreat, it was the views of ministers in Vienna led by the aggressive Foreign Secretary Berchtold that prevailed. On 23 July a stiff-termed ultimatum was sent to Belgrade, demanding a reply within 48 hours. None was expected. When a conciliatory reply was received, it was rejected by Berchtold, bent on war. Thereafter communications between the great powers were concluded in a headlong rush before they actually broke down.[38]

The 4th of August 1914 is one of the best documented days in British history. Nearly all the main protagonists wrote about their feelings on this day, including Mary who described it as

'An awful day of suspense. Several of the family came to see us at twelve. We sent an ultimatum to Germany and at 7pm she declared war on us. It is too dreadful that we could not act otherwise.'[39]

Mary was not alone in her feelings that the Germans might well back down and therefore war was still not inevitable. This day was also chronicled by Lloyd George, Asquith, Churchill and the Foreign Secretary, Sir Edward Grey. It was this last character that uttered the famous phrase: 'The lamps are going out all over Europe; we shall not see them lit again in our lifetime.'

I've left Sir Edward Grey out of the story completely because he seemed to me to be a disappointingly dull character, and there was just no space for him. But the sense of dread and foreboding that he expressed was shared by several members of the government and the royal family. There was a sense of excitement as well as the palace was surrounded by an increasingly excited crowd of spectators pressing themselves ever closer to the palace railings.

I have not dramatised the crowd because unless we had possessed an unlimited budget, it would have seemed profoundly theatrical. However I've tried to convey the adrenalin flowing among the characters through the scene of them congregating in the passage just before the ultimatum to Germany runs out. The image of the clerks all standing with their notebooks ready comes from Winston Churchill:

It was 11 pm when the ultimatum expired. The windows of the Admiralty were thrown wide open in the warm night air. Under the roof from which Nelson had received his orders, were gathered a small group of Admirals and Captains and a cluster of Clerks, pencil in hand, waiting. . . . Along the mall from the direction of the Palace the sound of an immense concourse singing 'God Save The

King' floated in. On this deep wave there broke the chimes of Big Ben and, as the first stroke of the hour boomed out, a rustle of movement swept across the room.[40]

The entry in George V's diary for 4 August 1914 reads:

I held a Council at 10.45 to declare War with Germany . . . An enormous crowd collected outside the Palace; we went on the balcony both before and after dinner. When they heard that War had been declared, the excitement increased and May and I with David went on to the balcony; the cheering was terrific.[41]

But the essential chaos of the opening sequences is based most of all on Lloyd George's remark: 'We all muddled into war.'[42]

The image of Mary's labelling all the different objects in the royal collection comes from several sources including:

There is hardly a piece of furniture, picture or print in the remotest bedroom or back passage of the royal palaces and houses on which a label is not to be found in Queen Mary's handwriting describing its subject and origin.[43]

She always had her 'one great hobby' to fall back on. And her 'one great hobby' was the care and collection of royal treasures . . . Now she spent endless hours cataloguing, matching up and reorganising and started to fill notebooks with details.[44]

Young George's desperate desire not to follow his older brothers David and Bertie into Naval College, is well documented. He was sent in 1916, just before his fourteenth birthday. Queen Mary realised that he was much more sensitive than his older brothers and tried to persuade George V to change his mind. But in the end there was nothing she could do.

The railway station

In this scene I wanted to dramatise the two brothers going their separate ways. I also show the fact that not everybody was rushing off to war in those early months in the images of the fat, surly young men watching the soldiers waiting on the platform.

There was a railway station at the bottom of the Sandringham estate, a few miles from the main house, where the King had his own private waiting room, in fact a suite of rooms. And Johnnie would have been able to hear the sound of the trains going off and indeed of the royal train arriving from his seclusion at Wood Farm. Because this station has now been converted into flats, I have chosen to locate this at King's Lynn station. I also wanted to show Hansell's increasing desire to get away from his imprisonment with Johnnie.

Johnnie moves to Wood Farm after the outbreak of war

Johnnie was moved to Wood Farm during the First World War. Most accounts that mention this give the date as 1916, although some make it as late as 1917. Young George went to Naval College in 1916. For narrative reasons, I have made these two incidents happen a year earlier – in 1915 – so that we can have a major change happening in both their lives early in Part Two.

As we have seen, Johnnie's garden and Hansell's sense of isolation are both firmly based on fact. The character Fred is a creation of mine based on somebody that Johnnie mentions in his letters.

Ernest often goes out with me . . .[45]

Ernest and I go to the fields on Sundays . . .[46]

The whole atmosphere of Lalla's frustration with the lazy servants is based on a description of the Sandringham servants who were used to enormous Edwardian meals and were shocked by the new atmosphere of austerity which began at the outbreak of war.

Breakfast was the meal at which the greatest economies of the day were practised by Queen Mary . . . the most wasteful aspect of Edwardian life had seemed to her the eight-course breakfasts . . . It was not only the Royal Family who had eaten heavily at the beginning of the day; it was the hundreds of servants as well . . . The old Edwardian servants had enormous appetites as a result of their years of good living, and rationing almost broke their hearts. This ban on alcohol came as a great blow to the lower servants and to the lords- and ladies-in-waiting, for everyone was accustomed to drinking with meals, and some of the lower servants had as fine palates as many of the Royal Family.'[47]

The Naval College passages

The Royal Naval College, Osborne, was a very Spartan place. It was even worse than Young George had imagined it would be. The following quotes are from a contemporary of his at the Naval College:

In wartime the lights were low and we had blue lights along the corridors . . . In the morning you started off by rushing into the plunge room where you washed, cleaned your teeth and then at a signal you plunged into about 6ft of absolutely ice cold water, which in the winter was covered with ice.[48]

Most of the teaching there was awful but there was one inspirational teacher, Callender, eccentric but dynamic, who imitated Queen Elizabeth and Sir Francis Drake and had written a book called The Sea Kings.

The only tutor remembered with respect and affection was Professor Geoffrey Callender. He taught naval history and English, and impressed the cadets the most. He was the author of Sea Kings of Britain which was his principal book in the classroom . . . He was good at teaching. He had a keen sense of humour and a very attractive voice, which made history extremely interesting to us . . . He would throw his academic gown over his shoulder and become Queen Elizabeth knighting Francis Drake and that sort of thing . . .

Two boys were 'discovered experimenting' with what are called the facts of life. Class teachers were instructed to find out what the boys knew about sex. Callender . . . unfortunately used long scientific words and no one could make out what he was talking about. He tried again: 'Has anybody in this class ever slid down the banister?' All hands rose in the affirmative. 'Let any boy who, whilst sliding down the banister, felt a guilty but pleasurable sensation hold up his hand.' Nobody moved. Callender smiled and remarked, 'You will be well advised not to slide down banisters. The class is dismissed. [49]

I have also used Callender as a way of showing the extent of anti-German feeling during the war which was whipped up by the propaganda stories about German atrocities that were circulating widely at the time. Young George did very well in his initial term at Naval College, but then things began to deteriorate rapidly. A former pupil described young George as 'a charming, very shy but delightful chap and sometimes we used to tease him a bit and he used to be so confused. He, of course, was extremely good at French and History but otherwise he was not high up in term.'[50] Prince George fared no better than his brothers in the naval classroom. Prince Albert wrote of him, 'He has kept up the best traditions of my family by passing out of Dartmouth one from bottom, the same place I did.'

Hansell leaves for the war

Hansell did go off to the war, leaving Lalla alone with Johnnie and the servants. He was extremely old to enlist and it must have been because of his handsome face that he was able to pass himself off as slightly younger. The image of him disappearing over the horizon to an uncertain fate suggests that he may well become one of the countless casualties of the war. In fact Hansell did survive the war.

Hansell continued as mentor to Prince Edward when, as Prince of Wales, he was an undergraduate at Magdalen College, Oxford, and later during his residence in France as guest of the Marquis de Breteuil. He served with gallantry and distinction in the First World War and died in 1935 aged seventy-two.[51]

The mustard water treatment administered to Johnnie during this scene is based on the following passage from a contemporary medical book on epilepsy:

Should a patient feel unwell between dinner and tea, instead of eating his tea he must empty his bowels by an enema or croton oil, and his stomach by drinking a pint of warm water in which has been stirred a tablespoonful of mustard powder and a teaspoonful of salt. After vomiting, drink warm water . . . after the stomach has been empty ten minutes, the patient should take a double dose of bromides and go to bed.[52]

Johnnie goes out on his pony with his household

Johnnie did make excursions out of Wood Farm with his household. The image of Mary and her ladies-in-waiting going foraging for chestnuts for the munitions workers is described in the following passage: 'Queen Mary and her ladies-in-waiting spent afternoons picking up chestnuts for munitions factories and supervised collection of jam jars and scrap iron from neighbouring villages.'[53]

Mary's extraordinary burst of activity during the war is described in many of the royal biographies. Her energy and inability to remain still found a natural focus: 'Her country's needs were great and Queen Mary filled her days with visits to hospitals – often as many as three or four in one afternoon – munitions factories and soup kitchens.'[54]

Mary's visit to the farmhouse

As mentioned above, Mary had a powerful need to remain occupied at all times:

> She was never able to relax nor did she want to. She had a strong aversion to wasting time, 'I like energy and doing and seeing things, but the way people fritter away their time and their vitality doing absolutely nothing makes me furious.' She was always very punctual, in complete contrast to her mother-in-law, Queen Alexandra, who was late for everything.[55]

Mary's aversion to ivy was just one of the more eccentric manifestations of her love of order and discipline, even in nature. 'She used to cut down trees that were in the way and had an almost symbolic hatred of ivy, which offended her passion for order and tidiness. She would arrive at someone's house and seeing them out set to work stripping it off the walls.'[56]

I have invented the episode with the gramophone, but it is firmly based on one of the best-known aspects of Mary's behaviour, her habit of collecting things that had caught her eye from people's front rooms when she came to visit them. When Mary was visiting a town the antique shops would often all close rather than have to give her anything that she liked for free. And some of her hosts in great country houses would conceal objects that they felt she might covet in the most unlikely places such as the lavatory reserved for gentlemen visitors. Mary's legendary habit of expecting to be given objects from other people's houses have led to the accusation that she was a kleptomaniac, pocketing things behind people's backs whenever she felt like it.

There is no evidence that she shoplifted her way around the antiques shops and stately homes of England but she could be incredibly persistent when an antique caught her fancy and it was almost impossible to stop her leaving without it. The episode with the gramophone allowed me to dramatise two aspects of Mary's behaviour in one incident – her passionate desire to help the war effort and the near hopelessness of stopping her removing an object once she had set her mind on it.

We see in these scenes the intriguing contrast at the heart of Mary, her obsessive, neurotic energy that makes her in one way a peculiarly modern character and her deep desire to preserve and conserve the past.

George's education at Naval College

George began to slip rapidly from first place down the classroom until he was second from bottom. He was completely bored by the place and alienated by everything that went on there. It was only his ability in French that stopped him becoming the bottom of the class. Eventually his boredom turned to despair as he became more and more lonely at the college.

The visit to wartime Sandringham

The gardens of Sandringham were transformed during the War and I wanted to show the impact this would have had on the gardens that Johnnie knew so well:

> Maids, while listening to the gramophone after tea, heard a whizzing drone of aircraft cross the park. A bomb dropped forming a crater. Flower gardens disappeared under rows of vegetables.[57]

The description of Queen Alexandra in this dark and shut-away world, are based on contemporary descriptions of her as 'an old lady of ghostly and tenuous beauty'. Another describes her during an audience at Marlborough House as 'a mummied thing, the bird-like head cocked on one side, not artfully but by disease, the red-rimmed eyes, the enamelled face, which the famous smile scissored across, all angular and heart-rending'. But '"The ghosts of all her lovely airs" remained; "the little graces, the once effective sway and movement of the figure." Still, the image of "her bony fingers, clashing in the tunnel of their rings, fiddled with albums, penholders, photographs, toys upon the table . . ." is one of wizened age and becomes more and more terrible when one recalls how much youth and beauty were prized by Queen Alexandra'.[58]

Queen Alexandra suggesting that they find a ball for Johnnie to play with is based on the following letter that Alexandra wrote after visiting Johnnie at Wood Farm: 'I found him playing football with Charlotte and the other ladies of his household! He is very proud of his house but is longing for a companion . . . he came rushing up to see me.'[59]

Johnnie coming across the image of the Fine Looking Woman consumed by anxiety in the dark garden, is clearly intended as an image of the grief and suffering caused by the War and how it touched everybody irrespective of class and position. It is also a harbinger of the transformed atmosphere at the court which, as we will see, became extremely frugal and austere.

George V and Alexandra alone together

George V cut back on his shooting greatly during the First World War, but he did have a few much-scaled-down shooting parties. He went to the Front several times and on one occasion was thrown by his horse:

> It was while inspecting troops in France on 28 October 1915 that the King suffered one of the cruellest misfortunes of his life . . . He mounted a chestnut mare . . . What had not been foreseen was the extraordinary noise emitted by 20 flying men trying to cheer. The wretched animal reared up like a rocket and came over backwards.[60]

The incident caused him a great deal of pain and did nothing for his temper. He made the Tsar a Field Marshal on 27 December 1915, writing to him:

> 'King George V to Nicky – 27 December 1915 –
> Buckingham Palace.
> Emperor of Russia: On the occasion of our New Year, when our two Armies are fighting against a Common Enemy, I am anxious to appoint you a Field Marshal in my Army as a mark of my affection for you. If you accept, it will be a great pleasure to me, and an honour to the British Army.'[61]

War propaganda

The anti-German propaganda started immediately war was declared. There was a secret meeting in September 1914 between members of the government and some of Britain's most famous authors including Arnold Bennett, Conan Doyle and Kipling who were encouraged to write anti-German propaganda. They were taken to the war zone and then wrote reports about their experience, which were full of praise for allied soldiers and generals but concealed the real conditions of trench warfare.

The government set up a commission to investigate alleged German outrages under the chairmanship of Lord Bryce in December 1914. The Bryce Report, published in early 1915, was the origin of most of the gruesome stories about German atrocities – mass rapes, babies being bayoneted, the cutting off of children's hands and women's breasts, hostages being murdered, etc.

The story about a German corpse factory that is referred to later in the script was reported in *The Times* thus:

> One of the US consuls, on leaving Germany in February 1917, stated in Switzerland that the Germans were distilling glycerine from the bodies of their dead.[62]

Mary's hospital visit

Mary visited hospitals regularly during the War and was very conscientious in her duties. She saw hundreds of wounded men, some of them in the most appalling condition and she must have been more aware than many of her subjects about the reality of life in the trenches. Although seeing all these young men in pain obviously saddened her, it did not for a moment lead her to question the wisdom of the war. She began to see it as a fight to the death which if the British were to loose would result in the collapse of the monarchy. She recorded this in her diary:

> Went to Milbanke Hospital to see 214 of our badly wounded soldiers who were prisoners in Germany & have been exchanged. It was very pathetic seeing so many men without arms, legs, eyes, etc. They were all wonderfully brave & patient & so thankful to be home again.[63]

The anti-German feeling that was soon to drive the Royal Family to change their name manifested itself in all sorts of ways. Dachshunds were stoned on the street (which we see mentioned in the previous scene) and the shop windows of those with German names were smashed.

The scene of Mary alone in her study, and her deep sense of Englishness is based, amongst other things, on the following letter that she wrote to her Aunt Augusta after the Coronation: 'To me who love tradition & the past, & who am English from top to toe, the service was a very real solemn thing . . . The foreigners seemed much impressed and were most nice and feeling . . .'[64]

We also know that these feelings were shared by George: 'In spite of an ancestry that for centuries had thrived on infusions of German blood, the King considered himself to be wholly and impregnably British. When HG Wells spoke of "an alien and uninspiring Court", the King retorted, "I may be uninspiring, but I'll be damned if I'm an alien."'[65]

The scene between Mary and Young George is based on the following sources, which clearly show a touching shared interest between them. He was the only one in the family to be interested in the same things as she was. Nevertheless Mary was extremely inhibited with her own children and found it very difficult to express any kind of emotion verbally.

From his earliest years he showed that he had inherited his mother's amazing memory . . . Dancing and music lessons were no difficulty to him. He was a born dancer and he is naturally musical, having a gift for composing as well as being an accomplished and sympathetic pianist . . . He loved beautiful things, harmonious colours, artistic effects of all kinds and of all her children it is Prince George who has shown the deepest interest and understanding of Queen Mary's hobby of collecting antiques.[66]

The royal family changes its name

The royal family instigated an extremely frugal regime during the First World War in contrast to what was going on elsewhere among the upper classes. According to the memoirs of the Royal Chef Gabriel Tschumi, 'Every member of the Royal Family has a ration book, and it is rarely possible for more than four courses to be served.'[67]

I have dramatised this in the banquet scene, which is meant to be a shadowy, ghostly reprise of the great banquet in Part One. I needed to bring several images of Spartan living into one scene, hence the heating being switched off and the rain dripping through a ceiling in one of the rooms. But I also needed to show the depression that was beginning to take its grip on the adult world. We are seeing this sequence through Young George's eyes, who has been shut away in Naval College and is seeing some of these characters for the first time in a long while. The sequence dramatises both the austerity at the court and the huge stress the characters were beginning to feel. The king and queen had reduced the number of courses served at all royal functions. But George V still hankered after his favourite dish.

King George loved Bombay Duck and curry which was served every day at lunch if there were no guests . . . He was miserable during the War when it was no longer available. In 1916 I tried as a substitute providing a chicken curry with a very dry grilled kipper, which I had prepared to resemble Bombay Duck as much as possible, but it was not a success. Then came the order '. . . there was to be no wine served with royal meals . . . M Cedard . . . sent up a note asking what was to be served at mealtimes. The answer came back, boiled water with sugar.' [68]

It was during a meal at Buckingham Palace that a character called Lady Warrender made a fateful intervention which led to our present royal family being called Windsor. The change was made with lightning speed in a matter of seven days, although the King's initial reaction was extremely hostile:

At a small dinner party at Buckingham Palace towards the end of May, Lady Maud Warrender confided to Queen Mary that rumours abounded that the royal family must be pro-German since their surnames were German. King George, who overheard this remark, 'started and grew pale'. Moments later, he left the gathering, quite disturbed; and shortly after, the Queen made a polite but early departure. Lady Maud had inadvertently propelled the King into an historic decision.[69]

Lalla's life with Johnnie at Wood Farm

Johnnie's fits became progressively more severe during the First World War. 'We tried everything,' Lalla Bill remembered, 'but nothing would stop those fits…We dare not let him be with his brothers and sister because it upset them so much, with the attacks getting so bad and coming so often.' [70]

There is very little recorded of Lalla's comments about life in Wood Farm for obvious reasons – they were isolated from the rest of the family and received few visitors. But we do know of Lalla's undying devotion to Johnnie and can clearly feel her sense of vocation from the remarks she made towards the end of her life.

> All the York children were mischievous but Lalla Bill often referred to as Mrs Bill, [as was the custom in royal service, even though she was unmarried] remembered Prince John as a well behaved child in general. He was always her favourite. A no-nonsense countrywoman who understood the particular needs of a royal child. Lalla Bill trained her charges carefully. She tried to overcome their shyness. Royalty must recognise and remember people they meet so she invented memory games to play with the children on walks.[71]

The royal family's change of name

Stamfordham played a crucial role in changing the name, as we see from the following quote. The actual change of name happened surprisingly late in the War, in May 1917. This was a few weeks *after* the decision not to allow the Russian royal family into the country. I have reversed the order of these two episodes because clearly the story of the Russians is so very much more dramatic than the royal family changing their name. It also helps to dramatise how vulnerable the royal family felt in the face of considerable hostility and republican feelings amongst some sections of the population.

> Since the Saxe-Coburg family belonged to the House of Wettin in the District of Wipper, Wettin or Wipper might be more appropriate . . . but both were considered 'unsuit-ably comic' . . . In the end, Lord Stamfordham had the final distinction of christening a dynasty. Edward III, he recalled, had been known as Edward of Windsor . . . And

certainly, the name 'Windsor' was 'as English as the earth upon which the castle stood . . .'[72]

The bizarre fact that the Kaiser was honorary head of certain British regiments at the very moment these regiments were locked in bloody battle with the Germans, is one of the most overlooked facts about the First World War. There was strong resistance initially from the King that the Kaiser should be relieved of his honorary posts for, I suspect, the reasons that Mary gives in the scene. And it was in fact Queen Alexandra (who despised the Kaiser) who prevailed upon George that it would be a good idea.

Queen Alexandra, who never forgot or forgave Prussian aggression against her native Denmark, wrote of him [the Kaiser] to Prince George in 1888, 'Oh he is mad and a conceited ass – who also says that Papa and Grandmama don't treat him with proper respect as the Emperor of old and mighty Germany. But my hope is that pride will have a fall some day and won't we rejoice then!'

He [George] also objected to proposals that the Kaiser and his family should be deprived of their honorary commands of British regiments; that their Garter banners should be removed from St George's Chapel, Windsor; that they should be stripped of their honorary appointments to British orders of chivalry . . .

Queen Alexandra, in a letter to her son, echoed the wide resentment of his subjects: 'Although as a rule I never interfere, I think the time has come when I must speak out . . . It is but right and proper for you to have down those hateful German banners in our sacred Church, St George's at Windsor.'[73]

Young George's escape to Wood Farm

Young George's flight to Wood Farm is dramatic speculation on my part. I feel certain that Young George would have visited there, because of all the children, he was most devoted to Johnnie. He also felt tremendously alone during the war. It is important perhaps to paint a picture of what occurred to Young George later on in order to understand why I felt free to characterise him as a rebellious spirit.

Young George, the future Duke of Kent, became a playboy after the First World War and was heavily dependent on drugs. He was bisexual and is widely believed to have had an affair with Noël Coward before he married Princess Marina of Greece, and died in a plane accident in the Second World War. There is amazingly no biography of this fascinating figure, somebody who was clearly far too intelligent and sensitive for the repetitive routine of royal life. From what happened to him afterwards, I have drawn inferences from how he would have behaved during these very dark days for him at Naval College.

The King changes his mind about the Tsar's arrival and Stamfordham visits Lloyd George

Lord Stamfordham kept notes of what happened during this crucial period, and Kenneth Rose, in his biography of King George V, was one of the first historians to tell the world how the Russian royal family was prevented from seeking sanctuary in England. Stamfordham's notes show unequivocally, who was responsible.

9 March 1917 – Buckingham Palace.
I pointed out the King's apprehensions entailed in the sea voyage from Romanov. The Prime Minister asked why the Emperor should not come to Bergen.'

Mr Lloyd George suggested that the King might be

able to place at His Imperial Majesty's disposal one of his houses, but I reminded the Prime Minister that the King had got no houses except Balmoral, which would certainly not be a suitable residence at this time of year.

After Stamfordham had tried hard to persuade Lloyd George there was nowhere in Britain for the Russian royal family to stay, he moved on to stress another of the King's concerns:

With regard to the Prime Minister's Message to the Russian Premier, which was dispatched yesterday, I said that the King thought it was a little strong to say 'that the Revolution is the greatest service which the Russian people have yet made to the cause for which the Allies are fighting . . . [The Prime Minister] explained that the message was framed to a considerable extent on the suggestions of Monsieur Nabokov at the Russian Embassy, who was anxious that we should emphasise the fact that responsible Government had been established, and that it was the establishment of a stable Constitutional Government, which appealed to us as one of the oldest Constitutional Governments . . . I answered that the word 'Revolution' had a disagreeable sound coming from a good old Monarchical Government, but good humouredly the Prime Minister replied, 'No, an old Constitutional Government,' and added that our present Monarchy was founded upon a Revolution, which I could not deny. Mr Lloyd George wished me to assure the King that the message was approved by the Cabinet, and he hoped His Majesty would interpret it in the sense above indicated.'[74]

Kenneth Rose in his biography of George V describes these events in a devastating passage:

Only once throughout four years of war did the King persuade Lloyd George to change course on an important matter of policy. It proved in retrospect to be the most perplexing act of his reign: the abandonment of a loyal ally and much-loved cousin to degradation and death.

In the contrasting attitudes of King and Prime Minister lay the seeds of a persistent myth: that it was the King who strove to rescue his cousin from the perils of the Russian Revolution, only to be thwarted by a heartless and opportunist Lloyd George. The late Lord Mountbatten, with all the authority of close kinship and apparent omniscience, gave currency to the legend. As a nephew of the Tsar – his mother and the Russian Empress were sisters – he continued to proclaim almost to the end of his life that Lloyd George's hands were stained with the blood of the Imperial family. Correspondence between the King and his ministers in March and April 1917 reveals a different chain of events leading to the murder of the Tsar and his family fifteen months later. It shows that the British Government would willingly have offered them asylum but for the fears expressed by Buckingham Palace; and that at the most critical moment in their fortunes they were deserted not by a radical Prime Minister seeking to appease his supporters, but by their ever-affectionate Cousin George.[75]

Lord Stamfordham wrote to AJ Balfour on 17 March:

My dear Balfour,
The King has been thinking much about the Government's proposal that the Emperor Nicholas and his Family should come to England.

As you are doubtless aware the King has a strong personal friendship for the Emperor and therefore would be glad to do anything to help him in this crisis. But His

Majesty cannot help doubting, not only on account of the dangers of the voyage, but on general grounds of expediency, whether it is advisable that the Imperial Family should take up their residence in this country. The King would be glad if you could consult the Prime Minister, as His Majesty understands no definite decision has yet been come to on the subject by the Russian Government . . . Yours very truly, Stamfordham.[76]

Young George's outburst to Lalla in the farmhouse

Young George's despair about his life at Naval College has already been mentioned and Lalla's high opinion of Young George's talent was a view held by many people who had known him as a young child.

George was a handful. He was academically, musically and culturally more gifted than the others.[77]

If intelligence, affability, cleverness and insight were necessary requisites for a monarch, this fourth son, fifth in succession, was the most qualified to be King.[78]

The idea of Johnnie taking such an interest in the Russian Royal Family and his daydreaming about them coming to live with him in exile is an invention on my part. However it is based on the documentary evidence of his great loneliness at Wood Farm, his yearning for the company of other children.

George V sends messages to the Prime Minister about the Tsar

George V kept up the pressure on Lloyd George, sending several messages, sometimes twice a day, about withdrawing the invitation to the Tsar to come to England. Lord Stamfordham wrote to AJ Balfour twice on the same day:

My dear Balfour,

Every day the King is becoming more concerned about the question of the Emperor and Empress of Russia coming to this country.

His Majesty receives letters from people in all classes of life, known or unknown to him, saying how much the matter is being discussed, not only in Clubs but by working men, and that Labour Members in the House of Commons are expressing adverse opinions to the proposal.

As you know from the first the King has thought the presence of the Imperial Family (especially of the Empress) in this country would raise all sorts of difficulties, and I feel sure that you appreciate how awkward it will be for our Royal Family who are closely connected both with the Emperor and Empress.

My dear Balfour,

The King wishes me to write again on the subject of my letter of this morning. He must beg you to represent to the Prime Minister that from all he hears and reads in the Press, the residence in this Country of the Ex-Emperor and Empress would be strongly resented by the public, and would undoubtedly compromise the position of the King and Queen from whom it is already generally supposed the invitation has emanated.[79]

The scene between George V and Mary at a very low point in the War

This is one of the very few scenes between Mary and George alone together in the whole story. They were devoted to each other but found it extremely difficult to put this devotion into words. Their most heartfelt feelings were expressed in letters to each other. Both of them were painfully inarticulate about their emotions except on paper, and even then George V's language was very limited and stilted when he tried to express his love.

Mary was sad to see less of her husband and was worried they were drifting apart due to the extra workload caused by the death of Edward VII. King George wrote to her: 'You have never left me for a single day since that sad event. I fear my darling, my nature is not demonstrative, but I want you to understand that I am indeed grateful to you . . . and to thank you from the bottom of my heart for all your love and comfort . . . My love grows stronger for you every day . . .'

Queen Mary replied the letter had given her 'such untold pleasure...What a pity it is you cannot *tell* me what you write for I should appreciate it so enormously.' 'I am glad my letter pleased,' answered King George '. . . somehow I always find it difficult to express what I feel except in a letter, especially to the person I love and am always with, like you darling.'[80]

On 1 March 1918, the Germans opened their final all-out offensive of the Western Front. For several days it seemed as though the offensive might prove successful and the King left for France to see the situation for himself. It was a truly dark time for both of them. Mary confided her deepest fears to George in a letter, and repeated them in her diary: 'I have never in my life suffered so much mentally as I am suffering now and I know you are feeling the same.'[81]

Mary meets Johnnie and the servants on the way to Sandringham

The encounter between Mary and Johnnie and his household on the road is a direct continuation of the fears expressed in Mary's diary. By this time the Russian royal family had been put under house arrest and their fate was very uncertain. It was very natural for the British royal family to feel distinctly uneasy about their own fate. In a few months, three of the great Royal Houses of Europe were to fall completely.

Johnnie's strange posy is based on his letters (see Part One), which are full of information about his garden and flowers that he is sending as gifts (one of the letters actually still contains some pressed flowers).

Mary continued to be desperately anxious for news from the Front and was informed about developments on a daily basis. She made terse and anxious notes in her diary as the news became more and more grave:

> March 23rd 1918 – Heavy fighting and many casualties.
>
> March 24th – Our troops have to go back a good way.
>
> March 25th – Not very good news from France. We all feel very anxious.[82]

George V and Mary are informed about the murder of the Russian royal family by the Bolsheviks

I have conflated time and dates, as I have done throughout the script, to bring the great offensive by the Germans and the death of the Russian royal family closer together. In fact, George V and Mary heard the news about the Tsar on July 24. They were in London at the time and heard about it in the morning rather than at night. But for sake of the right kind of dramatic movement in the last section of the script I needed them to be down in the country where Johnnie could pay them a visit.

Mary was horrified by the news but it was if this was just one other calamity that the war had caused. There is no evidence that she felt George V and her were in any way responsible for the fate of the Russian royal family.

Mary recorded receiving the news thus in her diary, 'I was

up and nearly dressed to receive him. The news were confirmed of poor Nicky of Russia having been shot by those brutes of Bolsheviks, last week on July 16th. It is too horrible and heartless.'[83]

And Mary listed the names of his wife and children in pencil with one of them rubbed out and rewritten when she realised she had written the same name twice.

The details of the murder of the Russian royal family are well known and several of the people involved in their execution wrote an account of it: What is more, both the Tsar and the Tsarina kept a diary of their last days:

28 June/11 July 1918 – Ekaterinburg

In the morning at 10.30 three workmen came up to the open window, lifted up a heavy grill and fixed it to the outside of the frame . . . Yurovsky [responsible for organizing the Russian Royal's murder] the commandant ordered that the corpses be stripped . . . When they started to undress one of the girls, they realised that in the places where her corset had been torn by the bullets – diamonds could be seen . . .[84]

So now we come to the question of whether George V felt guilty about his actions. For dramatic reasons I wanted him to question the role he had played. The truth is that he or those around him, managed to suppress his own involvement in the fate of the Russian royal family from being reported during his lifetime. On the other hand, he was advised not to attend a memorial service for the Russian Royal Family in London because of their extreme unpopularity amongst certain sections of the British public. But he ignored this advice and he attended the service with Mary.

Since George was a man of uncomplicated emotions, I think he would have been truly shocked by what happened, but not necessarily haunted by his own involvement. Mary's anguish is based on her diary entry (above) and also the fact that she clearly had fond memories of her days with the Russian children at the Isle of Wight. She was capable of great compassion, but her overriding concern was in preserving the British monarchy. Her belief that the world was near total collapse is best expressed by her passionate entry in her diary on the day of the armistice:

Monday, November 11th 1918 – The greatest day in the world's history! [85]

Johnnie's recital

Johnnie's recital is an invention on my part. It is a way of dramatising the extraordinary sense of grief and disillusion that the Royal Family and the whole country felt. It is also a way of illustrating the emotions that Johnnie aroused in all the main protagonists of the story when he died. The fact that he was totally uninvolved with the catastrophe that had overtaken their family and indeed the whole of Europe, made his sudden death both shocking and very upsetting for them. They'd had no time for him, but when he was no longer there they realised how much they missed him.

Mary had visibly aged during the war. By the end of 1916, she was going grey and she suffered from neuritis in one arm. Queen Alexandra was a mere shadow of her former self. All the older children had been made to do recitals throughout their childhood. There was, therefore, an irresistible dramatic logic in Johnnie ending his life by giving a recital.

The sense of grief for what had happened during the war that Queen Alexandra especially feels, is based not only on the previously quoted descriptions of her, but on her great anguish at Johnnie's funeral.

For Queen Alexandra, little Prince John's death was another great sadness to survive. She lingered at his small grave after his quiet funeral at Sandringham, heavily veiled and supported by Charlotte Knollys and Sir Dighton Probyn, and long after Queen Mary had departed.[86]

Johnnie's death

Johnnie died suddenly after a very bad fit on 18 January 1919. By extraordinary coincidence it was the opening day of the peace conference at Versailles. Mary wrote about the day of Johnnie's death and driving down to see his body. George V was in the car with her, but there is no mention of him actually going into the farmhouse to see Johnnie's corpse.

Mary records finding Lalla heart-broken in the parlour and she muses that although Johnnie might have found a release from his suffering, it was still a great shock. She describes the villagers and the household attending Johnnie's funeral and how pleasing and touching this was.

Saturday, May 18th 1919. At 5.30 Lala Bill telephoned me from Wood Farm, Wolferton that our poor darling little Johnnie had passed away suddenly after one of his epileptic attacks. The news gave me a great shock tho' for the poor little boy's restless soul, death came as a great release. I broke the news to George and we motored down to Wood Farm. Found poor Lalla very resigned but heart-broken. Little Johnnie looked very peaceful lying there.[87]

Tuesday 21st 1919. Canon Dalton & Dr Brownhill conducted the service which was awfully sad and touching. Many of our own people and the villagers were present. We thanked all Johnnie's servants who have been so good and faithful to him.[88]

And for a while in her utterances and the letters and diary entries she wrote immediately after his death one looks in vain for a sentence that describes her own feelings about Johnnie's death. Her language is very objective and one begins to suspect that she wasn't that affected, and then a single entry that she wrote a few days after his death leaps out from all the surrounding dry entries, a sentence that burns with sorrow:

Wednesday 22nd 1919 – *Miss the dear child very much indeed.*[89]

Mary's immediate diary entry on the day of Johnnie's death is more concerned with how racked with grief Lalla was, so I wrote the scene of them together in the parlour.

Lalla continued to be haunted by Johnnie for the rest of her life. In 1960 the Duke of Windsor reminisced about his childhood with her for his book, *A Family Album*. Aged 86 she is still as 'lively in her mind and as quick in her responses as ever.' Her recollections include the fact that she deplored the thick and bulky clothes the royal children were made to wear as babies. She also 'has a photograph, blown up to the dimensions of a sizeable oil painting of my youngest brother John, dressed like some beautiful doll, with the skirts of two voluminous petticoats, one of flannel and the other of muslin, emerging from beneath his cambric frock, and with thick white stockings and tight buttoned boots encasing his legs and feet.'[90]

Lalla sitting in retirement in her cottage in a room dominated by a giant photograph of Johnnie is a surreal and moving image of her life-long devotion. I did not wish to end *The Lost Prince* by flashing forward to modern times and showing Lalla with her photograph but I did try to express in the final scenes her powerful almost obsessive love for this special boy.

References

The permission of Her Majesty Queen Elizabeth II to include material from the Royal Archives is gratefully acknowledged.

1   Sydney Holland (2nd Viscount Knutsford), *In Black & White*, (Edward Arnold, 1926) 231-9 & 243

2   Ibid.

3   © Sarah Bradford, *George VI*, (Weidenfeld, 1989, Penguin 2002) 51

4   The Duke of Windsor, *A King's Story – Memoirs of HRH The Duke of Windsor,* (Cassell, 1951) 67

5   Ibid., 57

6   Richard Hough: *Born Royal, The Lives and Loves of The Young Windsors, 1894-1937,* (Deutsch, 1988) 52

7   Sydney Holland, 237

8   John Van Der Kiste, *George V's Children* (A Sutton, 1965)

9   Sydney Holland, 237

10 Charlotte Zeepvat, *Royalty Digest*, March 1998

11   Stephen Koss, *Asquith* (London: Hamish Hamilton, 1985)

12 The Duke of Windsor, *A King's Story*

13 Charlotte Zeepvat, *Royalty Digest*, March 1998

14 James Pope-Hennessy, *Queen Mary*, (Allen & Unwin, 1959) 77

15 Charlotte Zeepvat, *Royalty Digest*, March 1998

16 David Duff, *Queen Mary*, (Collins, 1985) 134

17 Anne Edwards, *Matriarch: Queen Mary & The House of Windsor*, (Hodder & Stoughton, 1984) 171

18 Letter to the Daily Mail from F. Hollingsworth, 2 February 1998

19 Charlotte Zeepvat, *Royalty Digest*, March 1998

20 *Lytton Strachey* Michael Holroyd (Vintage: 1995)

21 Harold Nicolson, *Diaries and Letters* (Collins: 1968)

22 Robert Lacey, *Majesty, Elizabeth II & The House of Windsor* (New York, Harcourt Inc. 1977)

23 Quoted in Kenneth Rose, *King George V,* (Phoenix Press, 2000) 92 & 173

24 Dennis Judd, *King George VI 1895-1962* (Michael Joseph, 1982)

25 Sir John Wheeler-Bennett, *George VI,* (Macmillan, 1965) 23-4

26 Quoted in James Pope-Hennessy, *Queen Mary,* 467

27 Quoted in Kenneth Rose, 157

28 Charlotte Zeepvat, *Royalty Digest,* March 1998

29 Queen Mary's diary, Royal Archive

30 James Pope-Hennessy, *Queen Mary,* 479-80

31 Prince John's letter, Royal Archive, 21 February 1916 (RA GV/AA 60/103)

32 Prince John's letter, Royal Archive, May 1918 (RA GV/AA 60/313)

33 Frederick Ponsonby, *Recollections of Three Reigns,* (Quartet Books, 1988) 283

34 Quoted in Kenneth Rose, 40-1

35 David Duff, 174-5

36 Kenneth Rose, *King George V,* 291-2

37 A.J.P Taylor, *British Prime Ministers and Other essays,* (Allen Lane, 1999) 201

38 Peter Young, *The International Impact of the Telephone,* (Granta Editions, 1991) 91

39 Queen Mary's diary, August 4, 1914, The Royal Archive

40 Winston Churchill, *World Crisis – an abridgement of the classic 4 volume History of World War 1* (New York: Charles Scribner's and Sons, 1992)

41 Quoted in Kenneth Rose, 168

42 A.J.P Taylor, 195

43 *A Crowded Life – the autobiography of Lady Cynthia Colville* (Evans Bros, 1963)

44 David Duff, 175

45 Johnnie's letter of May 1918, The Royal Archive (RA GV/AA 60/313)

46 Johnnie's letter of 3 June 1918, The Royal Archive (RA GV/AA 60/316)

47 Gabriel Tschumi, *Recollections of a Life in Royal Households from Queen Victoria to Queen Mary*, (Kimber, 1954)133-4 & 137

48 L. Cowland, interview in *Naval Life* (King Hall)

49 Ibid.

50 Ibid.

51 Sir John Wheeler-Bennett, 23-4

52 Isaac G Briggs, *Epilepsy, Hysteria & Neurasthenia* (1921)

53 *The History of Sandringham*

54 Anne Edwards, 244

55 James Pope-Hennessy, *Queen Mary*

56 James Pope-Hennessy, Ed. Peter Quinnell, *A Lonely Business – A self-portrait of James Pope-Hennessy* (London: Weidenfeld & Nicolson, 1981)

57 *History of Sandringham*

58 Anne Edwards, 278

59 Quoted in Anne Edwards, *Matriarch; Queen Mary & The House of Windsor*

60 Kenneth Rose, *King George V*, 180-1

61 Andre Maylunas & Sergei Mironenko, *A Life Long Passion – Nicholas and Alexandra, their own story* (Weidenfeld & Nicolson, 1996), 446

62 *The Times*, 16 April 1916

63 Quoted in James Pope-Hennessy, *Queen Mary*

64 Quoted in James Pope-Hennessy, *Queen Mary*, 442

65 Quoted in Kenneth Rose, 174

66 Keith V Gordon, *Their Royal Highnesses The Duke and Duchess of Kent*, (Hutchinson, 1941) 29 & 59

67 Gabriel Tschumi, 129

68 Ibid, 130-1

69 Anne Edwards, 263

70 Charlotte Zeepvat, Article in *Royalty Digest*, March 1998

71 Ibid.

72 Anne Edwards, 264

73 Kenneth Rose, 164 & 173

74 Andre Maylunas & Sergei Mironenko, 560

75 Kenneth Rose, 210

76 Andre Maylunas & Sergei Mironenko, 560-2

77 Keith V. Gordon, 23

78 Anne Edwards, 171

79 Andre Maylunas & Sergei Mironenko, 567-8

80 James Pope-Hennessy, *Queen Mary*, 426

81 Queen Mary's diary, Royal Archive

82 Ibid.

83 Ibid.

84 Andre Maylunas & Sergei Mironenko, 633 & 637

85 Queen Mary's diary, Royal Archive

86 Anne Edwards, 278

87 Quoted in James Pope-Hennessy, *Queen Mary*, 511

88 Queen Mary's diary, Royal Archive

89 Ibid.

90 Duke of Windsor, *A Family Album* (Cassell: 1960)

THE LOST PRINCE

Part One

INT. SANDRINGHAM. CORRIDOR BY STAIRWAY. NIGHT.

A boy of about five is walking towards us down the corridor of a great house lined by large clumsy lamps and tables covered in bric-à-brac. The boy is JOHNNIE. *He has a wide, rather handsome face and fair hair. He is dressed in the neat sailor costume of an Edwardian upper-class child. His small figure is dwarfed by the bulky furniture and ornaments.*

He pauses as he gets near to us. The passage he is in is quite dark, but ahead of him a lighted room is beckoning, and from it comes the sound of loud laughter.

JOHNNIE *moves towards the blaze of light.*

His entrance into the room is barred by the backs of royal servants, flunkies standing watching what is going on in the room. They have not noticed him.

JOHNNIE *squeezes through a gap between the tall servants and slips into the room.*

INT. SANDRINGHAM. LARGE ROOM. NIGHT.

In front of him in the middle of the room is a group of children, his siblings, HENRY, MAY *and* YOUNG GEORGE, *all older than him.*

They are clustered around a deep armchair in which is reclining a huge plump adult figure.

From JOHNNIE'*s point of view, as he moves round his siblings, he can at first only see the great thick legs of the adult.*

Next to the legs, a thin-faced servant is standing with a silver tray on which are several small pats of butter, just beginning to get slightly soft.

JOHNNIE *squeezes into a good position by the servant, and now we see for the first time the face of the old King,* EDWARD, *sitting in the chair.*

EDWARD: Everybody ready . . . Ready for the off?! . . .

EDWARD *pulls himself up with difficulty out of the chair, steadies himself, and stands very straight, his legs slightly apart. He commands the servant.*

EDWARD: Put them on, butchers, put them on! . . . Before they all melt too much . . . Everybody picked their runner . . . ?

The servant stoops by EDWARD'*s legs and applies a little pat of butter at the top of each crease of* EDWARD'*s trousers.*

As he does this, EDWARD *sees* JOHNNIE *is standing there watching.*

EDWARD: Come on, Johnnie – you're not too late . . . You can pick one too . . . Hurry though, they are already off – no stopping them now . . . !

The pats of butter begin to slide down the creases of his trousers. There is a race to see which pat of butter reaches the floor first. The King's voice barks out again.

Which one is yours, Johnnie?

The other children are urging their butter on – clearly this is a game they have played before.

JOHNNIE *watches the little dribbles of butter sliding down each crease. He refuses to be hurried.*

The servant is nervously cutting some more butter just in case EDWARD *deems that this is necessary for a second race.*

EDWARD: Come on, Johnnie – you'll be too late! Which one is yours?

JOHNNIE *smiles a relaxed smile.*

JOHNNIE: All of them are mine.

JOHNNIE *then helps himself to one of the spare pats of butter from the servant's silver tray and plops it in his mouth.*

EDWARD: This will be yours then! . . . I will choose for you . . .

EDWARD *points at the dribble of butter that is just a little bit in front of all the others as it slips down his leg. There are howls of protest from the other children, but* JOHNNIE *smiles*

4

as he watches his butter about to win.

At this very moment LALLA *appears behind him, her arms enveloping him firmly.*

She is his nurse, a cockney woman of about thirty, with a strong face and a natural forceful manner.

She looks relieved to find JOHNNIE, *as if she has been worrying about him.*

LALLA: There you are! . . . I didn't know where you'd gone, Johnnie . . .

We see her hand grip JOHNNIE's *hand tightly.*

We sense something extra protective about her manner.

INT. SANDRINGHAM. PASSAGE NEAR BALLROOM. NIGHT.

JOHNNIE *is standing by a large mirror in the passage as* LALLA *straightens his hair. She suddenly notices that he has a stain on his sleeve from the pat of butter he has eaten. She begins to clean it vigorously.*

LALLA: How have you managed to do that, Johnnie . . . ? The party is about to start – and look at you . . .

JOHNNIE (*remonstrating*): Grandpapa has butter on him . . . Grandpapa has butter all over him . . .

LALLA's *tone changes.*

LALLA: So, Johnnie . . .

Her voice is low, secretive, as if they share some private knowledge.

You will manage at the party? (*She turns his head towards her.*) You don't feel too tired?

JOHNNIE *shakes his head. He is staring at himself in the mirror.* LALLA *persists, her tone more intense.*

You are sure, Johnnie? . . . You promise me?

JOHNNIE *nods.*

5

At that moment PRINCESS MARY, JOHNNIE's *mother,*
passes them in the passage. A tall woman who holds herself
very straight, she has a very alert expression, as if she wants
to notice everything that is going on. She pauses by them.

LALLA: Your Royal Highness (*indicating* JOHNNIE's *clothes*),
we just had a little problem but it's gone now.

MARY *glances at* LALLA *and then at* JOHNNIE *in the mirror,*
the two contrasting women with the child between them.

MARY *can't resist rechecking her own appearance. She is*
wearing a fine but restrained evening dress and a few jewels.

MARY (*as she is glancing at herself in the mirror*): The Queen
has come down already – so we are starting on time this
year, which is almost unheard of I think . . .

JOHNNIE *stares back into the mirror at his mother. His*
manner is simple, direct.

JOHNNIE: It's nice. What you're wearing, Mama . . .
Grandmama will be wearing a prettier dress . . .

MARY *does not take offence. She smiles a distant smile. She*
touches JOHNNIE's *head very briefly.*

MARY: That is how it should be.

INT. SANDRINGHAM. LARGE DRAWING ROOM. NIGHT.
The room has been decorated for QUEEN ALEXANDRA's *birthday,*
with vines going halfway up the wall.

ALEXANDRA *is sitting in the middle of the room and there is a*
queue of guests lined up to give her her presents. She opens them
at once, letting out little coos of delight and surprise at the contents
of each box. It immediately becomes obvious that nearly everyone
has given her the same thing – the little animals made out of agate
that she particularly adores and collects.

We watch the scene through JOHNNIE's *eyes; he is standing at*
the back of the queue and slightly apart with LALLA.

He notices a line of almost identical small animals that is

6

beginning to form on the table next to ALEXANDRA, *and then he spots how many other agate animals are all over the room from past birthdays – monkeys, penguins, dogs, birds and chinchillas.*

All the guests are dressed in full evening splendour, the men wearing medals and the women in magnificent full dresses as they curtsy before ALEXANDRA. *The richness of the Edwardian court is on display. The women are weighed down with jewellery but still subtly less than* ALEXANDRA *who sits centre stage in an elaborate dress – just as* JOHNNIE *had forecast. As we get closer to* ALEXANDRA *we see how she relishes all the attention. She is still a beautiful woman, but has a fluttery rather girlish vanity, though she is in her mid-sixties.*

Next to JOHNNIE, *waiting his turn, is a sharp-faced rather animated man of about forty,* KNUTSFORD. *He has a large red spotted handkerchief hanging out of his trouser pocket.*

KNUTSFORD: Oh dear – we've all managed to get her the
    same thing . . . !
    He points to a large animal, an agate elephant, already
    opened that is sitting on the table beside ALEXANDRA.
    Except for the Germans of course . . . trust them to send
    the biggest one of all! (*He whispers.*) That's from your
    cousin Wilhelm . . .
    JOHNNIE *stares at the elephant – it is indeed much bigger*
    than anybody else's gift.
       We get a little closer still to ALEXANDRA. *She continues to*
    give her little laughs of pleasure.
ALEXANDRA: Goodness, we've got *three* giraffes now – how
    very charming . . . !
    We cut back to JOHNNIE *and* KNUTSFORD. KNUTSFORD
    drapes his red handkerchief over his present.
KNUTSFORD: If only I could make it disappear and turn it
    into a totally different present . . .
    JOHNNIE *laughs as* KNUTSFORD *does a conjuring trick, the*

box disappears from under the handkerchief but then
reappears in KNUTSFORD's *other hand.*

KNUTSFORD: Sadly it's still here! . . .

> KNUTSFORD *clearly enjoys* JOHNNIE's *company, for he*
> *seems to be getting more and more nervous the nearer he gets*
> *to* ALEXANDRA.

It's my first time here as a guest you know, it's quite
exciting . . . I never expected to see the ladies smoking
here – it's marvellous . . .

And indeed we see several of the women smoking vigorously,
clouds of cigarette smoke hanging around their tiaras.

And I hear the music is going to be very unusual . . . I've
been trying to guess . . . and all the clocks are set half an
hour fast . . . !

EDWARD: Every birthday she always gets the same thing and
she manages to sound surprised each time she opens a
parcel. (*Watching* ALEXANDRA.) Never understood what
she sees in those funny little animals, you can't do
anything with them! (*He smokes his cigar.*) She had a
clockwork hippopotamus one year which I liked but I
wound it up too much and broke it.

His mood darkens as he watches the queue with their gifts.

Is there no end to her presents?!

Suddenly the birthday cake appears, wheeled in by a
German footman. The wheels of the trolley get snared in the
carpet and the trolley pauses for a moment just by JOHNNIE.
The cake is an extraordinary structure with several tiers and
very elaborate icing. Between each tier is a bowl of water
with goldfish swimming in it. The cake is on JOHNNIE's *eye-*
level. He is staring directly into one of the bowls of goldfish,
and is able to examine the icing closely. He dips his small
hand into the water for a moment trying to touch one of the
fish. LALLA *pulls his hand back briskly.*

> JOHNNIE *catches sight of his mother,* MARY, *who is*

*watching something closely across the room. Then he sees
what she is staring at. The old King,* EDWARD, *is standing
slightly apart from everybody, a melancholy expression on
his face, a moment of private sadness, as if he is feeling his
age. He makes a striking contrast with the girlish laugh of*
ALEXANDRA *as she continues to express surprise at each new
animal.*

INT. SANDRINGHAM. THE BALLROOM. NIGHT.
*We cut to the concert. The women are smoking as well as the men
–* ALEXANDRA *is having a cigarette herself and lighting it with a
mechanical cigarette lighter that attracts much interest. Seeing
what a success her new lighter is,* ALEXANDRA *insists on lighting
a couple of the guests' cigarettes for them, much to their
embarrassment.*

*The guests and the royal party are all sitting in rows facing the
small stage. They are surrounded by the heads of animals,
trophies from the royal hunting expeditions all over the Empire.
The animals stare at them from the walls.*

MARY *and* GEORGE *are sitting together.* GEORGE, *the Prince
of Wales, is a short man of forty-four. He is watching his children
perform beadily.*

We move in on MARY's *face. We see her nervousness as she sits
watching her children recite to the guests. We see her desire for
them to perform well.*

As we cut into the scene DAVID *is reciting some lines of
Tennyson, from the* Morte D'Arthur. *He is delivering them in
an offhand sort of way as if he is indicating that he is far too old
to be made to perform in public. (He is fifteen.)*

*The other royal children are sitting in a line with ramrod-
straight backs, in order of age –* BERTIE, MAY, HENRY *and*
YOUNG GEORGE. *All except* JOHNNIE. *And then we cut to*
YOUNG GEORGE *who is only two years older than* JOHNNIE

taking the stage. He is a tiny, confident figure, with an extremely precocious manner.

EDWARD: We are getting the oldest and the youngest today I see . . .

EDWARD's manner is still gruff and troubled, the merry mood of the butter competition has vanished, but YOUNG GEORGE confidently reproaches him from the stage.

YOUNG GEORGE: I'm not the youngest, Johnnie is here . . . you've forgotten him . . . ! And I'm sure next year he'll be doing something too . . . a very long poem.

The guests turn to look at JOHNNIE who is sitting next to LALLA on a small settee at the side of the room. From there he has a very good view of all the guests. LALLA is watching them all too, with her sharp intelligent eyes, as they stare at JOHNNIE and her.

JOHNNIE smiles a calm unembarrassed smile, at the bejewelled throng.

At the same moment YOUNG GEORGE, standing on the stage, launches into a few lines from a poem by Victor Hugo. He has the most perfect French accent. He seems to glitter even at this early stage; he is a suave cosmopolitan little boy. YOUNG GEORGE and JOHNNIE's eyes meet, they exchange a private look, amongst all the adults.

And then there is an abrupt and powerful cut to the Russian band playing on their balalaikas. We cut to them in the middle of an extremely rhythmic, almost explosive passage of music. They are in full Cossack costume and look wild and uninhibited in comparison to their royal audience.

GEORGE is checking his father EDWARD's reaction, worried how the music is going down.

GEORGE: Amazing sound . . . never heard anything like it . . . !

We hear somebody whispering in a startled tone, 'It's the sound of the Tartars!' ALEXANDRA is fiddling with her cigarette lighter seemingly oblivious to the extraordinary music.

But the music has an effect on both JOHNNIE *and* EDWARD.

JOHNNIE *really responds to the wild rhythms, his whole body is shaking with excitement and enjoyment.*

LALLA *is watching him closely, warily. She moves her body even closer to him on the settee, her hand slips into his, she is holding him firmly, almost as if the two of them are tied together.*

EDWARD, *the King, stares transfixed at the Russians, unable to take his eyes off them. It is as if their wildness and energy and the alien music both repels and fascinates him.*

EXT. ISLE OF WIGHT. THE BEACH. DAY.
Some pennants are being driven into the sand in the foreground of the shot, flags fluttering, marking off an area of the beach. Burly Russian bodyguards are pushing the pennants into the sand with great energy. A carpet is also being rolled towards us along the beach as the Russian music from the preceding concert at Sandringham still plays over the image.

Then we cut to the Russian imperial family coming straight towards us along the beach, the TSAR *and* TSARINA *and their five children,* OLGA, TATIANA, MARIA, ANASTASIA, *and the tiny Tsarevitch* ALEXEI. *The Russian girls are in their beautiful white dresses and are holding crushed white handkerchiefs in their left hand. The* TSAR *and* TSARINA *are flanked by servants carrying fishing rods, fishing baskets and landing nets and by their large contingent of bodyguards.*

As the imperial family progress towards us along the carpet on the beach, we see the bodyguards move ahead of them and scoop up anything unsightly that is blocking their path, large shells and flotsam, a dog that is running on the beach, and they also send scurrying a few members of the British public that are on the sand.

We see the dainty feet, beautiful shoes of the TSARINA *moving gracefully along the carpet on the beach.*

We cut to LALLA, JOHNNIE *and* YOUNG GEORGE *watching from the hillside that overlooks the beach. They are gazing at the progress of the Russian imperial family from a distance, especially the ravishing Russian girls.*

JOHNNIE: I want to go down.

LALLA: You can't go down there now, they mustn't be
    disturbed. They want to get away from all the crowds . . .
    The TSAR *has chosen his place to fish and is casting his rod.*

YOUNG GEORGE: I don't know what they think they can
    catch so close to the shore . . .
    JOHNNIE *is staring, fascinated, at the girls.*

JOHNNIE: Why can't I go down, just for a moment?

LALLA: You will see your cousins when they come to tea,
    Johnnie, I promise.

YOUNG GEORGE: Nobody can have given them any advice
    about where to catch big fish on the Isle of Wight! We
    should go and help them, Lalla, tell them they won't
    catch anything there . . .

LALLA: I'm sure the Emperor doesn't need any fishing
    lessons from you, Georgie! . . . (*They stare down at them.*)
    Don't they look perfectly splendid, Johnnie?
    We stay on JOHNNIE'*s face as he stares at the Russian girls.*

EXT. ISLE OF WIGHT. BARTON MANOR GARDEN.
AFTERNOON.
We cut to GEORGE *and* MARY *and family waiting for the Russian royal party in the modest garden of Barton Manor. The house is an ugly late Victorian villa, a bit like a small school.*

MARY *is sitting poised outside by the tea which is already laid out.* GEORGE *is walking up and down constantly checking his pocket watch.* JOHNNIE *is sitting on a little grassy bank watching the scene with a cheerful expression. It is obvious his father is getting more and more tense.*

GEORGE: They are late! . . .

We see the long straight drive stretching out before us, no sign of the Russian royal party.

Then suddenly in the trees behind where JOHNNIE *is sitting on the grassy bank he hears something. He turns to see large men moving silently through the trees and in the bushes. He can see that they have guns in their holsters. One of them spots that* JOHNNIE *has noticed them creeping through the shadows and lifts his finger to his lips to indicate to* JOHNNIE *to keep silent.* JOHNNIE *smiles back at him, totally unafraid.*

And then we see all around the garden of Barton Manor the TSAR*'s bodyguards taking their places, a silent and rather sinister line of men encircling the edge of the garden.*

And then we see the cars carrying the TSAR *and his entourage approaching down the long straight road.*

GEORGE *immediately moves to the front of the house to watch them arrive. The cars stop in front of the house but for a moment nobody gets out except the chauffeur who stands by the rear door in anticipation.*

Then Nicholas, the TSAR*, climbs out with regal formality.*

TSAR: My apologies, my dear fellow . . . I thought for a moment we had come to the wrong place!

We cut to JOHNNIE *watching the Russian royal party move into the garden: he is fascinated by the sight of the Russian children, including the tiny and delicate* ALEXEI*. But he is still keeping his distance.*

GEORGE *is walking in front of the* TSAR *and* TSARINA*,*

13

gesticulating with slightly jerky movements towards the rest of the garden and the little wood.

GEORGE: We thought we would show you the garden first . . . it's not much but we rather like it – and it's not looking that bad at the moment.

The TSARINA *is moving like a tense racehorse, exuding a rather neurotic air.*

TSARINA: It's charming, absolutely charming (*She glances back at the house.*) – everything is in miniature, isn't it . . . how marvellous to have something so small . . . (*Then she repeats this remark in French.*)

As they move the TSAR's *bodyguards are moving with them silently in the shadows, a sinister accompaniment to the walk. The* TSAR *and* TSARINA *seem oblivious to them.*

Then suddenly the TSARINA *freezes as if she has been bitten by a snake. She is staring down at the grassy path.*
No, I have to stop I'm afraid . . . have the wrong shoes, because under foot – well you can see under foot it's not quite right for these shoes.

GEORGE *cannot stop himself replying.*

GEORGE: It's really quite dry – (*He pushes at the ground with his foot.*) you see it couldn't be drier in fact –

TSARINA: It's impossible! I can't take another step in these shoes . . .

TSAR: My darling – (*He says a phrase in Russian and then reverts to English.*) I don't think we have time to send somebody back to the yacht for some other shoes . . . (*He stops as she looks at him.*) I mean, of course we can . . . it's perfectly possible if you want –

TSARINA: That won't be necessary . . . (*She turns to* GEORGE *and* MARY.) I'm sure there are some overshoes here . . .

GEORGE *looks helplessly at* MARY.

GEORGE: Overshoes? . . .

INT. ISLE OF WIGHT. BARTON MANOR. CUPBOARD
ROOM. AFTERNOON.
*We cut to a cupboard room inside the house, where all the boots
and garden shoes are kept. The servants are going through all the
lines of wellington boots frantically to see if there is a pair small
enough, or if there are any galoshes remaining in the shadows of
the cupboard.* GEORGE *comes through the door of the room and
starts searching among the boots and shoes himself.*

GEORGE: Have we got any shoes? . . . Have we got the right
shoes? . . . There must be something here! . . . (*As he
searches.*) . . . Bloody ridiculous . . . it's absolutely dry out
there . . . it's bloody ridiculous!

EXT. ISLE OF WIGHT. BARTON MANOR GARDEN.
AFTERNOON.
We cut to JOHNNIE *watching a frog jump in the grass. As he is
playing with the frog the beautiful Russian girls appear staring
down at him and say in French, 'What a beautiful boy.'*
TATIANA *and* MARIA, *twelve and ten years old, start playing
with him and talking to him in English.*

TATIANA: If you like animals . . . (JOHNNIE *nods at this.*) we
will bring you a bear from Russia . . . or maybe a tiger
from Siberia . . . or maybe both a tiger and a bear!
The tiny delicate ALEXEI *is being watched closely by his
nurses and he tries to engage with* JOHNNIE *but* JOHNNIE
*only has eyes for the beautiful Russian girls who swirl all
around him.* LALLA *is watching the scene with a beady eye.*
   We then cut to the TSARINA *having some winter galoshes
put over her shoes as she sits on a chair at the edge of the
path. As this is being done she is speaking in a light way,
totally unaware of the commotion she has caused.*

We see the scene from YOUNG GEORGE*'s point of view: his parents seem small and nervous in the presence of the much grander* TSAR *and* TSARINA.

TSARINA: I cannot get over how different everything seems . . . even the big house seems to have got a little smaller . . . (*To* GEORGE.) I used to visit our grandmama there . . . but then I suppose as one gets older everything shrinks . . . and also it's a real surprise to me there are so many houses belonging to other people *so close*!

The group set off at last for their little walk down the grassy path. The TSARINA *walking extremely gingerly, the galoshes over her dainty shoes look rather strange.* YOUNG GEORGE *is following a few steps behind. The* TSARINA *stops by an azalea bush.*

Does this smell? I think this bush smells, doesn't it?

GEORGE *hesitates: seeing that she is not going to bend the few inches to sniff the flowers, he breaks off a little branch and hands it to her in a rather awkward manner. He realizes* YOUNG GEORGE *is watching all this and snaps at him.*

GEORGE: If you are going to follow, follow properly.

We cut back to the Russian children pushing JOHNNIE *in a wheelbarrow. He is gurgling with delight and* LALLA *is calling.*

LALLA: Not down the hill . . . You will *not* go down the hill! . . . I don't care *whose* children you are . . . !

The Russian girls ignore her completely and push him down the hill. We see from JOHNNIE*'s viewpoint their faces near him, the wind through their hair.*

And then we cut to a family photo that is being set up, first, the TSAR *and* GEORGE *together. The two cousins looking incredibly similar, the* TSAR *taller and so much grander in his demeanour, and* GEORGE *looking an awkward little man in comparison.*

The TSAR *suddenly breaks out of the photographic pose with his cousin before any photograph has been taken. He approaches the* TSARINA.

TSAR: Can you bear it my darling if we do this picture first? – Or maybe we should do the photograph with *you* in it first? . . . What do you think, my darling? . . . Or maybe it isn't the right time for any photograph at all? . . . Maybe that's what it is . . .

As they consult, the short figure of GEORGE *is left standing all alone, waiting in position against the wall.*

We see MARY *watching his embarrassment, but she is powerless to intervene.*

Then we cut to YOUNG GEORGE *who is standing next to his eldest brother* DAVID, *they are both observing how their father is being made to wait humbly by the wall.* DAVID *watches the* TSAR's *antics with a laconic gaze.*

DAVID: That's the way you behave when you are an absolute monarch is it?!

EXT. ISLE OF WIGHT. SEASHORE. LATE AFTERNOON.
We cut to the seashore and MARY *walking along with the Russian children.*

LALLA *is following them with* JOHNNIE *and* YOUNG GEORGE. *All three of them can see how the Russian children are charming* MARY *and making her soften, as they move on the broad expanse of sand picking up shells.*

LALLA: Your mother is having such a time with those children . . . (*And then she adds to herself.*) . . . I've never seen her have such a time with any children . . .

We see JOHNNIE *watching the Russian children, in their lovely clothes, going close to the edge of the sea, daring the waves to lap them. And his mother is with them. The cluster of girls are like glamorous sisters for him. And they keep glancing at him with warm looks.*

We then see JOHNNIE *gazing over the sand to where a group of the general public are watching the walk, being kept behind an invisible barricade, keeping their distance.*

OLGA, *one of the Russian girls, is standing on some rocks, beckoning her siblings to come and look at something and the children and* MARY *surge forward to join her.* MARY *is running too, for a moment completely relaxed.*

They stand with their backs to us, watching something.

We cut to JOHNNIE, LALLA *and* YOUNG GEORGE *joining* MARY *and the Russian girls on top of the rocks, and we see what they are staring at.*

They are peering down into a little bay which is encircled by rocks.

All along the shore and on the rocks opposite are standing the TSAR*'s bodyguards, armed men completely encircling the bay.*

A series of towels, forming a fine carpet on the sand have been spread in front of a bathing machine. Some Russian servants are clearing clumps of seaweed and other flotsam away from the whole area so it is pristine around the carpet of towels.

Below them, alone in the pool, is the TSAR *having a swim. He is swimming in a pompous way, showing off his handsome face, totally unaware that he appears deeply ridiculous swimming alone like this watched over by his bodyguards. There is something narcissistic and comic about his self-congratulatory swimming – as if the whole sea must be aware of his importance.*

JOHNNIE *stands watching the* TSAR *with fascination and chuckles to himself.*

JOHNNIE: He is like an emperor fish! . . .

One of the Russian girls, ANASTASIA, *overhears this remark*

*and repeats it to her siblings. They find it funny and laugh
at what* JOHNNIE *has said. They ruffle his hair.* JOHNNIE
smiles innocently at them, and then looks at LALLA, *a close
unspoken exchange between them,* LALLA *realizing how
struck* JOHNNIE *is by his Russian cousins.*

JOHNNIE *and* LALLA *stare down at the* TSAR *as he swims
and swims.*

INT. YORK COTTAGE. THE SCHOOLROOM. LATE
AFTERNOON.
The cold schoolroom on a dank afternoon. MR HANSELL, *the
schoolmaster, is standing in front of the blackboard on which the
words 'The Black Death' are written in large letters.*

Staring at the blackboard are YOUNG GEORGE *and* JOHNNIE,
*sitting at separate school desks in the tiny schoolroom in York
Cottage. The schoolmaster is a harassed pinched-faced individual
in his early thirties, talking in a loud formal manner as if he is
addressing a classroom of thirty-five children.*

HANSELL: Now how do you think it affected the power of the
     barons? – A plague across the whole of the country . . .
     Can anyone tell me that?
     *But the two boys are glancing out of the window across the
     large garden towards the big house which stands above them
     on a hill. They can see some servants scurrying, carrying
     provisions for the coming feast. It is the last hours of
     daylight, the lights are just coming on in the big house.*

     JOHNNIE *and* YOUNG GEORGE *exchange a pointed look.*
     HANSELL *is carrying on regardless in the background, as if
     he has grown to expect none of his questions to be answered.*
     I will tell you what happened with the Black Death – it
     had a devastating effect on everything it touched!

INT. YORK COTTAGE. PASSAGES. LATE AFTERNOON.
The cramped passages of York Cottage. It is a strange warren of a place, with tiny rooms in which the Prince of Wales and his family are squashed.

The two boys, YOUNG GEORGE *and* JOHNNIE, *are setting off together wrapped in their coats, when they are stopped by* LALLA.

LALLA: And where are you two going?
YOUNG GEORGE: We are just going up to the big house, and we can go on our own . . . We don't need anyone with us –
LALLA: That's what you think.

EXT. YORK COTTAGE AND THE GARDEN OF THE BIG HOUSE. LATE AFTERNOON.
LALLA *and the two boys set off from York Cottage, through the steep and lush garden towards the big house, Sandringham.*

We see York Cottage's exterior, a squat Victorian villa sitting on its own at the bottom of the garden.

JOHNNIE *is riding his tricycle through the gardens. And they catch glimpses of the security men that are dotted around the grounds.*

LALLA: All these new policemen . . . I'm not sure I like finding them all over the garden.
We cut to them going through the stables area, passing all the Queen's dogs who are about to be fed. Several liveried footmen are bringing the dogs' food on a series of trays.

INT. SANDRINGHAM. PASSAGE. LATE AFTERNOON.
We cut to them going through the back passages of the big house.

JOHNNIE *is merrily riding his tricycle down the passages until*
LALLA *stops him and makes him dismount.*

INT. SANDRINGHAM. SHUTTERED ROOM. LATE
AFTERNOON.
*Then we cut into a big cold shuttered room, full of bric-à-brac
that is being stored and banqueting chairs that are piled up
waiting to be used.*

*Two servants are standing on a short ladder retrieving a large
heavy box from high up on the pile. They are being watched by*
LALLA *and the two boys.*

LALLA: When I said you could play with them, I had no idea
    they had been put away up there! So this is to be a very
    short time with them, Georgie, only fifteen minutes at
    the most . . . (*She checks her large pocket watch.*) At the
    very most . . . You know what your mother is like about
    timing! (*She stares at all the bric-à-brac.*) And it's so
    freezing in here! . . .
*We cut to a vast platoon of toy soldiers arranged across the
floor of the shuttered room. Some of the old metal Victorian
soldiers have an arm missing, and several of the horses are
three-legged, and some of the gun carriages are missing a
wheel.*

 YOUNG GEORGE *is playing a game with the soldiers, a
fantasy battle, and as he does so* JOHNNIE *sits cross-legged in
the middle of the room watching the action.*
YOUNG GEORGE: So our commander is Sir Thomas Whitney
    Whatney with his three-legged horse – and this very
    small and very fat old chap here . . . (*he puts his fist round
    a soldier to make him look even fatter*) is the commander
    of the *French* Army –
LALLA: When your brothers played with those, they were all

so much shinier. The soldiers were spick and span – they would have passed any inspection.

We cut to the soldiers laid out in battle formation over the whole expanse of the floor, and the two boys are right in the middle of the armies. The door suddenly opens, it's the old King, EDWARD, *standing smoking a cigar, staring into the shuttered room.*

EDWARD: I thought I heard voices . . . So you've got the soldiers out . . . Well let's see what you can do with them – what's your position? . . . Is it a good position?!

EDWARD *stares down at the two boys on the floor, surrounded by all the metal soldiers.*

At this point GEORGE *enters. As soon as he sees his father his manner becomes very deferential.*

GEORGE: There you are, Papa . . . I was just coming along to our meeting . . . Am I a little early?

EDWARD (*showing no interest in the meeting*): I saw they had the soldiers out . . .

GEORGE *stares across the battlefield.*

GEORGE: And so they have . . . (*Then he suddenly barks at the boys.*) I hope you are not playing between countries?! You know my rules about that . . . (*He turns to his father.*) I told them they have to play between planets, not between nations . . . The armies are from Mars or Jupiter, that sort of thing, never the *French* or the *Germans* – (*Then he turns towards his sons.*) Have you been playing with the French? . . . Answer me!

YOUNG GEORGE (*very small voice*): No, Papa. We haven't been doing that, Papa . . . The armies are from Saturn and Jupiter.

YOUNG GEORGE *is desperately trying to avoid* LALLA's *gaze, as he lies to his father.* JOHNNIE *is watching all this from his position cross-legged in the middle of the room.*

JOHNNIE: We have been playing with foreigners.

GEORGE (*explodes*): I TOLD YOU NOT TO DO THAT! NEVER!

EDWARD *is sitting smoking his cigar staring across the expanse of soldiers.*

EDWARD: At least the boy is honest . . . Honest Johnnie . . .

EDWARD *begins to try to kneel on the floor among the soldiers and indicates* GEORGE *to follow him.*

Well, now they have got this far we might as well help them . . .

EDWARD *manages to get down on the floor, his great face is now much closer to* JOHNNIE*'s, the soldiers lined up between them.* EDWARD *is puffing from his exertions. He turns to* JOHNNIE.

EDWARD: God, that was difficult . . . I must be getting old, mustn't I?!

EDWARD *points at the soldiers directly opposite him.*

EDWARD: Are those the French then? . . . Certainly look like the French! (*He is on all fours among the soldiers.*) When I was young, the battles I won with these soldiers! Battles in the snow . . . In the jungle, even in the desert! . . . I won the lot . . . There was one little general always answering back, never did what I wanted, just refused to listen! So I eventually threw him out the window . . . (*He chuckles.*) That kept him quiet . . . Never heard from him again!

He stares at JOHNNIE *and* YOUNG GEORGE.

So shall we see what happens now? Who knows, I might still be quite good at it! Everybody ready then? . . . Let's find out who can get their men into the best position . . . Johnnie and I will be on this side – and we are going to have our cavalry lined up along here . . .

The two adults kneel with the boys surrounded by the soldiers.

INT. SANDRINGHAM. CORRIDOR BY STAIRWAY. LATE
AFTERNOON.

LALLA *is bustling along the passage by the kitchen leading the
boys out.*

LALLA: We are very late now. Goodness, if I had known how
long it was going to take I wouldn't have agreed to us
coming. My father gave me a good thrashing every time
I was late and it was the best thing that ever happened to
me . . .

*YOUNG GEORGE mouths this last line as if he is so used to
hearing it, as he watches the bustling LALLA leading them
on.*

*LALLA turns to encourage JOHNNIE to catch up with
them. She sees that he has stopped way down the passage
behind them and has pushed himself into a corner with his
face turned away. Immediately we see that LALLA is
concerned. She turns back to YOUNG GEORGE.*

LALLA: Georgie, go back to the cottage – we'll join you in a
few minutes –

*We see YOUNG GEORGE knows exactly what she means,
there is a complicity between them.*

*LALLA is moving JOHNNIE down the passage, trying to
find somewhere private for them to go. She is whispering to
JOHNNIE as she moves him, an intense confidential tone.*

*As she is doing this, grand-looking footmen are brushing
past them in the passage moving towards the dining room in
the distance, getting ready for the evening meal. Outside the
window are the security men.*

It will be fine, Johnnie . . . we will find somewhere to go
. . . Everything will be fine, we'll soon be there . . .

*As she is saying this she is trying the handles of the doors
that they are passing in the passage. Some are locked, some
are occupied. She opens one door only to find that they are in*

a pantry with people preparing food.

Finally, as JOHNNIE *is getting worse, she finds an empty room full of silver candlesticks, bowls, and cutlery.*

She closes the door behind her and takes JOHNNIE *in her arms. His whole body is shaking as he has a small epileptic fit. All the time* LALLA *talks to him softly.*

Johnnie . . . you are safe now . . . nobody can see you here . . . You're safe with me . . .

She holds his hand as he shakes, letting the fit take its course.

The door of the little room suddenly opens and a footman enters. LALLA *turns on him with real authority.*

We are just coming, the boy is upset about something. You will close the door and leave us . . .

The footman is gone. LALLA *turns towards* JOHNNIE, *her voice intense, private.*

Nobody else will discover us now, Johnnie. *(Softly in his ear.)* Nobody will see this . . . *(She kisses him on the forehead.)* And tonight we'll say our prayers twice and then maybe there won't be another one for a very long time . . .

We move in really close on LALLA *as she holds* JOHNNIE, *strongly, protectively.*

INT. YORK COTTAGE. MARY'S SMALL STUDY. EVENING.

We cut to LALLA *and* JOHNNIE *trying to slip back into York Cottage unnoticed. The cramped warren of dimly lit passages and tiny rooms. The door of* MARY'S *small study is open and* MARY *is sitting at her desk.* LALLA *and* JOHNNIE *move silently past the open door and* MARY *does not look up.*

But suddenly they hear MARY'S *voice summoning them back.*

LALLA *and* JOHNNIE *stand in the passage and* MARY *questions them from her desk in her cluttered room.*

MARY: Where have you been, Lalla? . . . I've been wondering
why you are so late . . .

LALLA: We were just a tiny bit longer than we expected,
ma'am . . . This young man has got a cold, he was
sneezing and coughing so very much . . . like a little
engine he was . . . (*She ruffles* JOHNNIE's *hair.*) But he is
so much better now . . .

MARY stares at her son, from her desk.

MARY: Good, Johnnie . . . I'm glad to hear you are better.

*JOHNNIE nods at his mother and he and LALLA move off
down the passage having not aroused MARY's suspicions.*

LALLA: She's got ears like a bat your mother – the very best
ears I've ever come across!

EXT. NORFOLK. THE SHOOT. DAY.

*We cut to the shoot, EDWARD's shooting party spread along the
ridge, firing into the grey winter skies.*

*The atmosphere is enormously intense. The guests are eager to
impress each other, anxious to show what good shots they are.
There is a huge line of dead pheasants on the ground.*

*But as we get nearer to the old King, EDWARD, we sense
something is wrong. His stout figure is all trussed up in his shooting
clothes and he is firing and firing. There is something almost
desperate about his shooting. We see he is not hitting anything.*

*His son GEORGE, the Prince of Wales, is shooting by his side,
his short figure like a pale reflection of his fatter more extrovert
father, but GEORGE is bagging an enormous amount of
pheasants.*

EDWARD: I'm not hitting nearly as much as I usually do . . .
can't understand what's happening . . .

*We see the clusters of rifles firing in silhouette against the
bleak skies, the servants scurrying around with the*

pheasants.

*The ground is muddy and the weather unpleasant, the
rain begins to lash.*

EDWARD: (*mutters melancholically*) Never hit so few . . .
never ever hit so few.

*He sits down for a moment on a tree stump, as servants
converge on him carrying chairs. The rain is dripping from*
EDWARD'*s beard.*

EDWARD: What's wrong? . . . One of my greatest pleasures
and I hate it today . . . (*He is staring ahead.*) Meaningless
. . . Completely meaningless – I have never felt that
before . . . and if I no longer enjoy shooting . . . not being
able to look forward to that as one goes to bed . . .

*He lapses into silence, staring at the others carrying on
shooting across the field.*

Look at them carrying on! . . . I'm not at all sure I
recognize half of them . . . Did I really invite some of
these people? Why is it making me so angry . . . Seeing
them here today?

*He suddenly rouses himself from the tree stump and resumes
taking part in the shoot. He fires again and again into the
sky.*

EXT. NORFOLK. THE MARQUEE. DAY.
*We cut to the women of the royal shooting party arriving outside
the marquee. They are milling about in the mouth of the marquee
in forlorn groups, as if the mood of* EDWARD *is affecting
everything.*

We then cut to YOUNG GEORGE *and* JOHNNIE *and* LALLA
*approaching the shooting party in a cumbersome-looking covered
motor, used for moving around the estate. This is being driven by
an estate worker.* JOHNNIE *stares through the rain-splattered
window at the servants standing grimly outside the marquee in*

the rain, with hundreds of dead pheasants and rabbits laid out in
rows along the muddy ground in front of them.

INT. NORFOLK. THE MARQUEE. DAY.
We cut to inside the marquee, where the royal hunting party is
eating at formal tables. The food is quite a grand spread.
EDWARD *is sitting in the middle of the table.* ALEXANDRA *is next*
to him beaming in an aimless way, completely oblivious to her
husband's dark mood. MARY *however has noticed* EDWARD*'s*
mood, and is watching him with concern. GEORGE *is not looking*
up from his plate, eating relentlessly, not knowing what to do
about his father.

    The disjointed atmosphere has affected all the guests, as
EDWARD *is just sitting hardly eating at all, chewing*
despondently, talking to no one.

    The flap of the tent is pulled back. It is pouring with rain
outside and LALLA *enters with the two small boys,* YOUNG
GEORGE *and* JOHNNIE. LALLA *apologizes to* EDWARD.

LALLA: I'm sorry we're so late . . . the motor got stuck in the
    mud.

    EDWARD *grunts in recognition, hardly looking up at*
    them.

EDWARD: About time they got a feel for shooting – those
    children . . .

    LALLA *is looking for the place setting for the boys before she*
    takes up her position watching from the side, standing with
    the waiters.

    But JOHNNIE *does not sit down, he stands looking at the*
    women in their dresses and the men in their hunting
    costumes.

    JOHNNIE *suddenly points at one of the guests sitting close*
    to EDWARD.

Queen Mary at the garden party in Sandringham

George V and his cousin, the Tsar pose for a photograph
during the Tsar's visit to the Isle of Wight in 1909

Queen Mary on the Isle of Wight with the Tsar's children

Edward VII and Johnnie play with toy soldiers

Edward VII at the shooting party a few months before his death

Johnnie's encounter with the Kaiser at the funeral of Edward VII

The nine kings pose for a photograph the day after
Edward VII's funeral, 1910

Johnnie on his trip to London to see the doctors

Johnnie with the scaly anteater at the doctors

Johnnie with his father's parrot Charlotte

Lalla, trying to reassure Mary as Johnnie has a fit after the banquet

JOHNNIE: Look, the silly man has got food stuck in his
beard . . . !

*The party falls quiet, staring at the boy standing in front of
them all, not sure how to react. But the embarrassed silence
is broken by* EDWARD *who seems prompted out of his deep
gloom. He chuckles, and a nervous laughter spreads round
the marquee.*

JOHNNIE *sees* KNUTSFORD, *the man with the red
handkerchief.*

JOHNNIE: You can make the food you don't like disappear
can't you?

KNUTSFORD *grins back at him.* JOHNNIE *is now holding
the floor, the whole shooting party looking back at him.*
JOHNNIE *seems to enjoy the audience.*

MARY: Johnnie, it's time for you to sit down now.

JOHNNIE *does not seem to hear her.* LALLA's *eyes are
darting, she wants to intervene. But* JOHNNIE *has
EDWARD's attention.*

JOHNNIE: Have you ever shot a crocodile, Grandpapa?

EDWARD: I have indeed . . . but not today . . . not today.

He shakes his head sadly.

JOHNNIE: After lunch you will all shoot a crocodile each.

YOUNG GEORGE *hisses, trying to stop* JOHNNIE.

YOUNG GEORGE: Don't be silly, Johnnie . . . don't be
ridiculous.

But JOHNNIE *is not to be stopped.*

JOHNNIE: The ladies will shoot tigers after lunch and the men
crocodiles.

The nervous laughter continues round the marquee. LALLA
inches closer to JOHNNIE.

EDWARD: And so we shall – though whether I will be able to
hit even something as slow as a crocodile I don't know. I
used to be one of the best shots in England . . . but today
I couldn't hit a single thing.

29

JOHNNIE: Maybe it's because you are so old, Grandpapa.

> *There is a startled silence, the whole marquee goes quiet again. People cannot bear to look, they are peering down at the table, very anxious not to catch the eye of* EDWARD.
>
> *But the King smiles, looking straight at* JOHNNIE.

EDWARD: The boy is right . . . that boy is always right!

EXT. LONDON. ROOFTOPS. NIGHT.

We cut to the night rooftops of London. The first roofs we see are the towers of the Foreign Office. We are right on the roof. A cluster of men in top hats are standing with their backs to us staring up at the night sky. We then cut to another rooftop in central London where a group of women are standing in capes staring up at the sky.

Then we cut to a high shot looking down on a road running along the edge of one of the parks. A line of people are standing watching the sky, some of them have binoculars, some have telescopes, there are one or two wearing spectacles with very thick lenses.

Then we cut to the rooftop of Marlborough House, the Prince of Wales' London residence. We are right on the roof among the chimneys where there is a gathering of servants, members of the royal household, and LALLA, YOUNG GEORGE *and* JOHNNIE.

The two small boys and LALLA *are standing in long shot right at the far end of the roof, staring up at the night sky. We then cut to* LALLA *and the boys in close-up and we see that* JOHNNIE's *eyes are wandering all over the place, looking everywhere but the sky.*

LALLA: It won't be long, Johnnie, look up, come on . . . Can you see the comet coming? . . . Is that it up there? . . . Any moment it will come, I'm sure . . . a bright light in a great rush . . . it'll get bigger and bigger!

YOUNG GEORGE: It doesn't come like a train, right on time
and then it's gone . . . We should be able to see it already
– I don't think it's coming . . .

As he is saying this JOHNNIE *is staring down into the
courtyard below where a large car is waiting.*

JOHNNIE (*points*): Look, Mama and Papa!

We see down below where the motor vehicle is waiting.

GEORGE *and* MARY *are moving across the courtyard in an
urgent way.*

JOHNNIE *watches his father who is waving his arms and
shouting.*

GEORGE: Why isn't the engine started?! . . . We have to hurry
for God's sake . . . Hurry!

MARY *and* GEORGE *get into the car as the chauffeur cranks
the engine urgently.*

LALLA: They must have been called to the palace.

YOUNG GEORGE: Maybe Grandpapa is worse . . .

LALLA, JOHNNIE *and* YOUNG GEORGE *watch the car move
out, past the line of people and away into the night.*

YOUNG GEORGE (*staring down at the car*): The comet is
coming and Grandpapa is dying . . . Is it an omen?

*We cut into the car. It is moving past the crowd who are
oblivious to the royal couple leaving so urgently. They
are standing with their backs to the car, their faces turned
to the sky. Those with telescopes are training them on the
stars.*

We stay on MARY *looking very nervous, as if she realizes
what might lie ahead.*

We cut back to JOHNNIE *staring into the night sky as the
comet approaches.*

INT. MARLBOROUGH HOUSE. BEDROOM. MORNING.
We cut to the dark bedroom, the sunlight just piercing the heavy

curtains. There is a loud flapping, a sharp rather disturbing sound filling the room.

YOUNG GEORGE *gets out of bed and moves towards the heavy curtains. He parts them. We see that the room is high up, overlooking the rooftops of St James, bright sunlight beating on the roofs. The disturbing sound continues.* YOUNG GEORGE *looks up in the direction it is coming from. We see the flag is flying at half-mast flapping loudly and violently against its post. The rope holding the flag to the mast is creaking in the wind.*

YOUNG GEORGE (*whispers urgently*): Johnnie . . . Johnnie, wake up!

> JOHNNIE *looks up from the bed, his big innocent face looking happy. He walks over to the window. They both stare up at the flag flying at half-mast.*

YOUNG GEORGE: Do you know what that means?

JOHNNIE (*looking at his brother*): You are the son of the King now.

YOUNG GEORGE (*touches his head and laughs*): We both are . . . *We both are,* Johnnie . . . !

INT. MARLBOROUGH HOUSE. GEORGE'S DRESSING ROOM AND MARY'S DRESSING ROOM. INTERCUT BETWEEN THEM. DAY.

We cut to GEORGE, *now the King, getting ready, putting on his clothes for the funeral. His very short figure stands in front of a very big mirror. It is obvious that he is very nervous.*

We then cut to MARY *also getting ready in her funeral clothes. We move in close on her. We see that she is shaking with nerves, at this first public appearance as Queen.*

We cut back to GEORGE. *He is walking a few steps in the room, he turns to his valet.*

GEORGE: I'm not sure about the shoes . . . the shoes are very
tight.
*His voice is very quiet, his whole demeanour apprehensive.
He looks like a terrified understudy about to go on for the
first time.*

*We cut back to MARY, her hand hovering over a pair of
gloves that have been laid out for her.*
MARY (*her voice very quiet*): These gloves . . . maybe we
should try another pair . . .
*One of the women tending to MARY comes over with another
pair of gloves.*

MARY looks startled, reacts to them.
No, no, those are my mother's . . . those will not do at
all.

FLASHBACK. INT. FAT MARY'S RESIDENCE. PASSAGE.
DAY.
*We see the huge shape of MARY's mother, Mary of Teck (FAT
MARY) coming towards us, a truly obese woman, grotesquely
overweight.*

*This great fleshy figure is coming straight towards us down the
passage. A couple of servants moving in the other direction have
to retreat in her path. She moves with delicate lightness despite
her enormous body.*

FLASHBACK. INT. DANCING CLASS. DAY.
*Then we cut to a long uncluttered room where several teenage girls
in ballet costumes are dancing and the YOUNG MARY is staring
aghast as her huge mother bursts in late to watch the dancing class.*

*There is a row of parents sitting watching the display, but there
is only one spare chair which is not sufficient to take FAT MARY's
enormous weight. As she sinks on to the chair this becomes*

33

obvious, and the dancing class mistress rushes in to help and
another parent has to give up her chair, in order to allow FAT
MARY *two chairs. Many voices are saying, 'No, I'll stand', 'No I
can stand . . . I'm quite happy to stand . . . '*

    FAT MARY *beaming at them all, as she envelops the chairs.*

    YOUNG MARY *watches appalled at the spectacle her mother is
making.*

FLASHBACK. INT. FAT MARY'S RESIDENCE. DRESSING
ROOM. NIGHT.

And then we see the YOUNG MARY *all dressed up for a function
coming into her mother's dressing room and finding her mother
sitting, not at all ready, her hair down, and laughing away with
her maids in a totally unhurried fashion.*

YOUNG MARY: Mama we are over an hour late already!

FAT MARY: Don't fret, my dear – I'm always at least an hour
    late . . . That's what people expect from me . . .

    FAT MARY *gets up, and as she does so she knocks an
    ornament off her dressing table that breaks on the floor.*

INT. MARLBOROUGH HOUSE. MARY'S DRESSING ROOM.
DAY.

We cut back to MARY *sitting at her dressing table. Her mother's
broken ornament is staring back at her from among the collection
of objects in her room.*

    MARY *looks down at her mother's gloves.*

MARY: No . . . these will definitely not fit me . . .

    We stay on MARY, *in close-up. She mouths an almost silent
    prayer.*

    God give me strength for this . . .

34

INT. BUCKINGHAM PALACE. PASSAGE OVERLOOKING
COURTYARD. DAY.
We cut to a smooth-looking tall gentleman, STAMFORDHAM, *the
King's private secretary, standing by a first-floor window, peering
down.*

*We see into the courtyard, the black funeral horses, carriages
manoeuvring themselves into position to ferry visiting dignitaries
to the funeral.*

We see, from STAMFORDHAM's *point of view, various shapes
milling around in the room that leads on to the courtyard,
silhouettes of the guests.*

*Sometimes they appear on the steps to see if their carriages are
ready, then they either wait for a few seconds or withdraw back
into the shadows – a picture of the Crown heads of Europe fussing
and fluttering as they wait.*

YOUNG GEORGE *joins* STAMFORDHAM *in the window.*

YOUNG GEORGE: May I join you . . . ? And Johnnie wants to
    too . . .

STAMFORDHAM: Of course . . . you look very smart, young
    man.

YOUNG GEORGE (*turning to look at* JOHNNIE): Johnnie . . .
    come and join us.

    JOHNNIE *is walking in a leisurely way down the passage
    towards them. He is smiling and stomping along, his walk
    bearing no relation to the solemnity of the occasion.*

    STAMFORDHAM *greets* JOHNNIE *politely with a formal little
    nod.* YOUNG GEORGE *automatically straightens* JOHNNIE's
    hair, always acting as his protector and guardian. JOHNNIE
    *peers down into the courtyard with a smile, again making no
    concessions to the formality of the occasion.*

JOHNNIE: It would be better if all the people weren't in black.

    STAMFORDHAM *smiles at this, and points towards the
    guests assembling in the shadows.*

35

STAMFORDHAM: You know who that is? . . . Can you see him? Standing just inside the doorway?

YOUNG GEORGE: Cousin Bill, the Emperor of Germany . . .

STAMFORDHAM (*chuckles*): And how about this one? The person there . . . He's just moved . . . The one by the vase?

Another shadowy figure is peering out to see if it is the right time for him to make his entrance and climb into his carriage.

YOUNG GEORGE: The King of Greece . . . Papa's uncle . . . And there is Uncle Fritz . . . The Grand Duke of . . . Mac . . . I nearly got it! It's very difficult –

STAMFORDHAM: The Grand Duke of Mecklenburg-Strelitz.

YOUNG GEORGE: And who's the one making all the fuss over there?

We see a shadowy figure chastising one of the footman while he is waiting.

STAMFORDHAM: That is the Grand Duke Michael Michailovitch of Russia . . . A member of your family . . . Just moving over now to talk to His Serene Highness the Duke of Teck, another of your relations . . .

YOUNG GEORGE: Johnnie – it's all the family together . . . !

We stay on the Crown princes restlessly moving, looking very edgy.

JOHNNIE: Why are they all fidgeting?

STAMFORDHAM: I think somebody has called them much too early.

YOUNG GEORGE: I wonder who decides which carriages go first . . . And who walks behind the coffin . . . Do you have to arrange that?

Their voices are beginning to fade away as we move in on JOHNNIE. *A flick of tension crosses his face. We hear* STAMFORDHAM's *voice continuing.*

STAMFORDHAM: It's partly up to me . . . problems of

protocol can be surprisingly tricky . . .

We see JOHNNIE *beginning to breathe quicker. He instinctively senses he needs to move off, find somewhere private. He sets off along the passage; his brother does not notice that he is gone.* JOHNNIE *turns a corner and begins to run. We stay on him, urgently running along the big passage. He collides with the legs of a tall severe-looking adult. It is Cousin Bill, Kaiser* WILHELM.

WILHELM: Oh no, not today, you don't run today . . . where are you running, young man?

JOHNNIE *stares up at the glinting small eyes of* WILHELM.

JOHNNIE: I've got something to do . . .

WILHELM (*staring down at him*): You don't know who I am?

JOHNNIE: Let me think . . .

WILHELM: You and I have not met . . . but I know who you are! I am your cousin Bill . . . (*He addresses the child firmly.*) Today we all have something to do . . . we are preparing to say goodbye to your grandfather . . . I myself feel great sorrow because I loved your grandfather . . . the whole of Germany loved him . . . He was my family after all . . . !

As he is saying this, JOHNNIE*'s eyes are fixated on* WILHELM*'s withered arm which he is holding very straight.*

So, now you understand – no running anywhere today . . . you walk carefully now! You don't want to do anything to disturb the family or the proceedings now do you?

WILHELM *stares down at* JOHNNIE, *who is desperate to get away.*

JOHNNIE: No . . . I won't disturb them, sir . . .

JOHNNIE *is beginning to breathe faster but he cannot move quickly away from the German Emperor. So he moves off walking at a dignified pace,* WILHELM *watching him go beadily.*

As soon as he goes around the corner and WILHELM *is out of sight,* JOHNNIE *begins to run down the passage furiously.*

He finds he has to pass through a group of dark clustered guests, the women, including some elderly dowager duchesses, wearing their great black dresses. He has to push his way through this crush to get to the stairs and safety. As he moves, one or two of the grand dukes pat him on the head or ruffle his hair. 'Where are you going in such a hurry, young man?' . . . 'There is no rush, little fellow . . . We are all here much too early!'

In the distance, the Queen, ALEXANDRA *is sitting surrounded by people.* JOHNNIE *is very keen to avoid catching her eye in his present state.*

WILHELM *is pushing his way towards* ALEXANDRA. JOHNNIE *sees* ALEXANDRA *flinching away from* WILHELM *as the Kaiser bends towards her to whisper his condolences.*

JOHNNIE *begins to climb the stairs. He is breathing very heavily, his heart is beating faster too and it takes a lot of effort to get up these stairs – he is fighting hard not to collapse in public. One or two of the grand mourners glance with idle curiosity towards this child pulling himself along with difficulty up the stairs.*

For JOHNNIE *it seems to take an age to get up the stairs and out of sight. His face full of determination as his breathing gets more and more violent.*

He turns a corner and is out of sight on the landing where he sinks to his knees in a corner, and then curls up, shielded from anyone seeing him by the banister.

He begins to have a terrible fit, the convulsions ripping through his body.

We cut to the mourners lining up for their coaches, many of the royal families of Europe gathered in one courtyard.

INT. BUCKINGHAM PALACE. MARY'S DRESSING ROOM.
EVENING.
We see JOHNNIE *lying in the foreground of the shot on a small settee,* LALLA *is standing close by. He smiles at her, and looks much better.*

In the distance the door of the room is opening. We can see MARY *standing in earnest conversation with a couple of ladies-in-waiting.* LALLA *whispers to* JOHNNIE.

LALLA: Johnnie . . . we are going to tell your mother what happened . . .
The ladies-in-waiting withdraw. MARY *is moving forward, the light of the palace passage behind her. She is still wearing her full black dress that she has worn for the funeral.*

LALLA: He had a very bad turn, ma'am. (MARY *stares down at* JOHNNIE.) I thought it best to wait to tell you until after the funeral.
JOHNNIE *tries to sit up but* LALLA *makes him lie down again.*

JOHNNIE: Mama . . .
MARY *stares down at him. Her manner is not cold – it is as if she does not really know how to address him.*

MARY: Has this happened before?
JOHNNIE *leans forward as if he wants to reply, but* LALLA *quickly intervenes.*

LALLA: Never as bad as this, ma'am. He's had a few little turns before . . . but that is normal for a child . . : I didn't want to worry you.
MARY *gives* LALLA *a sharp look, and then looks down at the child.*

MARY: We will make sure the doctors see him tomorrow.
MARY *indicates to* LALLA *that she wants a word with her.* LALLA *moves up to* MARY. *They talk in the doorway.*

MARY: You must make sure that there is somebody with him at all times.

LALLA: Of course, ma'am. *I'm* usually with him all the time – it was just today . . . because it was a special day, he was with his brother.

MARY: It's even more important when there are other people around . . . I'm sure you understand that, Lalla . . .

LALLA meets MARY's eye.

LALLA: Yes, ma'am.

MARY (*begins to move off*): For this to happen today of all days . . .

JOHNNIE is watching from the settee.

JOHNNIE: You're all in black, Mama.

MARY: Yes, Johnnie . . .

She continues to move off.

JOHNNIE: What happens to dead people . . . ? Where are they now?

MARY: They go to heaven . . . you know that.

JOHNNIE: Yes . . . But how do they get to heaven?

MARY stops and turns, unsure how to answer this question.

MARY: God makes it possible . . . (JOHNNIE *keeps staring at her.*) Their spirit leaves their body and inhabits the wind . . .

JOHNNIE (*looking back at her*): They go in the wind . . . ?

INT. BUCKINGHAM PALACE. STUDY OVERLOOKING GARDEN. MORNING.

We cut to JOHNNIE sitting at the end of a polished table in bright sunlight during the following morning. He is sitting very erect, dressed in a sailor suit, smiling a little to himself.

Two doctors, HETHERINGTON and LONGHURST, are watching him closely. In front of JOHNNIE lying on the polished

table are a series of illustrated cards of animals – an elephant, a
spider, a whale and a lion.

HETHERINGTON: Now, John, can you arrange the animals in
the order of their size? If you put the biggest one first
and the smallest one last. Can you do that for me?
JOHNNIE stares at the cards, his hand hovers for a moment,
as the doctors look expectant. Then JOHNNIE *leans back and*
smiles, having not chosen a card.
LONGHURST (*slowly*): The biggest? . . . Which is the biggest?
JOHNNIE (*looks up*): I like all the pictures.
MARY enters, the doctors bow. MARY *can see immediately*
from their faces that their examination of JOHNNIE *is not*
going well.
MARY: Please carry on . . . I will just sit here . . . carry on,
gentlemen.
LONGHURST: Ma'am . . . we have asked John to arrange these
animals in order of size . . . The whale . . . And then all
the way to the insect.
HETHERINGTON: There! . . . Now we have given you a big
clue, young man . . . Let's see you try again!
JOHNNIE's hand hovers over the animals. MARY *tries to look*
absolutely controlled and impassive, but we can see that she
is really willing him to succeed.
JOHNNIE's hand stops by the whale, everybody leans
forward. His hand moves on to the insect, then to the lion.
He leans back and looks at the doctors, having not moved
a single card.
JOHNNIE: I used to have a spider . . . I used to keep it.

INT. BUCKINGHAM PALACE. STATE ROOM. DAY.
We intercut with some ornate chairs being arranged in a state
room ready for a formal photograph to be taken. The servants are

41

*scurrying around as a courtier nervously barks out instructions,
as the room is being made ready to receive the heads of state.*

EXT/INT. BUCKINGHAM PALACE. STUDY
OVERLOOKING GARDEN. DAY.
We cut back to the doctors and MARY *standing at a window
staring out at* JOHNNIE *as they watch him play with* LALLA.

We cut outside. JOHNNIE *is standing stock still on the path in
the garden.* LALLA *is standing a little distance from him calling
him softly, an intense whisper, trying to encourage him to act
normally. But* JOHNNIE *stands rooted to the spot.*

LALLA: Come on, Johnnie, please!! Do something, don't
    stand there like that . . . Come on, play . . . Let's play
    with this ball . . . Come on, catch it Johnnie, please . . .
    LALLA *tosses the ball gently,* JOHNNIE *makes no attempt to
    catch it.* LALLA *pleads with her eyes.*
    Oh Johnnie, please . . . don't be like this now . . .
    The wind is blowing some leaves along the path. JOHNNIE
    *suddenly moves off and leaps in a strange way, trying to
    catch the leaves.*
    We dissolve to see JOHNNIE *has built a small mound of
    leaves in an eccentric shape.*
    MARY *opens the door as* JOHNNIE *is moving with the
    leaves, waving his arms, adding to his mound.*
MARY: What are you doing, Johnnie?
JOHNNIE: I'm gathering Grandpapa's pieces . . . he's on the
    wind . . . I'm gathering all the pieces of Grandpapa . . .
    *The two doctors exchange a meaningful look. We close in on
    * LALLA*'s face, her eyes anxious, as she sees the doctors
    forming their judgement.*

INT. BUCKINGHAM PALACE. STATE ROOM. DAY.
We cut to the cluster of nine kings in the state room lining up for their group photo, as YOUNG GEORGE *is watching through a half-opened door. The Kaiser,* WILHEIM. *is making a terrible business about whether he will be in the front row or stand at the back.*

WILHELM: No, no I am quite happy to be right at the back, no do not alarm yourself, I'm quite content with my position here at the back . . . !
The tiny figure of the King, GEORGE, *is sitting right in the middle of the front row, glancing around, not at all sure if he should change the formation or not.*

INT. BUCKINGHAM PALACE. PRIVATE DRAWING ROOM. DAY.
HETHERINGTON *and* LONGHURST *are addressing* MARY *in a secluded drawing room.*

HETHERINGTON: Ma'am, it is clear his brain has not continued to grow as it should . . . showing it must have suffered some damage at some stage . . . and the description of the fits clearly indicates epilepsy –
LONGHURST: Further tests will be necessary of course –
HETHERINGTON: Of course – But we have to prepare ourselves . . . it is more than possible that John's natural life may be cut short . . . The brain is very unlikely to develop further –
MARY: I can assure you, gentlemen, that Johnnie is not an imbecile . . .
HETHERINGTON: The brain is damaged, ma'am . . . whatever label we use.
LONGHURST: We are recommending complete isolation –

HETHERINGTON: Complete, ma'am.

LONGHURST: Where he can be given round-the-clock supervision.

HETHERINGTON: John will have regular fits, and for anybody witnessing those fits – whether it is the immediate family (*pointedly*) or people from outside the family . . . the effect will be most traumatic for anybody witnessing those.

LONGHURST: For the child and for the family this is best . . . a quiet place . . .

HETHERINGTON: A fit in public, ma'am . . . would not be . . . (*His voice tails away.*)
We stay on MARY*'s face.*

MARY: He is *not* going to be sent to a hospital.

INT. BUCKINGHAM PALACE. PASSAGE/STATE ROOM. DAY.

We cut to JOHNNIE *walking unconcerned down one of the ornate corridors. He stops, his small figure standing on the red carpet.*
YOUNG GEORGE*'s face turns sharply, as he stares at the solitary figure.*

   YOUNG GEORGE *is watching through the doorway the photograph being taken of the nine kings who are still shifting and rearranging themselves.*

YOUNG GEORGE: Johnnie? I thought you were with Mama . . .

   JOHNNIE *joins him in the doorway just as the first big flash goes off, as the photograph is taken. The sight of the nine kings all together, and the noise of the flash going off makes* JOHNNIE *laugh with delight.*

   At the noise of the second flash going off, we cut to –

44

EXT. NORFOLK COUNTRYSIDE. AFTERNOON.
A shot of the remote Norfolk countryside stretching out in front of us in a mist. Then we cut to the exterior of York Cottage.

INT. YORK COTTAGE. TINY BEDROOM. LATE AFTERNOON.
We cut to a small door opening right at the very far end of the warren of passages in York Cottage. LALLA *and* JOHNNIE *stand staring at a tiny bedroom.*

LALLA: Well it's very clean . . . So this will be your new room, Johnnie, and I will be next door . . .
    JOHNNIE *moves around his new room, puts one single toy soldier that he has been holding on the bare shelf above the bed. He seems to accept his new isolation.*
LALLA: It's only a few weeks until the family will be coming down and you will all be together again . . . for a little while at least.
    JOHNNIE *stands by the small window staring out across the landscape.*

EXT. YORK COTTAGE. THE GARDEN. DAY.
We cut to JOHNNIE *standing with* LALLA, *who is holding an umbrella, outside York Cottage.*
    JOHNNIE *is standing between two uninspiring looking shrubs and is staring at the rather sad bit of soggy lawn.*

JOHNNIE: I think I should have my own bit of garden . . . We will start to make my garden here.

INT. YORK COTTAGE. TINY BEDROOM/PASSAGE.
NIGHT.

We cut to night time inside York Cottage. JOHNNIE *is lying in bed, there is the sound of piano playing down the passage at the far end of the house. The door opens and* YOUNG GEORGE's *head appears round the door.*

YOUNG GEORGE: You're so lucky you don't have to do the recital!

We hear a voice calling YOUNG GEORGE.

Time cut. We cut outside into the passage. Far away somewhere in the house, YOUNG GEORGE's *voice is reciting Shakespeare in a clean crisp voice. We see* JOHNNIE *leaving his isolation quarters and creeping along the passage until he can see* YOUNG GEORGE *clearly, reciting to his parents. They cannot see* JOHNNIE, *but* YOUNG GEORGE *turns his head and smiles at* JOHNNIE *as he recites in his loud crisp voice. We cut to* JOHNNIE *lying back in his bed and staring at his single toy soldier on the shelf which has now been joined by some of his other toys including a parrot and a Russian doll. The bedroom door is opening slightly. We see* MARY *standing with* LALLA.

MARY: He is asleep . . .

LALLA: No I don't think he is, ma'am.

JOHNNIE turns and smiles at her.

JOHNNIE: Mama . . . ?

MARY stands in the doorway awkwardly. She seems almost nervous of talking to her child in front of LALLA.

MARY: Go to sleep, Johnnie . . .

The two women leave and close the door.

MARY turns to LALLA.

MARY: Will this work . . . this arrangement?

LALLA: Oh yes, ma'am, it will work I promise you . . . I will make it work . . . I will be here with him all the time –

MARY: Are you quite sure that it is all that's needed?

LALLA (*forcefully*): Nothing else is needed, Ma'am – it really isn't . . .

MARY stares at LALLA.

MARY: Very well.

We cut back inside the darkened bedroom. JOHNNIE *is lying in bed.* YOUNG GEORGE *has slipped into the room and is standing in the shadows. He lifts his finger to his lips to keep* JOHNNIE *from talking.*

We cut back to the two women outside the door.

MARY: It must be understood that any visitors, either coming to the cottage here or just walking in the garden, no visitors must ever see him. For their sake and his –

LALLA *surprised at the severity of the restriction.*

LALLA: That is any visitor at all is it, ma'am?

MARY: Yes.

We cut back to the two boys together in the darkness. They can hear the women moving away.

YOUNG GEORGE: Don't worry . . . I will always be here . . .

JOHNNIE *gets out of his bed in his pyjamas and stares down from his window into the darkness below.*

JOHNNIE: I'm making a garden . . .

YOUNG GEORGE: I can't see it, Johnnie . . . it's night now.

JOHNNIE: It's not very much at the moment, but I'm sure it will be . . .

YOUNG GEORGE (*suddenly*): I will never let them send you away!

The two boys stand together by the lighted window. A crane shot moving away from them, JOHNNIE'*s face staring out.*

INT. YORK COTTAGE. THE SCHOOLROOM. DAY.

We cut to the tutor, HANSELL, *looking several years older, standing in front of the blackboard. He is not just older but his manner has grown more harassed, more intense.*

For a moment we stay on him addressing the classroom, we do not see who he is addressing.

HANSELL: So now we come again to the outbreak of the Black Death . . . Can you tell me the name of one of the more important victims of the Black Death?

We cut to his point of view and we see the schoolroom is entirely empty except for one solitary pupil – JOHNNIE. *He is now four years older. He has a big handsome head and is tall for his age. He is nine years old.*

JOHNNIE *is staring back at* HANSELL *with a polite expression, but he does not respond at all.* HANSELL *suddenly raises his voice.*

So who was one of the important victims of the Black Death?! (JOHNNIE *stares back.*) Can anybody tell me that?! . . . John – we have done this again and again . . . I really must insist on an answer . . . Give me any kind of answer . . . !

JOHNNIE: I don't like the Black Death.

LALLA *is standing in the doorway watching.* HANSELL *swings round as he sees her.*

HANSELL: I give up . . . There is nothing more I can do!

LALLA: I thought you were going to teach him some family history . . . Johnnie likes that –

HANSELL: Oh, for goodness sake, I can't just teach him the last few years – he has to know it ALL! . . . (*He slams his book down on the desk.*) And he knows nothing and I'm locked up here . . . I'm as much shut away as he is and nobody listens to me – nobody could care less! . . .

He storms out.

INT. YORK COTTAGE. PASSAGE. MORNING.

We cut to the sound of children's voices laughing somewhere outside the house calling to each other in a vibrant way. JOHNNIE's *face turns with a sharp movement towards the noise.*

The blinds are shut all along the ground-floor passage. JOHNNIE *is moving along the passage lifting himself on tiptoe to see if he can catch a glimpse of what is happening through the shut blinds. He tries to open the blinds but he can't.*

He can hear the voices loud and clear and the noise of a car's engine seems to be moving along the side of the house. He starts to run down the passage, leaping high to see if he can catch any glimpse at all. The voices are really close. JOHNNIE *is excited and frustrated.*

He gets some boxes, piling them on top of each other, and then he pulls himself up so he can see from one of the top windows. The boxes teeter in a tall tower with him on top.

JOHNNIE *can see a huge new car right outside the back of York Cottage. And there is* KNUTSFORD, *the man with the red handkerchief, showing off his new car, tapping the shiny bonnet. Some of* JOHNNIE's *siblings,* MAY, HENRY, *and* YOUNG GEORGE, *who is now eleven and a suave-looking boy, surround the car excitedly.*

KNUTSFORD: So everybody in! – This is the fastest, the most elegant car in the whole kingdom . . . anybody who disagrees can stay behind!

The engine is running, the children pile into the car with excited laughs. KNUTSFORD *is sitting at the wheel. He glances up at the windows of York Cottage, as if he senses someone is watching. He searches the windows but he can't see anything.*

I never see that nice little chap Johnnie any more . . . Always busy at his lessons is he?

The car rolls away with a roar of its engine and squeals of excitement from its passengers.

EXT. YORK COTTAGE. THE GARDEN. AFTERNOON.
JOHNNIE *is working his garden, leather apron covering his sailor suit.* YOUNG GEORGE *is standing watching him and* LALLA *is sitting knitting nearby.*

JOHNNIE'*s garden is now a rich exotic place of flowers and colours, big tall foxgloves and sunflowers.* YOUNG GEORGE *is staring about the garden.*

YOUNG GEORGE: Johnnie . . . Your garden is really very impressive indeed now . . .

LALLA (*glancing up*): It's time for us to go in now, Johnnie . . . Before the guests from the big house come out into the garden.

As she gets up, a stout middle-aged servant, FRED, *comes running out into the garden rather frantically.*

FRED: Come quickly! . . . There's been another accident in the kitchen . . .

LALLA: Not more broken china – I don't believe it! . . . (*She moves off, calling out to* YOUNG GEORGE.) Bring Johnnie in now, Georgie –

But YOUNG GEORGE *and* JOHNNIE *don't move.*

And as they stand alone in the garden they catch a glimpse of a patrician-looking gentleman with an enormously self-important manner walking in the garden of the big house, accompanied by a younger man and a very pretty young woman.

Instead of going in, the two boys decide to follow them. We see them moving among the foxgloves and sunflowers, keeping pace with the adults but remaining out of sight.

The patrician man is ASQUITH *and he is in the middle of*

telling anecdotes, his laugh ringing round the garden.

ASQUITH: They couldn't believe their eyes – I promise you
. . . They just couldn't believe what they saw . . .

YOUNG GEORGE: You know who that is?

JOHNNIE: A very old general . . .

YOUNG GEORGE: No, no, don't be silly, Johnnie, he's the
Prime Minister.

They move to the very end of JOHNNIE*'s garden as they
follow the adults, and then slip through the gate into the
forbidden territory – for* JOHNNIE *– of the larger garden.*

ASQUITH *has stopped with the young couple on the path just
above them, and is glancing down towards York Cottage.*

ASQUITH: Amazing, isn't it, that they still live there – the
King and Queen – in that house?! It wouldn't look out of
place in Norwood or Surbiton . . . would it?! (*The young
couple are laughing away.*) And his mother all alone in the
big house . . . She won't move out! His advisers beg him
to give the place up – and so do we . . . What do you
think foreigners make of it?! They come to visit the King
on his country estate – and find him squashed into one
of the most suburban dwellings in the land! And the
King won't hear a word against it! . . .

YOUNG GEORGE *watches the Prime Minister move off.*

YOUNG GEORGE: You go in, Johnnie . . . I'll be back later . . .

YOUNG GEORGE *follows the adults along the path, leaving*
JOHNNIE *alone in the big garden.*

JOHNNIE *can just catch sight of people through the trees,
ladies in their long dresses moving with their parasols, men
in summer suits, glimpses of the royal gathering.*

He decides that he will take a closer look.

*We cut to him rounding a corner and seeing a ravishing
woman in her thirties standing all alone in the shadows
smelling flowers.* JOHNNIE *slips behind some foliage to watch
her. She seems to* JOHNNIE *to be a glowing, wonderful*

creation. The woman sees him looking at her through the
foliage. She is startled to find this big boy gazing at her.

FINE-LOOKING WOMAN: Hello . . . ? (JOHNNIE *smiles.*) What
are you doing in the bushes, young man? . . . (JOHNNIE
just watching her.) Who are you . . . ?

JOHNNIE: I'm Johnnie. I've just left my garden . . .

The FINE-LOOKING WOMAN *cannot stop herself touching*
his hair, drawn towards him by his natural warmth.

FINE-LOOKING WOMAN: Well, good afternoon, Johnnie . . .
Isn't it a blissful day?! The most perfect garden – the
most perfect day.

We cut to JOHNNIE *somewhere else in the garden. There is*
the sound of laughter, the whole garden seems to be echoing
with high spirits and adult laughter.

We cut to JOHNNIE *staring at a small wiry man sitting on*
a bench with a young woman. He is flirting with her in a
very overt, totally shameless way. The wiry little man is
LLOYD GEORGE; *his hair is not white yet. He is waving a*
cheap-looking novel at the lady.

LLOYD GEORGE: No no no – it is my *normal* reading matter –
absolutely! You will be surprised quite how many of
these I devour a month – tales from the Wild West . . .
And I love looking at the pictures too . . . just like a small
boy!

He hands the book to the woman for her to examine more
closely and as she takes it, he touches her hand, entwining
his fingers with hers.

EXT. SANDRINGHAM. TEA PARTY. AFTERNOON.
We cut to the royal party having tea out of doors under a
specially erected canopy. The old Queen, ALEXANDRA, *is sitting*
in the shade eyeing the biscuits. YOUNG GEORGE *is sitting close*
to her.

52

ALEXANDRA: Choose one for me, Georgie . . . No, careful now . . . You know the ones I like . . . The little pink ones, that's right . . . That's a clever boy.

We see ALEXANDRA *very conscious of her looks as she is sitting in the middle of this tea party containing* ASQUITH *and other important guests. She has an incessant self-obsession, her hand fluttering round her neck adjusting her necklace.* GEORGE *and* MARY *are also at the tea being watched by the politicians,* ASQUITH *and* LLOYD GEORGE. *There is a palpable tension between the diffident figure of the King and the confident politicians who ooze self-belief.*

GEORGE: Not bad, are they . . . The grounds at the moment . . . Did you see what has been done by the lake?

ASQUITH: It all looks splendid (*A tiny flick of his eyes.*) We walked all the way to York Cottage – a charming view, as always . . .

YOUNG GEORGE *is noticing how his parents are deeply conscious of the politicians' presence.*

FINE-LOOKING WOMAN: Mr Asquith, I'm sure this is a very misguided question . . . a silly thought . . . (ASQUITH *smiles indulgently.*) But I heard somebody say the other day, there could be a war before Christmas . . .

STAMFORDHAM *is sitting slightly behind the* FINE-LOOKING WOMAN *with his teacup balanced on his knee. He is watching everything with an eagle eye.*

ASQUITH: War? . . . (*He smiles breezily.*) Not as far as we know . . . Nobody has had the courtesy to tell us!

LLOYD GEORGE *smiles charmingly at the* FINE-LOOKING WOMAN.

LLOYD GEORGE: Put it out of your mind, please . . . There is no conceivable way that we'd agree to participate in a war in Europe . . . No foreseeable circumstances . . . I would be totally opposed to our involvement – and so would the Prime Minister . . .

YOUNG GEORGE: Because they are all our family? . . . Is that the reason? . . . (*The politicians all look at him.*) I mean not France of course but the other heads of state . . .

GEORGE: He is an absolute devil with his questions, that boy –

YOUNG GEORGE: Is that the reason?

ASQUITH: I think we'll just say, how could we argue with that!

LLOYD GEORGE (*chuckling*) That is absolutely true . . . an interlocking arrangement that binds us all together . . . an added safeguard!

During this last exchange MARY *has been galvanized by something she has seen. Behind the tea party she has caught a glimpse of a shape moving among the bushes in the distance. For a moment she just sees the movement, can't quite work out who is there. Then she sees that it is* JOHNNIE: *instinctively she looks worried about what might happen next. Almost at the same moment* ASQUITH *sees the shape in the bushes.*

ASQUITH: Who is that child over there?! . . . I thought for a moment it was some sort of animal watching us . . .

JOHNNIE appears out of the bushes and heads towards them across the lawn. MARY *watches his approach with apprehension, his eccentric but peculiarly confident walk.*

MARY: It is our son, Johnnie . . . It's a little surprising to see him over here, he should be at his studies –

GEORGE: Good Lord . . . . Why is he out of the cottage?

JOHNNIE walks straight past the politicians and heads directly for the plate of cakes in the manner of a much younger child.

ASQUITH: Hello, young man . . .

JOHNNIE ignores the greeting and with a cake in his hand turns to face them all. He peers at LLOYD GEORGE *for a moment, his face very close, much closer than a normal greeting, practically rubbing noses. Then he addresses them all.*

54

JOHNNIE: You know, Mama, we live in a really stupid house
... Which is a disgrace, an absolute disgrace! What's
more, everybody thinks that, the servants, the foreigners,
everyone ... ! This fat man here said so ...

ASQUITH *lets out a bark of a laugh, an extremely
embarrassed one.*

GEORGE: Be quiet at once, Johnnie!

MARY *tries hard to control her face, not to convey her
anguish at* JOHNNIE's *behaviour.*

JOHNNIE *chews his cake for a moment.*

JOHNNIE: Our house would not be out of place in a country
called Surbiton or Norwood. And Grandmama, silly old
thing, lives all alone in the big house when she ought to
know better!

ALEXANDRA *is laughing away merrily, and wiping her
mouth with her napkin. But we return to* MARY *and see just
how painful the situation is for her.*

INT. YORK COTTAGE. MARY'S SMALL STUDY.
NIGHT.
We cut to LALLA *knocking on the door of* MARY's *study. She is
obviously nervous, but there is also a determined look in her eye
as she enters. The room is very small and crammed with
ornamental objects. The two women face each other in this tiny
space.*

LALLA: Your Majesty ... ?

MARY: So why was Johnnie alone in the garden?

LALLA: I got distracted for a moment and he just slipped out
... I'm so sorry, ma'am ... He has never done that
before – all this time ....

MARY: I thought we had an understanding.

LALLA (*leaping in*): Yes, ma'am, we do ...

MARY: That Johnnie was not to be left alone, particularly
   when there are guests present –
LALLA: I know, ma'am! It will never happen again –
MARY: It *cannot* happen again. I know his father was very
   angry too . . . (*She moves an ornament on her desk.*) When
   Johnnie was small it was different, but now these things
   cannot be allowed.
LALLA: Yes, ma'am, I know. (*Very anxious.*)Was it terrible
   what he said? I do hope it wasn't too terrible?!
MARY: It was unfortunate in the extreme. If Johnnie cannot
   be controlled – we may have to consider an institution as
   the doctors advised. (LALLA *looks startled.*) I know we
   would rather not.
LALLA: That isn't necessary is it, ma'am?! . . . Surely not!
   MARY *looks at* LALLA. *She sees the strength of her feeling.*
MARY: You try very hard with him, Lalla, I do realize.
   (*Indicates photos of her children scattered among her
   ornaments.*) Each of my children have their strange ways
   I've found . . . (*Before* LALLA *can say anything.*) All
   children do, I know yes. And when they grow it becomes
   easier . . . or it should . . . But Johnnie will not grow in
   that way – we know that now – and we have to accept it.
LALLA: With respect, ma'am, I do believe Johnnie can grow, I
   mean in his mind, most certainly he can –
MARY: There's no sign of it so far, Lalla.
LALLA: There will be, ma'am! I'm sure he won't need to be
   shut away for the rest of his life . . . (*Before* MARY
   speaks.) I will be with him, all the time, like I said. But he
   will progress in his own way . . . You will see! He's
   working so hard at his studies – he really is!
   We stay on MARY's *face. We see she is unconvinced.*

INT. YORK COTTAGE. THE SCHOOLROOM. DAY.
We cut to JOHNNIE *standing by the window in the schoolroom with his back to the blackboard, rocking backwards and forwards, and tapping the window with a rhythmic knock.*

HANSELL *meanwhile is sitting at his desk beneath the blackboard, his head buried in his hands. Neither of them are talking to each other.*

LALLA *enters just after we cut into the scene.*

LALLA: Well, you make a fine pair, you two, don't you!
(HANSELL *groans without looking up.*) This just won't do
– this won't do at all!

INT. YORK COTTAGE. KITCHEN. DAY.
We cut to JOHNNIE *sitting at the kitchen table in front of* LALLA *surrounded by maths books and jars of different sorts of jam.*
FRED, *the plump servant, is sitting in the corner eating some large slices of ham.*

LALLA: Come on, Johnnie . . . You can do this sum . . .
(JOHNNIE *shakes his head.*) *Yes you can* . . . If I have ten
jars of blackberry jam and I take away three, how many
do I have left?!
JOHNNIE's *eyes are flashing towards* FRED *in the corner who
is biting into his thick slices of ham.*
(*Intense.*) Johnnie, you are able to do this . . .
JOHNNIE *staring back, giving no sign of an answer.*
If you do your arithmetic and some of your other
lessons, all sorts of things may happen . . .
JOHNNIE: I can't do it . . .
LALLA *suddenly turns on* FRED, *taking out her frustration
on him.*

57

LALLA: And it's the last time I try to teach the boy in here –
with you making all your terrible noises!

INT. YORK COTTAGE. THE SCHOOLROOM. LATE
AFTERNOON.
We cut to HANSELL, LALLA *and* JOHNNIE *in the schoolroom. On
the blackboard is a simplified family tree with Queen Victoria at
the centre, and showing how the* TSAR *is a first cousin of*
GEORGE V, *the* TSARINA *is Victoria's granddaughter.*

HANSELL *is staring down at* JOHNNIE's *effort to copy the
family tree.*

HANSELL: Your great grandmother is up there . . . in the
middle yes . . . now draw . . . draw the line going down
to show the Tsarina is her granddaughter – a *straight*
line . . .
We see JOHNNIE *drawing a very long arm of the family tree
bending round in an unconventional shape.*
HANSELL: Straight – the lines must be straight!
LALLA: Sssh . . . That's good, Johnnie . . . Now try to do the
other one straighter.
HANSELL: I can't believe we're spending all our time just
drawing these lines – drawing his relations . . .
LALLA (*to* JOHNNIE): Now your mother's side . . . as straight
as you can . . .
JOHNNIE *draws a long spidery line leading to* FAT MARY
and his mother.
LALLA: Not too long . . . you won't be able to fit it in –
HANSELL: Why not let the child just be in his garden?! . . .
That's the only thing he has mastered . . . You're just
raising his hopes like this . . .
LALLA (*determined*): He wants to do it, don't you, Johnnie!
Write your grandmother's name . . . My she was a large

58

woman! . . . (*A big earthy laugh.*) The fattest woman I
ever saw!

HANSELL is staring at JOHNNIE's other attempts at family
trees that are stuck up along the wall.

HANSELL: I don't know . . . These drawings are so odd! Look
at this one – the line of succession . . . here are his father
and mother . . . done perfectly normally . . . and then the
children . . . Prince Edward David first, Albert George
second – so far so good . . . but now why on earth does it
go over there? May and Henry in a funny loop! And
Georgie and John himself . . . right down here . . . with
strange rabbit ears!

For one moment HANSELL remains staring at the peculiar
line of succession then he looks up to see JOHNNIE struggling
to draw a straight line.

This will end badly for the boy . . . He needs simple
things, just simple things . . .

LALLA: No, no, that isn't true . . . Is it, Johnnie? . . . That just
isn't true!

JOHNNIE with his pencil writing very slowly.

LALLA is by the window staring down the long straight
drive at the back of York Cottage that stretches to the
horizon.

LALLA: He so wants to be with his family.

INT. BUCKINGHAM PALACE. A LONG PASSAGE. DAY.
We cut to YOUNG GEORGE staring down at some railings in
front of the palace. Three suffragettes have chained themselves to
the railings and a fourth is just in the process of doing so.
Suddenly police converge on them from all sides trying to get them
off the railings, the suffragettes determined not to be moved,
writhing and fighting to stop the police dislodging them.

MARY joins YOUNG GEORGE at the window. They both stare
down at the scene.

YOUNG GEORGE: They're having difficulty getting them off,
Mama . . . They'll need to cut them away –
MARY: They will manage it I assure you. We won't have them
dangling there for days, looking at us every time we
come out . . .
*We see the passion in the women's faces, and the
incomprehension in* MARY*'s eyes as she watches them.*
It's quite beyond me how people can make such a
spectacle of themselves. How on earth do they think this
will do them any good?!

INT. YORK COTTAGE. THE SCHOOLROOM. LATE
AFTERNOON.
LALLA *is alone with* JOHNNIE. *They are sitting next to each other
at* HANSELL*'s desk beneath the blackboard.* JOHNNIE *is writing
very laboriously.*

LALLA: Small . . . Johnnie you can write smaller than that.
JOHNNIE: Why does it have to be small?
LALLA: Because you're such a big young man now and you
should write like one . . . *small* letters. When we get our
call from London to see the doctors, they will wish to see
neat writing – for the tests they will do.
JOHNNIE: Will the tests be important?
LALLA: Oh I hope so!
We see JOHNNIE *trying with an intense effort to make his
writing smaller. As he writes his letter to his Russian cousins
we hear his voice.*
JOHNNIE'S VOICE: My dear Russian cousins, Olga, Tatiana,
Maria, Anastasia, and Alexei. I am writing to you after
all these years because I think of you so often. I will write
about my garden.

INT. RUSSIA. LONG CORRIDOR. DAY.
We see MARIA, *now aged sixteen, walking towards us down a long passage. She is reading* JOHNNIE's *letter and smiling.*

INT. YORK COTTAGE. THE SCHOOLROOM. DAY.
We cut back to LALLA *and* JOHNNIE.

LALLA: *Smaller!*

JOHNNIE'S VOICE: My garden is a wonderful place. I feel very happy sitting inside it.
We see the tall flowers in the garden. The camera moves through them revealing the secret hidden places of the garden.
It is the best garden that I have ever seen.

LALLA: Even smaller! . . .

JOHNNIE'S VOICE: Many times at night I think of your father swimming and how funny he looked.
We see a reprise of the image of the TSAR *swimming and swimming alone in the rock pool.*

We intercut with JOHNNIE *writing and the beautiful* MARIA *reading.*
My father will see me soon, I hope. He is very busy being King at the moment . . . All the railways nearly stopped absolutely and everybody would have had to walk . . . And the angry women are doing all sorts of things . . . And so are the Irish people . . .

INT. BUCKINGHAM PALACE. CORRIDOR NEAR CONFERENCE ROOM. DAY.
ASQUITH *is walking down a passage in Buckingham Palace. He is addressing an aide in a low voice.*

YOUNG GEORGE *is standing in the shadows watching him pass.*

ASQUITH: It is becoming more and more obvious I shouldn't be here . . . this is clearly a bad idea, a ridiculous notion, trying to do this – but nothing I could do would make him listen . . . !

ASQUITH *sees* YOUNG GEORGE *in the shadows just as he passes him.*

But no doubt this young man would have it all worked out!

We cut to YOUNG GEORGE *moving to the doorway of the state room where the conference is being held. A round table in the middle of the room is surrounded by about twenty chairs. The room is ringing with the sound of Irish voices. Groups of Irish politicians are clustered on separate sides of the room. Nobody is sitting down.*

STAMFORDHAM *is standing in the doorway.* YOUNG GEORGE *stands next to him staring at all the Irish politicians.*

YOUNG GEORGE: Why is this such a bad idea?

STAMFORDHAM (*not unkindly*): What have you been overhearing now?

YOUNG GEORGE: I'm just interested.

STAMFORDHAM: I know you are . . . (*As they both stare at the swirling groups of Irish politicians.*) Your father wanted to see if he could make a difference . . . by bringing together the different parties in Ireland. So he's holding this conference . . .

YOUNG GEORGE: But people don't think he can make a difference . . .

STAMFORDHAM *smiles at the boy's keen interest.*

STAMFORDHAM: I think that may be the general view, yes . . .

The King, GEORGE, *is approaching down the passage, with a determined walk.*

STAMFORDHAM *begins to move away.*

I have to join your father –

GEORGE *passes* YOUNG GEORGE *without acknowledging his presence. All the Irish politicians turn as the King enters.*

GEORGE: Gentlemen! . . . I thought you would all be in your places by now . . .

YOUNG GEORGE *sees how small his father appears, everybody else in the room seems to tower over him.*

The door shuts in YOUNG GEORGE's *face.*

YOUNG GEORGE *stands for a second listening to the muffled noises, extremely curious. After a moment he pushes the door open, just a few inches, so he can see through a tiny crack.*

He can see his father now seated in the middle of the round table. The group of politicians are all sitting down now, but they have left big gaps at the table to preserve their two distinct groups.

GEORGE: Gentlemen . . . it's very good of all of you to make yourselves available . . . Now I just have to see . . . I thought we'd begin . . . (*Turns to* STAMFORDHAM *and snaps.*) No, not that one, I want the other file! . . . No – *the other one . . .*

GEORGE *is shuffling his papers in total confusion.*

STAMFORDHAM *whispers in his ear.*

GEORGE: Are you sure we're going to begin with that? . . . It's not what I was expecting . . . I was given the wrong information . . . I don't know . . . I will need a moment before I'm ready . . .

YOUNG GEORGE *sees his father lost in a mountain of papers, shuffling them desperately.*

YOUNG GEORGE *closes the door, not wishing to watch any more, feeling for his father's embarrassment.*

INT. YORK COTTAGE. THE LANDING. DAY.

JOHNNIE *is at an upstairs window, staring down the long straight drive. His face is pressed right up to the glass. There is nothing coming towards him down the drive.*

FRED *sees* JOHNNIE *kneeling by the window, desperately peering out.* FRED *is eating an apple.*

FRED: Expecting news, Johnnie? . . . I'm not sure if it will be coming today . . .

    JOHNNIE *presses himself even closer to the glass. He is like a cat at the window.*

    It won't be coming today Johnnie!

    JOHNNIE *sees a distant shape coming over the horizon. For a moment it is so far away it is a blur – and then he sees it is just a horse and cart.*

    We see the disappointment in his eyes.

    LALLA *appears on the landing.*

LALLA: No it won't be today, Johnnie – but it will be soon . . . (FRED *looks doubtfully at* LALLA.) It definitely *will* be soon . . .

    We return to the road stretching towards the empty horizon.

INT. YORK COTTAGE. TINY BEDROOM. LATE AFTERNOON.

JOHNNIE *is sitting on his bed. He is pulling some books off his bookshelf to reveal a jar of blackberry jam hidden behind them.*

    He sticks his finger in the jam to get a big dollop out.

    We see the walls of his bedroom are covered with his family trees, several of them now, with their strange curving spidery lines.

    The door flies open and LALLA *is standing there flourishing a letter.*

LALLA: It's come, Johnnie! . . . It *has* come. The date for you to go to London.

JOHNNIE *grins, his mouth completely smeared with*
blackberry jam.

EXT. YORK COTTAGE. DAY.
A very fine motor car, one of the royal cars, stands outside York
Cottage. JOHNNIE *and* LALLA *moving to get into it.* JOHNNIE
looks exceptionally smart.

 Just as they are about to get into the car, JOHNNIE *moves*
round to inspect the bonnet, as he saw KNUTSFORD *do to his car.*
He gives the bonnet a little tap, and also the black and white tyres
a little prod. He salutes the chauffeur and gets in.

EXT/INT. ROYAL CAR. DAY.
We cut inside the car as it drives along. LALLA *is all dressed up*
sitting on the plush back seat. JOHNNIE *is sitting next to her,*
relishing the exquisite interior of the car with all its polished fittings.

 LALLA *is obviously tense, whereas* JOHNNIE *just looks like he is*
setting out on a great adventure.

LALLA: Now we are going to go over a few questions, Johnnie
 . . . So we are prepared. If they produce those animal
 cards again, the doctors, I'm not sure they will, because
 you're so much bigger, but if they produce the animals
 . . . you will remember the insect will always be the
 smallest . . . It is quite safe to put that last every time.
JOHNNIE: Yes.
 We can see JOHNNIE *pressing his nose to the car window, as*
 they leave the gloomy environs of the royal estate
 Sandringham, with its heavy pine forest. And then he sees
 the flat arable fields spreading out. They pass a group of
 agricultural workers who glance up from their work and
 watch the royal car pass, with this beautiful child staring

back at them from the car window.

LALLA: Listen to me, Johnnie . . . We have to do more
　　questions . . . Geography now – they're bound to ask
　　some geography questions . . . And you *do* know
　　geography . . . What is the capital city of France? . . .

JOHNNIE (*giving it a heavy French accent*): Paris! Or Paree . . .

LALLA: That's right . . . And the capital of Russia? . . .

JOHNNIE: St Petersburg . . . (*He stretches the word out.*) a
　　German name!

LALLA: You can say . . . 'My cousin the Tsar lives there' –
　　that will sound impressive –

JOHNNIE: Yes . . . (*He stares out of the window.*) I will say my
　　cousin Bill has a withered arm –

LALLA: No don't say that . . . I'm talking about cities, I
　　shouldn't have mentioned that, I'm muddling you now,
　　Johnnie . . . We must do some spellings of course as well
　　. . . Like 'sincerely', spelling that – and we must go over
　　all the sums we've learned of course –

JOHNNIE: I know all the questions . . . They will be happy
　　with me, the doctors.

*There is an abrupt cut to an industrial landscape. A large
expanse of dark brick walls, and sweaty muscular workmen
glimpsed through smoke, labouring at roadworks that
surround the car. They loom out of the smoke of the fires and
glance through the window of the car.*

　　LALLA *leans over and pulls the blind down on* JOHNNIE's
*window, then she pulls the blind down on her window, and
then on the dividing partition.*

　　JOHNNIE *can no longer see the outside world at all. He
can hear the sounds of the city, and we stay on his face,
peering around, desperate to see this new world.*

LALLA: Now we are in London – we must have the blinds
　　down . . . That was one of the messages I was sent . . .
　　About this trip . . .

JOHNNIE *does not reply, but he puts his face really close to the blind. When* LALLA *is straightening her hair in the mirror next to her seat,* JOHNNIE *lifts the blind just a little.*

He can see a confectionery shop plastered with advertisements for Bovril, chocolate and a big Union Jack advertisement trumpeting the delights of Empire toffees. Two stout clerks are standing outside the shop eating, their mouths full of toffee.

JOHNNIE *lets the flap go down, and then can't resist sneaking it up again. Another car is very close, just overtaking them, a couple of fashionable women peer back at him with interest.*

We cut outside, and see JOHNNIE *from their point of view. A crucial image of* JOHNNIE *staring out from the half-parted blind in his car, as he surveys the outside world. A glimpse of the hidden prince as others might see him.*

We cut back to LALLA.

LALLA: We're nearly there Johnnie . . .

We cut back to JOHNNIE. *He lifts the blind again. And sees a crocodile of children in school uniform walking down the street, in a neat disciplined formation.* JOHNNIE *watches their regimented progress with fascination.*

INT. BUCKINGHAM PALACE. THE BALLROOM. DAY.
We cut to the great long banqueting table stretching out in the ballroom. Two servants in stockinged feet are crawling on the surface of the table on all fours, one at each end, polishing. They are slowly moving towards each other down the length of the table.

INT. CONSULTING ROOM. DAY.
We cut to JOHNNIE *sitting in a large chair in front of a big desk.*

LALLA *is sitting in the background. Behind the desk is*
LONGHURST. HETHERINGTON *is standing.*

LONGHURST: Now, John . . . We want you to take your time
over every question we ask . . .
JOHNNIE: I will not need any time.
LONGHURST: Who is the Prime Minister of this country?
HETHERINGTON: The Prime Minister of England.
It is obvious JOHNNIE *doesn't know the answer but he
remains poised.*
JOHNNIE: He is a very fat man . . . a man of great importance
. . . Nearly as important as my papa.
LONGHURST: And do you know his name?
LALLA *mouths the name in the background.*
JOHNNIE: When I met him I was not allowed to say his name
– because he'd been very rude . . . and he wanted to
remain my friend . . .
*The doctors are puzzled by this answer but after glancing at
each other they feel it makes some kind of sense.*
    LONGHURST *starts writing elaborate notes with a heavy
black pen. The nib of the pen scratching menacingly across
the paper.* JOHNNIE *watches for a moment, then glances
anxiously at* LALLA.
JOHNNIE (*suddenly*): The capital city of Russia is St
Petersburg and my cousins, the Romanovs, live there . . .
The capital city of Greece is Athens and my uncle the
King of Greece lives there . . . the capital city of
Denmark is Copenhagen and my grandmama comes
from there . . . The capital of Germany where my cousin
Bill, the Emperor, lives –
LONGHURST: Please, John, you must wait for the questions.
JOHNNIE: My name is Prince John.
LALLA *sits bolt upright, completely surprised by* JOHNNIE'*s
tone.*

HETHERINGTON (*smiles*): Your Highness . . . you must allow us to go through the list of questions we have prepared.

JOHNNIE: Very well . . . . While I'm waiting I will get down.

JOHNNIE gets off his chair. He surveys the room which is decorated with various pompous pieces of furniture and a couple of stuffed animals on the mantelpiece. JOHNNIE moves around the room doing an exaggerated grand walk. When he speaks he mimics his father for a moment.

This room is not bad . . . not bad, gentlemen . . . (*He stops by the mantelpiece.*) This stuffed creature here – (*he indicates the specimen*) is called a spiny anteater and is quite a small animal . . .

He stares at the two surprised doctors and announces in a loud voice:

A *small* animal that lives in holes!

INT. BUCKINGHAM PALACE. THE BALLROOM. DAY.

We cut to the tablecloth being rolled down the full length of the banqueting table. And then we cut to the silver beginning to be laid, and the table decorations being put in place.

YOUNG GEORGE is sitting watching this happen, as the footmen and waiters scurry around the empty ballroom preparing the banquet. STAMFORDHAM pauses in the doorway to survey the scene. He calls across to YOUNG GEORGE.

STAMFORDHAM: What are you thinking about, young man? . . .

YOUNG GEORGE: I was thinking how difficult it must be to work out where everybody is going to sit at a banquet like this . . . (STAMFORDHAM's *eyes flick*.) With so many ambassadors, from all sorts of countries, and bishops and generals coming –

STAMFORDHAM: Not to mention politicians . . .

69

YOUNG GEORGE: Yes the politicians! . . . It must be hugely taxing . . . Do you do it?

STAMFORDHAM: Yes, I do it, in consultation with the King . . . And tonight is an interesting one . . . We've had several goes at it. There were a few little tricky corners.

YOUNG GEORGE: How do you decide?

STAMFORDHAM *moves among the tables, surveying his handiwork.*

STAMFORDHAM: Ah . . . There are the rules of protocol, of course – the smaller countries further down the table . . . and then you decide you might just bend the rules a little – because you know for instance the Russian ambassador has a passion for bird-watching and so does the Duchess of Bedford . . .

YOUNG GEORGE: I expect you're brilliant at that.

STAMFORDHAM (*smiles*): If nobody takes offence . . . if the banquet goes smoothly – then I'll be pleased. I always feel a slight flutter of apprehension as they start.

YOUNG GEORGE: Apprehension? . . . What could go wrong?

YOUNG GEORGE *has sat himself at the head of the long table. He stares around imagining the spectacle to come.*

STAMFORDHAM *smiles as he watches him do this.*

STAMFORDHAM: It's a pity you're not coming tonight, young man!

We stay on YOUNG GEORGE*'s eyes.*

INT. BUCKINGHAM PALACE. CLOAKROOM. LATE AFTERNOON.

We cut to some white gloved hands laying out beautiful soaps and stiff long brushes for the gentlemen's cloakroom.

We move over to the windows of the cloakroom and see security police taking their positions around the perimeter.

INT. BUCKINGHAM PALACE. PASSAGE. EARLY
EVENING.
We cut to JOHNNIE *and* LALLA *coming towards us down one of
the formal passages.* JOHNNIE *is stomping along having reverted
to his normal ungainly walk.*

They round a corner to see YOUNG GEORGE *standing in a
doorway down the other end of the passage.* JOHNNIE *rushes
towards him, his arms flailing.*

YOUNG GEORGE: Johnnie! . . . At last you've come.
    JOHNNIE *swings his arms around* YOUNG GEORGE.
JOHNNIE: George . . . I had my own motor car . . . I rode in
    my own car!
LALLA (*following behind*): Yes, I managed to see to it that
    we're staying here tonight . . . (*She ruffles* JOHNNIE*'s
    hair.*) I said he was too tired for the long journey back to
    Norfolk – and so here we are!
    LALLA *begins to move past* YOUNG GEORGE, *about to enter
    the drawing room*
YOUNG GEORGE: Lalla . . . I just want a moment alone with
    my brother.
LALLA: Alone?! No.
YOUNG GEORGE: Just for a moment . . . please . . . *please*,
    Lalla!
LALLA: Why do you need to be alone?
YOUNG GEORGE: Because I haven't seen Johnnie for ages! . . .
    (LALLA *looks sceptical.*) And I have a present for him –
    some pictures of our latest battleship. Papa will be so
    pleased if he knew I was talking about ships to Johnnie!
    (*He looks straight at* LALLA.) You can be here – right
    outside . . .

INT. BUCKINGHAM PALACE. DRAWING ROOM. EVENING.
We cut to some pictures spread all over the floor of the drawing
room. But instead of a battleship, they are of a great liner sinking.
The two boys are kneeling on the floor looking at the pictures.

YOUNG GEORGE: So what do you think?

> JOHNNIE *is staring at the dramatic pictures. We see they are*
> *a mixture of photographs and drawings from the* Illustrated
> London News *of the sinking of the* Empress of Ireland.

JOHNNIE: It's a great ship – falling down . . .

YOUNG GEORGE: Yes . . . It's the biggest ship of the
Canadian Pacific Line . . . The *Empress of Ireland*, it
collided in the St Lawrence river with another ship, it
just happened – two weeks ago.

> *We see the pictures of the wonderful interiors of the ship, both*
> *photographs and drawings. There is a picture of a concert in*
> *progress in the first-class saloon, and of children playing on a*
> *sandy beach created on the deck of the ship, and a game of*
> *cards being played in the smoking room, and people playing*
> *deck golf – 1914 society besporting itself across this great*
> *ship.* JOHNNIE *is staring closely at the pictures.*

JOHNNIE: It crashed? . . . The boat?

YOUNG GEORGE: Yes, it was an *enormous* boat, Johnnie . . . it
was nearly as big a ship as the *Titanic* and almost as
many people died. (JOHNNIE *is staring at the dramatic*
drawing of the ship sinking.) I knew you'd be interested,
Johnnie . . . It's better than a boring battleship!

JOHNNIE: Why are all the big boats crashing? . . . At the
moment? . . .

YOUNG GEORGE: I don't know . . . I don't know, Johnnie . . .
Something in the stars maybe.

> YOUNG GEORGE *suddenly flicks* JOHNNIE'*s hair in a*
> *spontaneous gesture.*

YOUNG GEORGE: I've missed you . . . a lot . . . (*Laughing*

72

teasingly.) I never thought I would, of course! (*He moves*.) I'm going to stop you being shut away – for tonight at least . . .

JOHNNIE *looks up sharply. Their eyes meet. At that moment* LALLA *appears round the door.*

LALLA: I have to get you to bed, Johnnie – right now!

INT. BUCKINGHAM PALACE. PASSAGE/MARY'S DRESSING ROOM. EVENING.

We cut to LALLA *sitting outside* MARY'*s dressing room. A lady-in-waiting comes out.*

LADY-IN-WAITING: The Queen will see you now.

Before she finishes the sentence LALLA *is pushing her way into the room.* MARY *is sitting at her dressing table in full evening dress.*

MARY: Lalla . . . There you are –

LALLA *cannot wait for* MARY *to finish her greeting, her words come tumbling out in a torrent.*

LALLA: Your Majesty, he did so well! You should have seen him, ma'am, seen Johnnie! You know how he usually finds it difficult, he finds talking a little hard sometimes . . . how to reply to people – in a way that is correct conversation . . . Well, he did it marvellously today, ma'am – he answered all the questions and more. He was quite the proper prince, he was – it was a wonderful thing to see, if only you had been there, ma'am –

MARY: Now now, slowly, Lalla . . .

LALLA: I'm sorry, ma'am . . . I've been waiting to tell you this – and it's rushing out of me . . .

MARY: Yes, so I see. (*It is obvious* MARY *is immensely pleased by the news, but she is keeping it firmly in check.*) And the doctors?

LALLA: The doctors were *stunned* . . . I think that's right, they were *stunned*.

MARY: They thought he had made progress did they? They said that?

LALLA: They did seem quite pleased, ma'am . . . I really think they were . . . Of course I don't know what they will say in their report to you – but they *must* say that! If only you'd been there, ma'am . . .

MARY: They wouldn't have been able to do their proper tests if I'd been there.

LALLA: No, I know that of course ma'am . . . I just meant it as a wish! If you *could* have seen it –

MARY: Well you're giving me a very good account, Lalla. I'm very surprised they let you stay in the room during the tests.

LALLA: I insisted on it, ma'am . . . I said I had to be there – I said I was *required* to be there.

MARY looks at her surprised, LALLA *meets her gaze unflinchingly.*

MARY: And Johnnie is here now?

LALLA: Yes, he's safely tucked up in bed. Fast asleep. He needed his sleep so much – he's worked so hard today –

MARY: Good.

LALLA: If you had heard him today, ma'am – you would have heard something different . . . I've never seen him speak like that –

MARY suddenly becomes more severe, keen not to become carried away.

MARY: There's still his *other* illness Lalla . . . The fits . . . Those will never go. They cannot be wished away.

LALLA: I know . . . But we haven't had one for such a while now – such a while . . .

We see a tiny private moment of excitement in MARY's *eyes, of real hope.*

74

MARY: Let us pray that is the case . . .

LALLA: I can only tell you what I witnessed – when you next –

MARY (*cutting her off*): I will see the child tomorrow. We have an important occasion tonight.

LALLA: Of course, ma'am . . . Of course. (*Backing out of the room.*) I just wanted to bring you the news . . .

MARY *alone with her ladies. She has now completely recovered her public poise.*

MARY: She is devoted, Lalla . . . completely devoted to the boy. But how she talks . . . How that woman talks! One needs to set aside an extra hour for all her talk.

MARY *stares at herself in the mirror.*

INT. BUCKINGHAM PALACE. UPSTAIRS BEDROOM. EVENING.

JOHNNIE *is alone in his spacious upstairs bedroom. He is standing in his pyjamas. The shadows of a summer evening fall across the room.* JOHNNIE *staring out of the window. He can see across the walls of the palace to the street beyond. A couple of carriages are going round in circles in the little square beyond and just to the left we see a motor car driving in circles too.*

Suddenly YOUNG GEORGE *is standing next to him.*

YOUNG GEORGE: I knew you wouldn't be asleep. (*Indicating the carriages going round in circles.*) They were worried about arriving too early (*He moves to the other window.*) And look here!

We see, half obscured by trees, the end of a queue of three carriages and two cars trying to get into the palace. The two forms of transport are mingled together in the queue.

And *those* people are worried about being too *late*!

JOHNNIE *watches the queue, and then the carriages going round in circles.*

75

JOHNNIE: What silly people!

YOUNG GEORGE: No Johnnie, it's because Papa has decided to introduce Sandringham time to here as well – you know how all the clocks are set half an hour fast in the big house – well now they are doing it here too! . . . And nobody knows what time it is! (*He turns*.) Coming?

JOHNNIE: Where am I coming?

YOUNG GEORGE: We're going to find a way of seeing the banquet.

JOHNNIE *accepts this as perfectly sensible. He moves off in his pyjamas.*

YOUNG GEORGE: Johnnie? (JOHNNIE *stops*.) Isn't there one thing we have to do?

JOHNNIE (*looks blank*): What?

YOUNG GEORGE: I think maybe we need a change of clothes for you.

JOHNNIE: They have taken my clothes away!

YOUNG GEORGE: Well we'll have to see what we can do . . .

INT. BUCKINGHAM PALACE. CORRIDOR NEAR
BALLROOM. NIGHT.

MARY *is walking down the passage accompanied by her ladies, moving towards a state room where people are milling before the banquet, blurred shapes in the distance. The passage is lined by footmen and a few guests admiring pictures.*

The camera picks out a YOUNG WOMAN *standing among the guests watching the Queen approach. The* YOUNG WOMAN *is obviously very tense.* MARY *stops for a moment unexpectedly, seeing some guests admiring an ornate clock sitting on a table. The* YOUNG WOMAN'S *face becomes even more tense as she waits for the Queen.*

MARY: Charming isn't it . . . this clock has just rejoined the

collection as it happens . . . It had been given away
inappropriately as a gift – but we managed to retrieve it.

MARY *smiles and moves on.*

Suddenly the YOUNG WOMAN *lunges forward and falls
to her knees in front of* MARY.

SUFFRAGETTE: Oh, Your Majesty . . . please . . . stop
torturing the women . . . why are you torturing the
women? . . .

MARY *is terrifically calm. She is not tempted, even for a
second, to reply to the* YOUNG WOMAN. *She glances down
at her with an imperious stare, totally composed.*

And then she steps around the YOUNG WOMAN *and
moves on as if she was walking round a chair that had been
suddenly put in her path. Footmen converge on the* YOUNG
WOMAN *from all sides bundling her away.*

*There is consternation round the Queen, her ladies swarm
round her buzzing with anxious queries.*

MARY: No need for alarm . . . Everything is simply fine.

*We cut to the doorway of the state room, guests are craning
to see what has happened, bunching up in an excited group.
We hear the gossip spreading through the throng about the
incident. 'Was the Queen attacked? . . .', 'Was there a
knife?! . . .', 'I think there was a knife! . . .', 'She was
magnificent . . .', 'She was so calm, it's amazing how calm
she was . . .', 'Was the woman foreign? . . .', 'They will
never get the vote now! . . .'*

INT. BUCKINGHAM PALACE. PASSAGE/STAIRS.
NIGHT.

We cut to JOHNNIE *and* YOUNG GEORGE *moving along the back
passages.* JOHNNIE *is dressed in one of* YOUNG GEORGE'S *suits
wearing it over his pyjamas, the jacket a little too big,
occasionally hanging open to reveal the pyjamas underneath.*

The two boys are moving along a dark passage and then a subterranean corridor, surrounded by old pipes.

YOUNG GEORGE: Come on . . . we're nearly there! . . .
We cut to YOUNG GEORGE *moving up some hidden very steep stairs which are squashed into a corner of the basement. As the boys climb higher and higher we can hear the sounds of the guests, the adult world, ringing out all around them, and getting louder.*

    YOUNG GEORGE *opens a small concealed door at the top of the stairs and the two boys disappear through it.*

INT. BUCKINGHAM PALACE. THE BALLROOM. NIGHT.
Suddenly the boys emerge high up in the ballroom, in a gallery below the musicians gallery, hidden from the ballroom by a screen. Below them they can see the spectacle of the banquet through a latticed screen. There are a few discreet viewing holes in the screen where people can watch what is going on below.

    The banquet is in full flow. There are all the ambassadors of Europe, of the USA and Russia and the Empire, there are the bishops and the politicians, and a sprinkling of favoured aristocrats.

    YOUNG GEORGE *looks at* JOHNNIE *triumphant at getting them in.* JOHNNIE *beams.*

YOUNG GEORGE: Now, Johnnie . . . Stand here . . . Be careful you're not seen –
We can see below them STAMFORDHAM *in earnest conversation with an ambassador covered in medals. We see all the different orders and decorations which festoon the guests, clanking as they eat, getting in the way. We see several army generals looking very merry and confident, cheeks flushed, drinking happily.*

JOHNNIE: I think the generals have got too many medals on
them . . .

We see MARY *at one end of the great banqueting table and*
GEORGE *at the other.* YOUNG GEORGE *surveys the scene,
his gaze moving from* STAMFORDHAM *to where some of the
important guests have been seated.*

YOUNG GEORGE: I just want to work out how he's done it.
There's the Russian ambassador next to that bishop who
never stops talking – look Johnnie, Russia is opposite
Germany, Cousin Bill's ambassador . . . and there's the
Austrian ambassador opposite France . . . And look at
those ladies between them. (*We see some very beautiful
women sprinkled in among the ambassadors.*) And look, Mr
Asquith is sitting opposite the Tories, so they can gossip
together . . . Politicians only like talking to each other!
(*Admiringly.*) It's a perfect plan . . . everybody pleased
with where they have been put . . . It's ideal!

JOHNNIE *staring at the adults below him, he starts to mimic
the bishop's vigorous chewing – the bishop chews so fast
because he wants to go on talking.*

*We cut down to the level of the banquet. We see the boys'
faces just visible through the screen staring down at the great
table. So far nobody has spotted them.*

We cut back to the boys. YOUNG GEORGE *pulls* JOHNNIE
back slightly into the shadows.

YOUNG GEORGE: Careful, Johnnie . . . You mustn't be seen . . .

*Suddenly a hatch opens in the floor of the gallery above
them. One of the musicians stares down at them. The two
boys glance back anxiously at the musicians who are waiting
with their instruments on their laps. The boys are not sure if
their position is about to be given away.* YOUNG GEORGE
decides to wave confidently.

YOUNG GEORGE: Gentlemen!

VIOLINIST: Your Royal Highness . . . Quite a hubbub, isn't it?!

YOUNG GEORGE: A hubbub indeed.

VIOLINIST: We'll have to play loud tonight – they are in a rather excited mood . . . !

YOUNG GEORGE: And why are they like that, sir?

VIOLINIST: Haven't you heard? . . . There was an incident between your mother and an intruder . . . And she was magnificent, the Queen, so they say . . . And that is what everybody is talking about . . . ! Everybody is thrilled no harm came to the Queen . . . We'll have to play rather too loud tonight . . . No adagios at this banquet . . . You'll have to hold on tight!

We cut back to the children's point of view of the banquet and we indeed see MARY *sitting at the head of the table sparkling, seemingly more confident then she has ever been. She can hear people's comments from the other end of the table, various stray remarks – 'It was marvellous the way she reacted', 'Just stepped over her'.*

GEORGE, the King, looks at MARY *from his position at the other end of the table and smiles admiringly at her. The whole banquet is in a euphoric state, with relief, and determined to enjoy themselves.*

We cut back to YOUNG GEORGE.

YOUNG GEORGE: Doesn't Mama look different . . . She is smiling . . .

JOHNNIE: She looks very pretty.

YOUNG GEORGE *suddenly looks at* JOHNNIE *concerned.*

YOUNG GEORGE: You will remember, Johnnie, if the music is too loud – or anything else happens – if you feel ill . . . you will tell me *at once.*

JOHNNIE: I'm not ill.

YOUNG GEORGE: You must tell me as soon as you feel it – if you think anything's coming . . .

JOHNNIE: Nothing is going to happen to me . . .

JOHNNIE *suddenly sees the* FINE-LOOKING WOMAN, *the*

*one he saw in the garden, sitting among the guests. He
smiles, thrilled to see her and presses his face even closer to
the screen. There she is in a magnificent dress.*

At this very moment we cut to the FINE-LOOKING
WOMAN. *She looks up towards the musicians as if she senses
something.* JOHNNIE *moves back just in time and disappears
into the shadows. The* FINE-LOOKING WOMAN *is puzzled –
did she see a young boy up there staring out?*

And then a moment later JOHNNIE *dares to step out of the
shadows and he can see her clearly. And she can recognize
him. She looks surprised and then delighted to see him. He
beams back, he moves into the shadows again and then back
out, like playing a game of hide-and-seek with her. The*
FINE-LOOKING WOMAN *laughs, this beautiful boy moving
in and out of the light, just for her, a private moment between
them, among the hundreds of guests. The* FINE-LOOKING
WOMAN *blows him a discreet kiss, and then waves.*

MARY *notices the* FINE-LOOKING WOMAN *staring up to
the gallery.* MARY *follows her gaze, but* YOUNG GEORGE
pulls JOHNNIE *back into the shadows just in time.* MARY *is
not sure if she saw something or not. She keeps watching the
space for a moment but* JOHNNIE *does not reappear.* MARY
returns to her guests.

YOUNG GEORGE: We you seen?

*He sees the senior footmen staring up at them and giving a
signal, pointing vigorously.*

*Suddenly there is a deafening eruption of music above their
heads, a piece of Handel. The senior footman was signalling
for it to begin. The music seems to shake the whole gallery.*
JOHNNIE'S *face turns towards* YOUNG GEORGE. *He reacts
very strongly to music, he looks excited, his body responding
physically.* YOUNG GEORGE *is suddenly alarmed.*

Johnnie? . . .

But JOHNNIE'S *eyes are shining. He stares down at his*

*parents' banquet, the adult world looking magnificently
confident, supremely sure of their place in the world and of
the future. We see a series of images, intensifying with the
music, the ambassadors, the politicians and the royals
laughing and gossiping with each other and sneaking careful
judgemental looks at each other's appearances when they get
the chance. The music is accelerating in tempo all the time,
getting more agitated.* JOHNNIE *stares up at the musicians,
at their fingers moving over the instruments, especially the
woodwind and the trumpets. He moves his fingers like he is
playing an imaginary instrument.* JOHNNIE *is revelling in it,
his body begins to move in a strange little dance.* YOUNG
GEORGE *is holding* JOHNNIE's *hand really tightly as*
JOHNNIE's *body is shaking.*

YOUNG GEORGE: Maybe we should leave? . . .

JOHNNIE: No . . . I like it . . . there's nothing to worry about
. . . I won't spoil the banquet . . .

*Suddenly we see a tall dark man, an official government
messenger, standing in the doorway of the ballroom. He gives
a note to a footman, talking to him in a very agitated way.
We follow the footman, picking his way reluctantly round
the table to give the note to* ASQUITH. ASQUITH *looks
surprised to be bothered.*

At this very moment we see STAMFORDHAM *glancing up
idly at the musicians and seeing the boys behind the screen.*

YOUNG GEORGE *meets* STAMFORDHAM's *gaze, gives
him a charming smile and lifts his finger to his lips.*

JOHNNIE *is doing his excited leaps in the air to the music.*

We see ASQUITH *get up, move along the table, making
profound apologies. He stops by* LLOYD GEORGE *and
indicates they must leave the room at once. We cut back to*
STAMFORDHAM *who is watching this with concern.*

YOUNG GEORGE: We've got to go, Johnnie . . . we've got to
go now . . .

INT. BUCKINGHAM PALACE. CORRIDOR NEAR
BALLROOM. NIGHT.
*We cut to the two boys rushing through the back passages. We cut
back to the banquet, a piece of Handel reaching a climax. We cut
back to* JOHNNIE, *glancing over his shoulder as he runs, reluctant
to leave the spectacle of the banquet.*

*The boys go round a corner and collide with a conspiratorial
group of* ASQUITH, LLOYD GEORGE, *the dark messenger and
two other aides.*

ASQUITH: We have to have this confirmed – before we tell the
King . . . Confirmation is essential . . . but this news
might change everything, everything, gentlemen . . .
*The boys move past the politicians, the adults barely register
their presence.*

*We cut to a high shot of the banquet, glowing with such
tremendous confidence.*

*We dissolve to an empty ballroom after the banquet. As
the music cuts abruptly we cut to a floor-level shot tracking
under the table, as footmen crawl on all fours under the great
table, picking up things people have dropped. Pieces of food,
gloves, a pocket watch, pieces of a necklace that has
disintegrated – the detritus of the banquet is being laid out in
front of the head footman.*

INT. BUCKINGHAM PALACE. MARY'S STUDY. MORNING.
We cut to morning light, MARY *sitting at her desk writing. The
door opens,* LALLA, YOUNG GEORGE *and* JOHNNIE *are in the
doorway.*

MARY: There you are, Lalla, exactly on time, admirable.
YOUNG GEORGE *is staring straight at his mother,
wondering if she saw them at the banquet.*

LALLA: This young man (*smoothing* JOHNNIE'*s hair*) was up
    very early.

MARY: Come here, Johnnie . . . (JOHNNIE *advances towards
    her.*) I hear you did very well when you saw the
    doctors . . .

JOHNNIE: The doctors were funny.

MARY: They were funny, were they? . . . And I hear your
    garden has made great progress . . . You must send me
    some pressed flowers from it. Will you do that?

JOHNNIE: Yes, Mama.

MARY: Now I have news. Your father wants to see you,
    Johnnie. So we'll go –

    STAMFORDHAM *enters escorted by one of* MARY'*s staff.*
    YOUNG GEORGE *meets his look.* STAMFORDHAM *gives
    him a private smile before moving over to the Queen. He is
    holding some newspapers.*

STAMFORDHAM: Ma'am . . . I just wondered if you'd like to
    see these? Descriptions in the newspapers of the incident
    last night –

MARY: If they're nice – I'll look at them.

STAMFORDHAM: Well just to pluck one at random – *The
    Times* for instance says your behaviour was 'a
    masterpiece of dignity and composure'.

MARY (*slight smile*): I think I might glance at them, yes –

STAMFORDHAM: Also, ma'am . . . I understand Johnnie is to
    see the King at any moment –

MARY: Yes . . . ?

STAMFORDHAM: Well, we have received some rather
    unexpected news, ma'am, which I'm expecting
    confirmation of any moment . . . If that comes through –
    I will need to see the King at once.

MARY: Johnnie will see the King. It's been too long . . . I'm
    very keen that the appointment is kept and not
    interrupted.

INT. BUCKINGHAM PALACE. THE KING'S
LIBRARY/STAMP COLLECTION. MORNING.
We cut to the large door of the library opening and JOHNNIE
looking in cautiously.

GEORGE *is right at the other end of the library staring down at*
some stamp albums. We see that most of the bookshelves are not
full of books but albums of stamps. And there are stamps in glass
cases.

GEORGE: Come in . . . Come in, Johnnie . . . I've got some of
the stamps out . . . here . . . some of the best I've got . . .
I thought we could have a look at the stamps . . . Come
here, child . . .
It is obvious that JOHNNIE *has absolutely no interest in*
stamps. He looks bewildered at the idea, but dutifully
advances towards his father.
You see how my collection has grown – we have special
rooms for it now! Now look at these ones . . . A whole
page from Persia . . . from Persia, my boy . . .
JOHNNIE *glances down for just one quick second at the*
stamps, and then looks at his father's face – he's much more
interested in studying his father's expression.
JOHNNIE: Very nice . . .
GEORGE: Look properly, child! You didn't look for long
enough . . .
Some of the stamps fill the screen, exotic designs and colours
from the far corners of the Empire.
This one is very rare . . . Very rare indeed . . . This one is
especially pleasing – it's from Fiji . . . I have a glance at it
every day at the moment . . . I come in here and have a
look at it –
As GEORGE *is saying this there is a strange sound from*
behind the display case. JOHNNIE *moves round the corner to*
look at the noise and finds himself staring at a large parrot.

85

What are you looking at? . . . Ah, the bird, haven't you
seen her yet? . . . That's Charlotte . . . I let her fly about.
(*Slight laugh to himself.*) She talks a lot more sense than
most people I meet!

JOHNNIE *smiles with delight at the parrot.*

GEORGE *is moving another large album in front of them
eager to show off his best stamps.*

Now what about China?! . . . Have you ever seen a
stamp from China? . . . How much do you think that one
there is worth? Come on, take a guess! . . . To the
nearest ten guineas.

It is clear that JOHNNIE *has no idea what his father is
talking about. He just stares at him.*

There is a knock on the door. STAMFORDHAM *appears
looking very grave.*

STAMFORDHAM: Sir, my apologies, sir . . .

GEORGE: What! Can't you see I'm busy?!

STAMFORDHAM: I have the Prime Minister on the telephone.
It is most urgent –

GEORGE: What? Why is he calling at this hour? I only saw
him last night – (GEORGE *moves off.*) Look at the stamps,
Johnnie – I'll come back and see what value you guessed
at!

JOHNNIE *is left alone in the big room. He stares at the
parrot, thrilled to be so close to the bird. The parrot is looking
at the clock near the stamp album.* JOHNNIE *opens the clock
face and carefully puts the minute-hand back half an hour.
He looks up. They are still alone.*

The parrot suddenly flies off to the far end of the room.
JOHNNIE *follows.*

*He opens the door at the end of the library. The parrot
looks at him and then flies through the door.* JOHNNIE
*laughs delightedly and chases after the parrot as it sails in
front of him through the palace.*

INT. BUCKINGHAM PALACE. LONG CORRIDOR.
MORNING.
We cut to LALLA *in the passage talking urgently to a maid.*

LALLA: What do you mean nobody can find him?! . . . He is
     with his father – and the Queen said they must not be
     interrupted.
MAID: Nobody can find Prince John, he is not in the library
     . . . The Queen wondered if you knew where he was . . .
     LALLA *looks up alarmed.*

INT. BUCKINGHAM PALACE. KITCHEN/MAIN PASSAGE.
MORNING.
We cut to JOHNNIE *following the parrot further and further along
the back passages. He is beginning to breathe faster and faster. He
follows the parrot into a dark area where food is laid out under
muslin. The parrot perches in the shadows and* JOHNNIE *looks
up.*
  We cut back to LALLA *approaching* MARY *outside her study.*
YOUNG GEORGE *is also there.*

LALLA: Ma'am – Johnnie must have gone on one of his
     wanders . . . I haven't seen him –
MARY: We will go and look for him together then, Lalla.

INT. BUCKINGHAM PALACE. KING'S STUDY. MORNING.
GEORGE *is on the phone,* STAMFORDHAM *is standing near him.*

GEORGE: Are you sure? . . . In that case this is the most
     shocking news . . . It's been totally confirmed? (*He looks
     at* STAMFORDHAM.) The Archduke Ferdinand has been
     assassinated . . . (*Back into the phone.*) Where was it?

87

Sarajevo . . . (*He looks at* STAMFORDHAM.) You don't look very surprised – when did you know about this? (*He turns back to the phone, and addresses the Prime Minister in a sharp tone.*) I'm beginning to suspect quite a few people knew about this before I did –

INT. BUCKINGHAM PALACE. KITCHEN/MAIN PASSAGE/SCULLERY AREA. MORNING.
We cut to MARY, LALLA *and* YOUNG GEORGE *moving urgently through the subterranean passages and into the kitchen area. Servants getting to their feet rapidly as they see* MARY *coming. A scullery maid is standing at the far end of the kitchen beckoning to them.* MARY, LALLA *and* YOUNG GEORGE *approach and go into the darkened room.*

We see their startled faces. And then we see JOHNNIE *lying on the floor in the darkened pantry watched over by the parrot that has retreated into the shadows.*

JOHNNIE *is having a severe epileptic fit, his body jerking violently on the floor, his face distorted.*

MARY *looks absolutely devastated at this sight, shocked and apprehensive. We see there are tears in her eyes. She is appalled to see her child in such a condition.*

MARY: The poor child . . . Is that what happens? I had no idea . . . The child . . .

LALLA *has run over to* JOHNNIE *and is kneeling by him.*
LALLA: Come on, Johnnie . . . I'm here now . . . Lalla is here . . . That's my boy . . . (*Her tone is fearless, totally calm. As he has this powerful fit, she holds him close.*) This is my fault . . . I got him too excited . . . He's overtired with everything –

YOUNG GEORGE *is staring completely stunned at seeing his brother like this. He has never seen a full fit before.* LALLA *instinctively feels she has to reassure them.*

I know it's a shocking thing to see . . . But he'll be so much better so very quickly . . . It's not as bad as it seems, ma'am!

We close in on MARY *who is clearly very shaken.*

INT. BUCKINGHAM PALACE. CORRIDOR NEAR KING'S STUDY. AFTERNOON.

We cut to the passage outside the King's study. It is full of officials with their notebooks at the ready swirling about in confusion, highly agitated. The door in the distance opens, and we can see STAMFORDHAM *and* GEORGE.

GEORGE (*furious*): It is clear there was a deliberate decision not to tell me last night – that was an absurd decision! It appears practically everybody knew about it apart from me – How can I work out what this means?! . . . How can I have an opinion on what we should do if nobody tells me it has happened?!

LALLA and YOUNG GEORGE *and* JOHNNIE *are moving down the passage in the opposite direction having to push their way through all the milling officials.*

YOUNG GEORGE: Nobody knows what this means . . . Nobody knows what's going to happen . . . The Archduke assassinated! Will all the armies start mobilizing? . . . Everybody is trying to guess who will make the first move.

Officials overhearing are startled at his grasp of events.

LALLA: Well, we have to get back to the country and make sure Johnnie gets better –

YOUNG GEORGE: They will let you stay with him? They're not going to send him away, are they?

LALLA: He did so well with the doctors. Just let anybody try!

EXT. BUCKINGHAM PALACE COURTYARD.
AFTERNOON.

*We cut outside into the palace courtyard. A motor car is waiting.
As* LALLA, JOHNNIE *and* YOUNG GEORGE *approach it, large
government cars appear and rumble past them. People are spilling
out of the cars, more government officials holding files and papers,
moving urgently towards the palace.*

*One of the officials drops the box he is carrying and the
documents scatter all over the courtyard in a snow flurry of
papers, being tossed in the wind. The official moves frantically
trying to pick them up.*

YOUNG GEORGE *gives* JOHNNIE *an intense passionate
embrace.*

JOHNNIE: Where am I going?
LALLA: Just back to the country, Johnnie . . .
YOUNG GEORGE: If they think they can take Johnnie away – I
will never let them! *Never!*

> JOHNNIE *and* LALLA *move off in the car, looking back
> through the rear window at the courtyard. A receding shot of*
> YOUNG GEORGE *waving them off emotionally – his small
> figure determined. All around him the official is scrabbling to
> retrieve the documents as the papers blow everywhere.*
> JOHNNIE *and* LALLA *watch the frantic official and the
> fluttering paper and the figure of* YOUNG GEORGE *receding.*

JOHNNIE: I liked the banquet . . . When will they be holding
another? . . .

> *We stay on* JOHNNIE'*s face staring out of the back window
> as he moves away from us.*

Credits.

90

THE LOST PRINCE

Part Two

The Russian princesses out boating shortly before the revolution

Johnnie goes on procession with his household

Queen Mary and her ladies-in-waiting gather chestnuts
to help the war effort

Johnnie with his precious gramophone, a gift from his brother

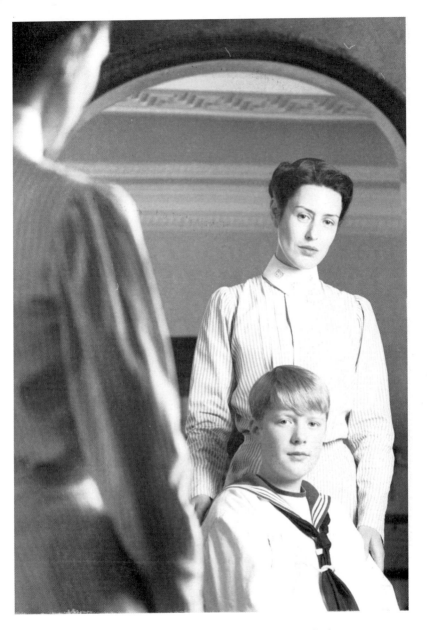

Johnnie and Lalla preparing for the recital

Maria, one of the daughters of the Tsar
during her imprisonment in the farmhouse

Johnnie giving his recital

Georgie shouting for Lalla when Johnnie is dying

INT. CREDIT SEQUENCE. DAY.
As the main titles finish we dissolve into a large close-up of
JOHNNIE *staring straight into the lens.*

His particular stare, his curious shining eyes are both innocent
and penetrating.

EXT. RUSSIA. A LAKE SURROUNDED BY FOREST.
AFTERNOON.
A high shot of a rowing boat drifting lazily on a lake which is
surrounded by woods.

In the rowing boat are three of the Russian royal daughters,
TATIANA *(aged seventeen),* MARIA *(fifteen), and* ANASTASIA
(thirteen). Their white dresses contrast with the dark water. Their
boat drifts gently past little ALEXEI *(aged ten), the Tsarevich, who*
is alone in his boat being rowed by his bodyguard.

On the bank of the lake the TSARINA *is sitting on a fine chair*
surrounded by servants and picnic baskets. It is an abundant
picnic with the food beautifully laid out. Everything is perfectly
poised, but the TSARINA *breaks the tranquil mood. She indicates*
with some ferocity that she wants the rugs that have been so
carefully laid out to be rearranged into a different configuration.

The servants scurry around trying to carry out her orders.

EXT/INT. BUCKINGHAM PALACE. THE TELEGRAPH
ROOM. AFTERNOON.
We see through a window down into the courtyard of the palace
in London.

It is raining, figures are scuttling urgently under their
umbrellas, criss-crossing the courtyard.

We move from the window to the interior of the small palace
telegraph room, which is manned by three stout clerks. They are
handling the incoming wires and are writing furiously. The

telephone switchboard is also contained in the room. It is polished and gleaming.

   STAMFORDHAM *is standing in the doorway watching the clerks' frantic activity.*

STAMFORDHAM: If the telephone rings from Austria –
   nobody can talk to the King, except the Emperor
   himself. Is that understood, gentlemen? If anybody
   telephones from Russia – you must find me where ever I
   am . . .
   We move in on the telephone switchboard, as if it is about to ring.

   STAMFORDHAM *staring at it anxiously.*

EXT. RUSSIA. A LAKE SURROUNDED BY FOREST.
AFTERNOON.
We cut back to the Russian royal party having their water picnic. The TSAR *is swimming directly towards the camera, his leisurely self-congratulatory swimming a reminder from the first part. He slips through the water towards us.*

   We see a high shot of the royal party, and the Emperor swimming.

   Some estate workers are passing on a trail through the wood. They stop to stare down at the TSAR *in the lake. They are immediately surrounded by some of his bodyguards and are moved on.*

   We see the royal children who are now sitting around the TSARINA *waiting for their father to finish his swim so they can start their picnic. And then we see some government cars, a convoy of four bumping along the trail to the lake. Officials clamber out – we see they are generals and chiefs of staff. They stand in a line waiting for the* TSAR *to finish his swim.*

   We see the TSAR *turn and start swimming on his back,*

absolutely oblivious.

We cut to the youngest girl, ANASTASIA, *watching the scene, the officials waiting by the car for the* TSAR, *eyeing the picnic hopefully, clearly expecting to be asked to partake.*

We cut from ANASTASIA's *face to* YOUNG GEORGE's *face, in London, from young adult to young adult.*

INT. BUCKINGHAM PALACE. STAMFORDHAM'S OFFICE. AFTERNOON.

YOUNG GEORGE *is standing in the doorway watching* STAMFORDHAM *who is hunched forward over his desk, staring at the silent telephone.*

YOUNG GEORGE: Waiting for it to ring . . . ?

    STAMFORDHAM *looks up with a start.*

STAMFORDHAM: Maybe . . . (*He then adopts his customary charming, detached manner.*) The Emperor of Austria has never used the telephone before . . . I'm told he has one on his desk purely for decoration . . . (*He moves his telephone slightly.*) He's eighty-four years old and he has to try to get the hang of it this week of all weeks . . . ! And what are you waiting for, young man . . . ?

YOUNG GEORGE: I'm trying to see my father . . . I've been trying all week – to discuss my future –

    He notices STAMFORDHAM's *eyes flick towards the telephone. He sees he is not listening.*

    Who's going to make the first move then?

    STAMFORDHAM *chuckles at his grasp of events.*

STAMFORDHAM: Have you got some money?

    YOUNG GEORGE *is flattered to be asked.*

YOUNG GEORGE: Of course. (*He takes three half-crowns out of his pocket.*) How much do you want? . . . Are we having a bet?

STAMFORDHAM: Oh no, I never bet . . . three will do . . . (*He slides the coins along the surface of his desk.*) If you've lost your heir to the throne – as Austria has – then you feel you have to do something, so you declare war on who you imagine is responsible – Serbia . . . but you don't really mean it.

YOUNG GEORGE: How can you not really mean it?!

STAMFORDHAM: All the Austrian generals are on holiday . . . so are all the German generals . . . so is the Kaiser and the Emperor –

YOUNG GEORGE: And so are we.

STAMFORDHAM: Absolutely! You don't declare war when everyone is on holiday and not have them return . . . So it is purely for show – a wrap on the knuckles . . . And that is how it will stay . . . (*He moves the third coin slowly across the desk, then spins it.*) Just so long as Russia doesn't get everybody excited, doesn't decide to mobilize its army, to come to the aid of Serbia –

YOUNG GEORGE: Because then Germany would feel it had to make a move – (*He pushes another coin into* STAMFORDHAM*'s neat pattern.*) And *we* wouldn't approve of that would we –

STAMFORDHAM (*chuckles*): Who knows what we would do . . . ! But there's really no chance of any of this happening –

He pockets all YOUNG GEORGE*'s money.* YOUNG GEORGE *looks very startled.*

Because as you might know, young man – your cousin, the Russian Emperor, finds it difficult to make decisions . . . (STAMFORDHAM *jangles* YOUNG GEORGE*'s money.*) I think we may have a bet after all . . . !

EXT. RUSSIA. A LAKE SURROUNDED BY FOREST.
AFTERNOON.
We see the TSAR *turn in a lazy circle in the water.*

*The generals on the bank shift from foot to foot. Then we cut to
the* TSAR *emerging from the lake and the servants converge on
him with his robes and towels.*

The TSAR *moves towards the generals waving his arms,
making decisive gestures.* ANASTASIA *stares across at the scene
and we see it through her eyes. It is obvious her father has
surprised everybody by suddenly giving orders.*

TSAR: We mobilize! . . . Of course we mobilize . . . ! NOW!
*The generals look startled. It is truly not what they were
expecting. Their hopeful glances towards the picnic have been
rudely interrupted.*

EXT. A HUGE CLOCK. NIGHT.
*We cut right inside the clock face of Big Ben, at night, as its
hands move. The bell is chiming, its customary ominous sound.*

INT. BUCKINGHAM PALACE. CORRIDOR OF CLOCKS.
LUNCHTIME.
We cut to YOUNG GEORGE *standing staring down a corridor of
ornamental clocks. Each one has a footman by it, and the clocks
are being carefully put back by half an hour.*

STAMFORDHAM *is coming along the corridor towards* YOUNG
GEORGE.

STAMFORDHAM (*indicating the clocks*): The end of
Sandringham time in London . . . all the clocks will show
the same time as everywhere else from now on . . . !
(*As he reaches* YOUNG GEORGE.) Don't look so worried,

young man, Germany will back down by the end of the
day – you will see . . . and you'll even be able to have
that appointment with your father – just as everybody is
celebrating . . . !

INT. BUCKINGHAM PALACE. THE TELEGRAPH ROOM.
AFTERNOON.
We see GEORGE, *the King, standing in the doorway of the
telegraph room looking across at the telephones.*

GEORGE: It hasn't rung yet . . . ?
*The clerks reply 'No Your Majesty' . . . startled to find
themselves being watched by the King.*
I like small rooms . . . they remind me of my time in the
Navy. You don't mind me keeping you company . . . ?
(*He sits staring across at the telephones.*) Any of you spent
a decent time at sea? . . .
The clerks shake their heads embarrassed. GEORGE *glances
out at the courtyard where more clerks are standing in a
group, all very tense, all holding notebooks.*
GEORGE *looks back at the silent telephones, almost
imploring them to ring.*

INT. BUCKINGHAM PALACE. SMALL DRAWING ROOM.
EVENING.
We cut to MARY *looking up very sharply as* YOUNG GEORGE
enters her study. MARY *is writing labels to be attached to
furniture, as a steward stands by her with a ledger. The room is
full of the sound of clocks.*

MARY: Georgie, you gave me such a start . . . ! I thought it
might be some news –

YOUNG GEORGE *sees through the window the palace clock in the courtyard, glowing out in the evening sun.*

YOUNG GEORGE: No I'm afraid I have no news, Mama . . . except I must see Papa about how I can't possibly go to naval college.

YOUNG GEORGE *sits at the piano in the corner of the room and plays a few effortless chords.*

I have to explain to him why I am totally unsuited to such a place –

MARY: I've told you I cannot change your father's mind. And neither will you. But today is not the day . . . (*She turns back to her labels.*)

YOUNG GEORGE: Today is certainly not the day, no . . . *He looks up to see his mother deep in her labels, with the steward standing close by.*

MARY: I'm making sure that every piece of furniture in the collection will have the right label, with the correct date and its place of origin . . . (*To the steward.*) And this list here is all the objects we wish to see returned – which were given away as gifts by our predecessors and now their owners must be asked to return them . . . There are terrible gaps in the collection . . .

YOUNG GEORGE *sees his mother concealing how anxious she is.*

YOUNG GEORGE: There will be good news, Mama . . . we will hear from the Germans . . . everybody seems to think there will be good news . . .

MARY *does not look up.*

MARY: There are only a few hours left for that to be possible . . .

INT. BUCKINGHAM PALACE. A STATE CORRIDOR.
EVENING.

YOUNG GEORGE *goes out into the passage. There are more clerks
and officials gathering all the time. In the distance he can see his
three elder brothers (*DAVID, BERTIE *and* HENRY*), staring out
nervous silhouettes standing by the window, pale and distant.*

INT. YORK COTTAGE AND BUCKINGHAM PALACE.
STAMFORDHAM'S OFFICE. LATE EVENING.
We cut to LALLA *calling* JOHNNIE *down the length of the
claustrophobic warren of passages at York Cottage, a striking
contrast to the great corridors of the palace.*

LALLA: Johnnie, Johnnie, come quickly! It's your brother, it's
Georgie, on the telephone.

JOHNNIE *moves at a steady unhurried pace towards the
telephone, and without waiting to hear* YOUNG GEORGE*'s
voice he immediately speaks.*

JOHNNIE: I can hear you!

YOUNG GEORGE: I haven't said anything yet – what are you
talking about?

JOHNNIE: I can hear you very well!

YOUNG GEORGE: I just thought I'd ring you . . . because there
is the most extraordinary business here – we might be
about to go to war . . .

No reaction.

Johnnie? . . . Did you hear that? . . .

JOHNNIE: When?

YOUNG GEORGE: When? . . . Well, now –

JOHNNIE: I see. When will the foreigners come?

YOUNG GEORGE: No, Johnnie . . . they are not coming! Not
at the moment! We have sent a message to Germany,
and if they don't back down . . . well, we'll be at war in

about two hours – maybe less . . . everybody is on
tenterhooks, waiting to see if a message is going to come
through! And I just thought I would telephone you
because I am thinking about you . . . I thought you
would like to hear . . .

A hand comes down on the telephone receiver.

STAMFORDHAM: Best not to use any of the telephone lines at
the moment . . . we don't want the Germans having
difficulty getting through . . .

YOUNG GEORGE (*shouting into the receiver as it is moved
away*); I will ring you back and tell you what's happened,
Johnnie –

INT. BUCKINGHAM PALACE. THE KING'S STUDY.
NIGHT.
*We cut to the King sitting at his large desk, staring at the
telephone.*

GEORGE: I hate looking at the machine . . . waiting for it to
ring!

INT. BUCKINGHAM PALACE. CORRIDOR NEAR KING'S
STUDY. NIGHT.
*We cut to the great passage outside the King's study. Through the
window we can see the headlights of the government cars rolling
into the palace courtyard, more and more government officials are
gathering. Prime Minister* ASQUITH *and* LLOYD GEORGE
emerge from their cars and cross the courtyard.

We see YOUNG GEORGE *at the end of the corridor watching
the gathering of the increasingly excited adults.*

*We see all the top army generals are in the passage and the
admirals too, all the chiefs of staff are gathered. We see through*

YOUNG GEORGE's *eyes, their faces flushed with excitement and adrenaline, as they sense the ultimatum is about to run out.*

STAMFORDHAM *is standing in the shadows. For a moment* YOUNG GEORGE *catches him off guard, for he is looking nervous and uncertain.*

As soon as he sees that YOUNG GEORGE *is watching, he smiles his charming smile.*

STAMFORDHAM: I'm still not at all sure you're going to win . . . the bet!

YOUNG GEORGE: I never did make a bet . . . . I don't know what needs to happen to make me win . . . (*He glances along the corridor at all the senior officials and chiefs of staff.*) Why are they making so much noise?!

STAMFORDHAM (*staring across at them*): I think the generals are itching to show what they can do – they want to give the Germans a short sharp shock! And the Prime Minister doesn't want to seem out of step with the people . . .

We see ASQUITH *laughing with his entourage as he waits in the corridor. He is clearly keen to seem in control and relaxed. But the excitement is building all the time in the passage.*

ASQUITH (*calling out to the throng in the passage*): Very little time to go, gentlemen!

YOUNG GEORGE *sees all the adults preening themselves, showing each other how in charge they are and on top of events. He can also feel the sense of exhilaration building as the inevitable line is crossed. The mood seems to pass from adult to adult.*

The door opens at the far end of the passage, and there is the small figure of his father, the King.

GEORGE (*very quietly*): Come in, gentlemen . . .

STAMFORDHAM: So this is it . . . (*He taps* YOUNG GEORGE *on the shoulder and slips him two sovereigns.*) I just lost . . . !

The adults in the passage begin to move towards the King,
who is standing right at the far end of the doorway.

We cut to MARY *sitting alone in her study, writing her*
labels. We move closer, as the pen moves across the paper,
and we hear her pray to herself.

MARY: Lord, make this war . . . a very short war . . .

We cut back to YOUNG GEORGE *as he watches the last of*
the adults disappear through the door at the far end of the
passage. The door closes, he is left alone.

We cut to him in close up as he whispers to himself.

YOUNG GEORGE: I never telephoned Johnnie back . . .

EXT. KINGS LYNN. RAILWAY STATION. DAY.

We see a station waiting room. A train is roaring through the
station. As the train finishes wiping past camera, we see a face
staring out from the waiting room. It is JOHNNIE. *We see from his*
POV various shapes on the platform opposite; couples waiting for
their train to arrive, some older men and several men in uniform.
There's the sound of whistles and activity. JOHNNIE *moves on to*
the platform, LALLA *just behind him.*

JOHNNIE: Let me get on the train . . . Let me get on his train
     and wait there!

We see other faces of his household in the doorway of the
waiting room. JOHNNIE *is looking imploringly at* LALLA
and then at the train standing a little way down the platform
on his side of the station.

We cut to JOHNNIE *entering the royal compartment on the*
train, followed by his household HANSELL, FRED *and*
servants. FRED *is impressed by the luxurious compartment.*

FRED: This is the way to travel!

The servants are all carrying baskets of food and luxury
goods like supplies of tea and preserves. As FRED *is admiring*

103

the compartment, JOHNNIE *is peering out of the carriage window, sticking his head right out to have a good look. He finds himself staring at a huge locomotive pulling an ammunition train that is coming straight towards him. We see the train thunder through the station, pulling trucks full of ammunition and dark objects covered by tarpaulins, a steam crane that is spewing its own black smoke across the station.*

As it finishes going past, JOHNNIE *sees* YOUNG GEORGE *standing in his shining naval uniform on the opposite platform, his tall bodyguard looming behind him.*

JOHNNIE: My brother! My brother is here!

We cut to LALLA *standing on the platform, looking upwards as* YOUNG GEORGE *crosses the bridge that spans the railway station.* JOHNNIE *is staring out of the window with a broad beam on his face.*

JOHNNIE: My brother! He is a sailor now!

We cut to some members of the public on the opposite platform watching the curious sight of JOHNNIE *leaning out of the window – his arms swinging in strange exuberant moves, a rare public glimpse of the hidden prince.*

Time cut: YOUNG GEORGE *has entered the carriage where all of them are waiting for him. They are sitting, having spread themselves around on cushioned seats, in the dark, plush interior of the royal carriage.* FRED *is admiring* YOUNG GEORGE'S *naval uniform as* GEORGE *is tucking into one of the treats that* LALLA *has brought.*

LALLA: We took the opportunity – when we knew we were going to be seeing you off – of going on a great shopping trip . . . (FRED *eyeing all the food they have brought.*) We've got our marching orders too, oh yes! We're moving to a new home – but it's not too far away.

YOUNG GEORGE (*staring around the carriage*): I wish I was staying with all of you . . .

HANSELL: We have taken the chance to escape today . . . Get away from the estate. This is a big adventure for us. (*Melancholic smile.*) A trip to the railway station, and then to actually sit on a train! . . . It is the highlight of the year.

JOHNNIE is back by the carriage window. Moving the blinds, he can see the excited faces of young soldiers waiting on the platform opposite. He can see aristocratic looking women standing together as if trying to separate themselves from other characters on the platform. They still have the poise and untroubled arrogance of the pre-war world. JOHNNIE is studying them from above at an oblique angle. In the shadows he can also see the fascinating sight of a young couple embracing passionately, their bodies entwined. Some of the waiting soldiers are grinning to each other as the couple embrace so sexually.

FRED is watching the soldiers from another window.

FRED: It has already gone on longer than they said . . . A few weeks, that's what they said . . . That's all it would take.

We see a shot of three plump, self-satisfied young men in civilian clothes sitting on a bench waiting for their train. They are eyeing the soldiers with complacent smiles. Clearly they have no intention of volunteering themselves.

JOHNNIE is still by the window. He is absolutely enthralled by the sight of the kissing couple. LALLA suddenly realizes what he is looking at.

LALLA: Johnnie! Come away! Come away from there at once! We haven't travelled all this way to look at that. Talk to your brother – the train is going very soon!

We can hear the sound of whistles and can see shots of activity in the station, other people clambering on to the train and the sight of another great engine parked in a siding, belching smoke.

JOHNNIE turns to YOUNG GEORGE.

JOHNNIE: Don't stay long at your new school – tell them you've had enough.

YOUNG GEORGE: I most certainly will, Johnnie. I'm going to get away from there as soon as I'm able!

HANSELL: Well try to shine a little bit first won't you, Georgie. Please show them I've managed to teach you something . . . !

YOUNG GEORGE: I will . . . I'll dazzle them – but I'll do it in a way that shows I don't fit in.

LALLA: You'll behave yourself, Georgie . . . (*She moves close to him and then hugs him.*) It will be tremendous . . . It will be exciting!

There's the sound of very loud whistles extremely close.

LALLA: Come on, we all have to get off now or we'll be going with him!

JOHNNIE embraces YOUNG GEORGE too, but as he does so he stares over his shoulder through the window at the passionate kissing couple on the other platform.

YOUNG GEORGE: Goodbye, old chap. (*He holds him tight.*) I will make sure they move you closer to me one day soon.

We cut to LALLA and JOHNNIE getting off the train and JOHNNIE's household spilling back on to the platform with extreme reluctance. As they do so, YOUNG GEORGE sticks his head out of a window further down the carriage and calls out to JOHNNIE.

YOUNG GEORGE: And Johnnie – there's a present waiting for you at home . . . A big present . . . Too big for me to carry!

INT. YORK COTTAGE. HALL. NIGHT.
We cut to LALLA, JOHNNIE, HANSELL and the servants returning to York Cottage late at night with all their shopping.
Sitting in the middle of the table in the hall is a large parcel

with a label saying 'For Johnnie'.

We cut to the parcel coming open and revealing a splendid gramophone with a very large brass horn, and a pile of gramophone records carefully packaged, each one individually wrapped in silk.

JOHNNIE *beams at the gramophone.*

JOHNNIE: A music machine . . . !

EXT. YORK COTTAGE. JOHNNIE'S GARDEN. DAY.
We cut to HANSELL *and* JOHNNIE *standing in* JOHNNIE'S *garden. It is raining heavily and as they stand among the tall plants big drops fall all around them.*

HANSELL: Say goodbye to your garden, Johnnie . . . I don't know when you will be seeing it again.
    JOHNNIE *is breaking off little cuttings from several of the plants.*
JOHNNIE: I'm going to take bits with me . . . Why are we moving, Mr Hansell?
    HANSELL *is staring out towards the garden of the big house which is looking lush and beautiful in the rain.*
HANSELL: So Lalla can look after you better . . . (*He adds to himself.*) And nobody need see us . . . We're going to be shut away even further from everything . . . (*We see the deep frustration in his eyes.*) How are we going to be able to bear it, Johnnie?!

EXT. YORK COTTAGE. AFTERNOON. RAIN.
A convoy of carts and a small carriage are lined up to make the move from York Cottage. It is still pouring with rain. The servants are strapping down the luggage on the carts, but

everything is packed in an untidy, unwieldy fashion. The
servants are moving slowly in the rain, grumbling and slipping.
    LALLA *is watching the scene with fierce impatience, as* FRED
stares at her.

LALLA: Come on!! Why are you looking at me?! . . . It's not
    my fault about the weather . . . ! I have no patience with
    all their complaining. (*She turns to* HANSELL *who is*
    holding an umbrella.) I insisted on taking a full household
    with Johnnie but look at them . . . ! They have all
    become so idle . . . with their grumbling and their
    moaning . . . I might have been better off starting from
    scratch!
    JOHNNIE *emerges from York Cottage holding his*
    gramophone tightly as the rain intensifies.

EXT. NORFOLK COUNTRYSIDE. AFTERNOON. RAIN.
We cut to the caravan of carts crossing the flat Norfolk
countryside in a big wide shot. The carts are tilting at alarming
angles, the wheels grinding through the mud. A noisy chaotic
scene.
    One of the ropes strapping down all the trunks on a cart comes
free and a waterfall of trunks descends on the muddy road,
spraying a collection of JOHNNIE's *shoes in all directions. The*
servants have to get off the carts and stumble on the track picking
up the individual shoes out of the puddles and the mud. They slip
all over the place as they do it. JOHNNIE *sticks his head out of the*
carriage window smiling in recognition at their clumsy
movements. But LALLA *climbs out of the carriage and berates*
them with real authority.

LALLA: Come on, gentlemen . . . will you hurry please! (*As the*
    servants stumble all over the place.) What a shambles they

are . . . they are going to be in for a shock when we've
settled in – I'm not going to stand for this any longer . . . !
*The caravan of carts arrives outside the isolated farmhouse.
It is surrounded by a sea of mud. The building looks glum
and unwelcoming.*
It's a little smaller then I was expecting . . .

INT. WOOD FARM. FRONT HALL. LATE AFTERNOON.
We cut to them entering the interior of Wood Farm – JOHNNIE,
LALLA, HANSELL *and the members of the household. The interior
is rather dank and very plain. The walls are stained with smoke.*

LALLA: Well, there's certainly a lot to do here!
   JOHNNIE *stands in the middle of the hall surveying his new
   accommodation.*
      HANSELL *is staring out of the window at the muddy
   farmyard and the dilapidated farm buildings.*
HANSELL: What a place to end up in . . . We're missing out
   on everything that is going on . . . and now this . . . (*He
   moves closer to the window.*) I'm going to go mad here . . .
   *The dingy hall suddenly vibrates with the sound of a
   gramophone record.* JOHNNIE *has wound up his gramophone
   and it is pouring out music.*

INT. NAVAL COLLEGE. DORMITORY AND PASSAGES.
DAWN.
We cut to YOUNG GEORGE's *eyes flashing open with a shock.
There is a crashing of bells, violent and incessant. For a moment
he cannot think of where he is, then he looks around to see he is in
a dormitory of about twenty boys. The room has a high ceiling
and enormous windows, all of which are wide open. It is barely
light outside.*

109

The boys are all leaping out of bed and charging out of the room, as disembodied voices are yelling down the passage 'Remember, at the double . . . at the DOUBLE!'

We cut to YOUNG GEORGE *standing at the end of a very long passage. He is dressed in his silk pyjamas. A strange and frightening sight greets him.*

The passage is lit by an eerie blue light that makes it look like the lower deck of a battleship or the inside of a giant submarine. All down the passage semi-naked boys are being made to run and run. They brush past YOUNG GEORGE *in his silk pyjamas and hurtle on down the long blue passage, to disappear into complete darkness.*

Two masters are standing in the shadows watching YOUNG GEORGE *with a beady stare.*

We cut to YOUNG GEORGE *standing in the washroom staring in fascinated horror as the boys have to leap into the low communal baths that are built into the floor. The water in the baths is covered in ice. And the boys are leaping in and then screaming as they hit the water.*

YOUNG GEORGE *stands for a moment teetering on the edge, and then reluctantly but with real poise removes the silk top of his pyjamas, but retains his trousers, as he leaps into the frozen water. As he hits the water, he too screams out.*

INT. NAVAL COLLEGE. CLASSROOM. MORNING.
We cut from YOUNG GEORGE*'s shout of shock to the face of* CALLENDER *addressing the classroom. He is an elderly teacher, with magnificent white hair, and wearing a gown which he constantly flicks over his shoulder. He is being watched from the corner of the classroom by his dachshund, Victor. His teaching style is eccentric but there is a frightening side to it as well.*

CALLENDER: Today will be marvellous . . . for we are doing

the Armada! What more could we want? We are going to be on the deck of those ships, we are going to be on those cliffs too – we'll be as close to Sir Francis Drake as one of his bowls rolling along the grass . . . We are going to be Queen Elizabeth as she knights Sir Francis.

He imitates Queen Elizabeth, sweeping his gown over his shoulder, as YOUNG GEORGE *watches from the middle of the class.*

We're going to feel the fire and excitement of those times – and they will impress themselves so deeply on all of us, we will find inspiration for what we have to do now! (*Suddenly, without warning, his tone changes.*) Who can tell me the name of the King of France at the time of the Armada?

A hand goes up at the back and an unfortunate boy volunteers 'Philip'.

No, boy, you were wrong, calamitously wrong – Philip of *Spain* . . . (*He stares at the blank boys.*) Somebody tell me . . . right now . . . or I will despair –

YOUNG GEORGE *reluctantly puts up his hand.*

CALLENDER: Yes, indeed, sir.

YOUNG GEORGE: The King of France was Henry III, son of Henry II and Catherine de Medici, he was the last of the House of Valois. A year after the Armada he was succeeded by Henry of Navarre, Henry IV.

The boys are all staring at him in astonishment.

CALLENDER: Move to the front of the class, sir . . . as fine an answer as I've ever heard in this classroom . . . (*As* YOUNG GEORGE *moves to the front.*) It is not who you are but *what* you are we salute . . . In the very *front* row, sir . . . !

YOUNG GEORGE *has to sit at the very front of the class, next to a pleasant-looking boy,* RUSSELL.

YOUNG GEORGE (*to* RUSSELL): That's *not* what I wanted . . .

CALLENDER: Now, gentlemen, we are ready – Hold on tight! The wind is up at last . . . we set sail with Sir Francis Drake –

INT. WOOD FARM. FRONT HALL/KITCHEN. DAY.
We cut to LALLA *looking up abruptly. We see real surprise on her face.*

And then we see in wide shot the front hall of the farmhouse, now much cleaner, the walls shiny white. It is decorated with flowers and with the furniture they have brought with them.

In the distance JOHNNIE *is listening to his gramophone, moving to the music. At first he is conducting an orchestra and then his hands mime playing a woodwind instrument, like he did at the banquet.*

But standing just by the front door, having entered at that very moment, is HANSELL, *who is dressed in military uniform.*

LALLA *is truly surprised to see he has joined up.*

LALLA: What are you doing dressed like that?

HANSELL: I would have thought that was rather obvious.

LALLA: Aren't you too old to be in the Army?

HANSELL: Absolutely not. (*He stares at himself in a mirror.*) Anyway I think my precise age is rather hard to guess . . .

Suddenly they both see that JOHNNIE *is beginning to breathe very fast. They rush over to him.*

We cut to LALLA *and* HANSELL *holding* JOHNNIE *on the bare kitchen table, his head is propped up, and* LALLA *has a pitcher of disgusting looking yellow water.*

LALLA: Come on, Johnnie . . . take a drink of this . . . it will be horrible . . . yes, but they told us to do this . . . each time we felt one coming on . . . It's mustard water – that's why it's yellow . . .

JOHNNIE *drinks as much of the water as he can manage. He immediately makes terrible retching sounds.* LALLA *puts her arms around him as we hear the sound of urine hitting the stone floor.*

No, no. (*As she holds* JOHNNIE.) I'm not doing that again, never – that's a terrible treatment . . . we'll never use it again . . .

HANSELL: I'm sorry, Lalla . . . leaving you with the boy at such a time . . .

LALLA *is in an emotional state because of* JOHNNIE's *fit.*

LALLA: Don't say you're sorry . . . you're not going to change your mind so please don't say anything . . .

HANSELL *tries to say something.*

LALLA: No, no, don't bother to explain . . . ! You've never shown any interest about going to the war before – but there we are! I will manage . . . I assure you I will manage. And when you come to visit us . . . Goodness what progress we will have made – you *will not believe* what progress we'll have achieved . . . !

EXT. WOOD FARM. MORNING.
We see HANSELL *setting off in a pony and trap which he is driving himself. He waves to them merrily and sets off towards the horizon.* LALLA *and* JOHNNIE *and the servants watch him go.*

HANSELL *disappears out of sight.*

INT. WOOD FARM. THE PARLOUR. DAY.
We see a record spinning round on JOHNNIE's *gramophone blasting out Beethoven, and then* JOHNNIE's *pencil sliding down the page.*

We cut wide and see he is drawing a strange map of the war – with Russia and Britain and France all joined together forming

113

*one massive island on one side of the English Channel, staring
across at Germany and Austria on the other side. Germany has a
giant stick man standing astride it labelled 'Cousin Bill', and the
massive island of Russia, France and England have two giant
stick men holding hands, 'Cousin Nicky and Papa'.*

EXT. WOOD FARM. AFTERNOON.
*The members of the household are all lined up outside the
farmhouse.* LALLA *stands in front of them staring at them for a
moment. Their clothes are much smarter and they are standing
ramrod straight in an orderly fashion. They look more like a
proper household for a prince.* JOHNNIE *emerges out of the front of
the farmhouse and does a mock salute to his household.*

EXT. NORFOLK COUNTRYSIDE. AFTERNOON.
We then cut to a huge wide shot of JOHNNIE *and his household
crossing the horizon.*

   JOHNNIE *is riding a pony at the head of the household, and the
servants and* LALLA *are following behind, in an orderly
formation, keeping pace with the slow walk of the pony. It is a
regimented progress.* FRED *is waddling slightly but the effect from
a distance is of discipline and a touch of majesty.*

   *We cut to another shot of their progress, coming towards us,
with* JOHNNIE *leading his household on his horse, the out of
condition servants beginning to puff a little.*

   *We then see the procession pass some villagers standing on a
country road, watching the strange group escorting the Prince.*

   We cut close to JOHNNIE *for the first time and we see he is
beaming and laughing to himself as he rides his horse. The
atmosphere is much less regal the closer we get to* JOHNNIE.

   *We then cut to them moving along a ridge at the edge of a great
wood. Suddenly* LALLA *stops. She holds up her hand and the*

114

whole procession stops too.

Below the ridge, through the trees, they can see a group of women on their knees picking things up off the forest floor. A foraging party. But these women are all in very fine clothes.

LALLA *suddenly realizes to her astonishment that one of the women is the Queen,* MARY.

LALLA: Johnnie! Look . . . it's your mother!

FRED: Yes, we're on the edge of the estate here . . . What on earth are they doing?

LALLA: Wait here . . . nobody move. Hold your positions just as you are everybody. Johnnie – stay on the pony!

LALLA sets off down the ridge, running towards the group.

As she approaches MARY *looks up, seeing* LALLA *plunging down the ridge, the brambles pulling at her long dress.*

LALLA reaches the Queen.

Ma'am, we were passing . . . and what a surprise it was . . . seeing it was you!

MARY: Indeed . . . I didn't know you came this far on your walks . . .

They both look up at the household and JOHNNIE *on the ridge, all of whom are remembering to look very poised.*

MARY glances at her ladies-in-waiting.

We're collecting food . . . food for the munitions workers, chestnuts, something additional for them to eat . . . mustn't let the natural food go to waste – (*with surprising intensity*) food is everything, without it we cannot win!

JOHNNIE *is staring down from his pony at the group of ladies-in-waiting foraging for chestnuts.*

LALLA is not sure whether MARY *has realized that it is* JOHNNIE *up there on the ridge.*

LALLA: Johnnie is there, ma'am . . . see . . . up there on his pony . . . Shall I have him brought down here, ma'am? –

MARY: No, I have not got the time today. I have to visit a
factory shortly . . . and then I have to meet some more
volunteers . . . I'm also collecting metal . . . any spare
metal objects, scrap metal. It's very useful for the war
effort. Anything made out of metal. So if you have any
of that at the farmhouse, Lalla, collect it together . . . you
will do that?

LALLA: Yes, ma'am. I will definitely do that.

*LALLA is staring at MARY. She is really surprised by
MARY's determination, her extraordinary focus. It is as if the
war effort is beginning to possess her.*

*JOHNNIE has dismounted from his pony, having lost
patience with sitting upright and poised. He is now doing his
strange walk and little skips.*

Both women are looking up towards the skipping figure.

LALLA: I could bring him down here for you, ma'am . . . just
for a moment! It's been a while since he saw you, and
he's made such progress –

MARY (*firmly*): I really do not have the time now, Lalla.

LALLA's face clouds. MARY suddenly turns.

I will see you tomorrow. I will come to the farm.

*She sees the doubt in LALLA's eyes, as to whether she really
means this.*

We will be there tomorrow at three o'clock exactly.

*We see JOHNNIE moving on the horizon of the ridge, with his
shambolic walk. He suddenly remembers and stands stock
still, poised and erect, staring down at his mother.*

EXT. WOOD FARM. AFTERNOON.

LALLA, JOHNNIE *and the servants are standing outside the
farmhouse staring towards the horizon. There is nothing coming
towards them.*

LALLA: It's three o'clock . . . (*Her voice full of disappointment.*)

. . . two minutes after three o'clock . . .

FRED: She's never late . . .

We return to the empty horizon. And then we cut to
JOHNNIE'S *face staring anxiously. Suddenly it breaks into a*
smile.

A royal car is approaching down the bumpy track.

LALLA: There she is . . . how could we have ever doubted!

INT. WOOD FARM. FRONT HALL. AFTERNOON.

MARY *enters the little farmhouse, with* JOHNNIE, LALLA *and*
FRED *and the servants of the household following behind.* MARY
stands in her very fine dress in the clean simple farmhouse hall.

LALLA: I'm so glad there's a little sun this afternoon for you,
ma'am, because as you can see it's really quite light and
pleasant –

But MARY *is moving briskly to the window that overlooks*
the dilapidated farm buildings. She points to the wall of one
of the buildings.

MARY: Why is there ivy growing there?

LALLA: Ma'am? . . . I'm sorry, I don't understand . . . what
do you mean?

MARY: You should never let ivy grow. It's a chaotic plant . . .
it makes everything untidy . . . I will not have ivy
growing on any of the estate buildings, I thought you
knew that . . . You must have it removed immediately.

LALLA (*very surprised*): Yes, ma'am . . .

We cut to MARY *sitting in the little parlour having some tea.*
A couple of the servants are moving towards her with a
basket of metal objects they have collected, old garden tools,
tin cans, etc.

MARY: Thank you. That's a reasonable amount. Well done.

We see MARY'S *extreme restlessness. It is as if she finds sitting still nowadays extremely difficult.*

She stares at JOHNNIE *for a moment, who is sitting opposite her trying to drink tea in a dignified genteel manner.*

You have grown, Johnnie . . . I had no idea . . . You've grown so quickly . . .

LALLA: I thought while we were having tea, ma'am – maybe you would like to see some of the things Johnnie has been doing . . . that's why I put all of his maps and drawings up . . . you will notice, ma'am, how small and neat his writing has become . . .

We see all around the parlour walls are JOHNNIE'S *maps of the war and his strange family trees and portraits of the* TSAR, *cousin Bill and his father.*

MARY: The maps are a little strange . . . . all the countries joined together . . . but quite well done, Johnnie, the colours are pleasant . . . is that really how you see your cousin Nicholas?

We see an extraordinary picture of the TSAR *swimming.*

We must make sure no Russian ever sees that picture . . . And your father wearing a giant crown . . . so much bigger than his head . . . how very odd –

MARY'S *eyes are flicking restlessly, she cannot relax at all.*

LALLA: We thought, ma'am, Johnnie might show you his piano playing . . . I've been trying to teach him a little.

LALLA *indicates to* JOHNNIE *to take his position by the piano.* JOHNNIE *opens the piano, lifts his hands up like a maestro preparing to play a great tune, but then only plays a couple of notes, repeating them woodenly.* LALLA *mouths encouragement to him.*

MARY: His brother Georgie plays the piano beautifully, of course . . .

JOHNNIE *continues to play single notes.* MARY'S *mind is racing on to other subjects.*

I have visited two factories already today – I don't mind the noise and the heat, I would happily do five a day if it could be organized – It is extraordinary though how few people are good at organization, and that's what we need above all at the moment . . . above everything . . . As you may recall waiting is something I hate to do.

LALLA *sees* MARY*'s energized state, how much* MARY *wants to get out of the farmhouse and continue with her schedule.*

LALLA: Ma'am . . . with respect, ma'am . . . if you take a moment to hear the child play . . .

MARY: I am listening . . .

JOHNNIE *plays a few more notes. His mother is not looking at him. It's as if she has no space for him.*

You will do something about that ivy, won't you, Lalla – and if there's any more –

MARY *suddenly stops in mid-sentence. Through an open door she has seen* JOHNNIE*'s gramophone with its great brass horn shining in the sunlight. She points towards it.*

Why haven't you included that with the other metal things?

LALLA: That is Johnnie's gramophone. His brother gave it to him . . . he gets such joy from it –

MARY: Everybody's making sacrifices at the moment. I'm sure he won't miss it. Bring it here and add it to the other things.

FRED *looks at* LALLA *stunned.*

LALLA: Ma'am, please . . . ! It's not spare metal – it's Johnnie's most special possession –

MARY (*to* FRED): Go and fetch it. We will take it with us.

JOHNNIE *watches* FRED *go to fetch his gramophone.*

LALLA: Ma'am, please! . . . The music helps Johnnie . . . helps his progress –

MARY: Lalla, you will stop this. (*Indicating the brass horn.*)

119

There's a lot of metal there . . . this is a good thing to take and we will take it.

Suddenly she spins around in her chair.

Why is there no clock in this room?! I have absolutely no idea what time it is!

EXT. WOOD FARM. AFTERNOON.

We cut to MARY *about to step into the car.* FRED *is placing the gramophone in the car and another servant is holding the basket of metal objects.* JOHNNIE *watches with despair his gramophone being carried away from him.*

LALLA (*to* JOHNNIE *passionately*): Ask your mother . . . go on, Johnnie . . . go on . . . ask her not to take it . . .

But JOHNNIE *cannot find the words.*

Suddenly LALLA *moves urgently over to the car.*

LALLA: Ma'am . . . I *implore* you not to take Johnnie's gramophone . . .

MARY *turns very startled at* LALLA'*s tone.*

It will, with respect, ma'am, make no difference to the war at all – not one bit . . . ! But for Johnnie it is of *such* importance . . .

MARY *stares at her.*

LALLA: Please listen, ma'am . . .

MARY *looks at* JOHNNIE.

JOHNNIE: I want the music . . .

MARY *suddenly realizes what she is doing. It is as if her extreme focus on the war relaxes for a moment.*

MARY: Of course, Lalla – if it means a lot to the child . . . You may have it, Johnnie.

We see JOHNNIE *taking his gramophone, embracing it tightly.*

I shouldn't have taken it . . . (*Watching* JOHNNIE *with the*

gramophone.) clearly I shouldn't have done . . .
She gets into the car surrounded by the metal objects, recovers
her poise and calls out to JOHNNIE *and the household.*
God willing next time we see each other there will have
been some real military results! For us to cheer!

EXT. NAVAL COLLEGE. COURTYARD. MORNING.
It is sleeting hard. We see a high shot of the naval cadets, dressed
only in shorts and barefoot, hurtling backwards and forwards
across the courtyard of the naval college doing some form of
intense drill, choreographed lines criss-crossing each other. The
speed the boys are being made to run is getting faster all the time,
as orders are barked from either side of the courtyard.

INT. NAVAL COLLEGE. CORRIDORS AND CLASSROOM.
DAY.
We see the boys hurtling along the blue corridor straight towards
the camera. They are never allowed to stop running for a second
while they are in the passage.

We then cut to CALLENDER, *the formidable old teacher, in the*
classroom watched by his dachshund, Victor.

Outside the window there is a view straight out to sea, and we
see the waves are rough, angry.

The boys are staring at CALLENDER *with pale white faces.*

CALLENDER: All these fellows, the great commanders, these
    sea kings and land kings share one thing – and I hope
    from all the months and months we have spent studying
    them it is obvious what that is . . . (*Suddenly he bellows.*)
    What is it, gentlemen?!
    The boys chorus back 'Belief and confidence . . . Confidence
    and belief . . . !'

Louder!

As the boys recite this louder the camera looks for YOUNG
GEORGE *and we see he is no longer anywhere near the front,
but about two-thirds back in the classroom. He is also barely
mouthing the litany.* CALLENDER *stares down at the boys.*

Indeed – belief in themselves, their God and their
Country! Confidence – from Drake, to Nelson, to
Wellington – they knew they could do it! No doubts at all,
it wasn't slippery arrogance but confidence based on their
native ability, and they never needed to stoop to achieve
their victories . . . (He adopts a strange hunched posture.)
Never needed to stoop to low brutality . . . It was clean, it
was clever, and it was decisive!

YOUNG GEORGE *is staring out through the sea mist and grey
waves, imagining the rumble of guns across the Channel.*

We cut abruptly to:

INT/EXT. SANDRINGHAM. ESTATE AND NORFOLK
ROADS/ROYAL CAR.

LALLA *and* JOHNNIE *travelling in a royal car with the blinds
drawn.* JOHNNIE *has been dressed in his smartest clothes. He
chooses his moment when* LALLA *is not looking and lifts the
corner of the blind to look out. He sees two teenage girls walking
along the country road together. We see from their point of view*
JOHNNIE*'s large head staring out eagerly from behind the blind,
the half-hidden boy peering at the world.*

*We see the car passing through the gates of Sandringham's
garden.*

We cut back inside the car, LALLA *checks they are indeed
travelling through the gardens and then lifts the blinds so*
JOHNNIE *can look out.*

JOHNNIE *stares out hopefully at the familiar landscape, but he
is truly surprised by what he sees.*

JOHNNIE: Where are we . . . ? I thought we were at the big house?!

For we see from JOHNNIE's *point of view sinister glimpses of the garden, the atmosphere completely changed. The garden is an austere place now. There is barbed wire running along the drive, and wire netting clambering round the plants, clusters of dark figures in the distance are digging, and a pall of smoke is blowing across the garden as something is being burnt.*

LALLA: We *are* at the big house, Johnnie!

We see York Cottage, and JOHNNIE's *garden which has been completely dug up and covered in wire netting.*

Suddenly a large vehicle full of estate workers, in uniform and with guns, roars towards them down the drive and passes them.

JOHNNIE *watches the dark shapes of the garden, and the figures in the distance digging.*

INT. SANDRINGHAM. LARGE DRAWING ROOM. AFTERNOON.

We cut to LALLA *and* JOHNNIE *approaching Queen* ALEXANDRA, *now in her seventies, who is sitting in the middle of the large drawing room with all the curtains drawn, even though it is only mid-afternoon.*

ALEXANDRA *is formally dressed in a fine dress and wearing many of her jewels. Behind her all her agate animals are clustered, twinkling in the half light of the room.*

ALEXANDRA *calls out as soon as she sees them in the doorway.*

ALEXANDRA: Come in, come in, my little one . . . here you are! . . . Come and kiss your grandmama . . . it's so long since I've seen the little tiny one . . . !

JOHNNIE *lurches over to his grandmother, his big shape nearly as large as this tiny birdlike woman.*

LALLA: He's so pleased to be here, ma'am.

JOHNNIE *allows himself to be kissed on the top of his head.*

JOHNNIE: It's very dark.

ALEXANDRA: It is, I know, my little one . . . I keep the curtains drawn because I hate what they have done to the garden. I know they probably had to do it – but most of the time I can't bear to look at it. (*She catches hold of* JOHNNIE's *hand.*) My tiny one . . . you must be hungry!

EXT. SANDRINGHAM. GARDEN OF THE BIG HOUSE. AFTERNOON.
We cut to more wire netting being unrolled, a huge wire ball slowly unravelling along the top of one of the lawns.

INT. SANDRINGHAM. LARGE DRAWING ROOM. AFTERNOON.
We cut to JOHNNIE *sitting eating a large cake. We see he is surrounded by silver trays containing a multitude of different food.*

ALEXANDRA *is not eating tea herself, but smiling benignly as* LALLA *shows her* JOHNNIE's *drawings.*

LALLA: He's just done these, ma'am, they are for you . . . of the family.

ALEXANDRA: They are so charming, delightful . . . and quite a good likeness . . . after a fashion!

We see JOHNNIE's *strange elongated pictures of the* TSAR *and* TSARINA.

There they are, Johnnie – you see the real pictures of them –

124

We see photos of the TSAR *and* TSARINA, *and the Kaiser dotted around the room.*

   LALLA *stares at the photograph of the* TSAR *and* GEORGE *taken at the Isle of Wight, standing close together looking like brothers.*

LALLA: I remember when they did that photograph, ma'am
   . . . it took ages to get right !

   ALEXANDRA *stares at the photograph of the* TSAR. *We see a reprise of the live action, of the* TSAR *moving in the garden on the Isle of Wight. It's as if the photo moves for a moment.*

ALEXANDRA: My sister brought him up so well . . . so very
   well . . . Nicholas's behaviour is always excellent. It's
   such a pity Vicky didn't do the same with Wilhelm . . .
   We see a picture of the Kaiser.
   But if only – don't you think, my tiny one – if only we
   could get the family together! Get your papa and Cousin
   Wilhelm and Nicky all together in a room . . . we could
   have it all sorted out . . . and there would be no need for
   this awful fighting, no need for battles at all . . . What do
   you think, my little one?
   JOHNNIE'*s mouth is full of cake.*

JOHNNIE: That would be very good. We should do it soon.
   (*He eats some more cake.*) Maybe next week.

   ALEXANDRA *claps her hands.*

ALEXANDRA: And now I think we should get a ball – because
   all boys must kick a ball, mustn't they?! I will ring and
   see if they can find us a ball somewhere.

LALLA: I'll go, ma'am . . . It will take them ages to find a ball
   – but I remember where everything is . . . No, I'll go . . .
   because time is so short I know.

   LALLA *makes a gesture encouraging* JOHNNIE *to talk to his grandmother and leaves. The old lady and* JOHNNIE *are alone.*

ALEXANDRA (*suddenly really heartfelt*): Oh my dear, what

125

times these are! (*She looks at* JOHNNIE.) But we have a plan, don't we . . .

JOHNNIE *beams back at her.*

Now . . . open that curtain . . . you can open that one, Johnnie . . . that will do no harm. Yes, my little one, pull it back –

JOHNNIE *pulls back the curtains on the French windows that open on to the garden. He sees the door is slightly ajar. He can also see glimpses of adults moving in the garden.*

Your father is having a shooting party – he hasn't had one for so very long . . . but this will do him so much good! Some of the guests are already here I believe –

As she is saying this JOHNNIE *has caught a glimpse of a dark figure moving on one of the paths. He feels certain he knows the figure. He slips through the French windows and out into the garden.*

EXT. SANDRINGHAM. GARDEN OF THE BIG HOUSE. AFTERNOON.

JOHNNIE *catches another glimpse of the dark figure moving ahead of him. He is walking along a parallel path trying to keep pace with the figure.*

He sees it is the FINE-LOOKING WOMAN *he saw in the garden that sunlit day before the war and also at the banquet. She looks older, much more intense and preoccupied, her joyful radiance has gone. She is whispering to herself as she walks along.*

Suddenly she catches sight of JOHNNIE *following her.*

FINE-LOOKING WOMAN: Oh, it's you! (JOHNNIE *smiles at her.*) Hello, stranger . . . you must forgive me, you caught me talking to myself . . .

JOHNNIE: I talk to myself . . . quite a lot. It's not bad, is it, people talking to themselves?

The FINE-LOOKING WOMAN, *responding to his warmth,
touches his hair.*

FINE-LOOKING WOMAN: One doesn't do it, no . . . if one can
possibly help it. I'm just waiting for some news . . .
waiting to hear some very important news about what's
happened to somebody – which must come . . . which
surely must come . . . !

JOHNNIE (*looking up at her*): It will come, I'm sure.
We hear LALLA's *voice ringing out, calling* JOHNNIE's
name. The FINE-LOOKING WOMAN *and* JOHNNIE *look up.*
*Two other guests are moving rapidly through the grounds,
not talking to each other, their shoulders hunched. There is a
sense of preoccupation in the garden.*

FINE-LOOKING WOMAN: Everybody's in a foul mood, aren't
they . . . (*She ruffles* JOHNNIE's *hair.*) Don't worry, it will
pass soon enough . . . !
LALLA *appears round the corner.*

LALLA: Johnnie . . . ! There you are . . . ! This is not a time
for you to go wandering . . . I'm taking you home at once
. . . (JOHNNIE *opens his mouth.*) No, *absolutely at once!*
JOHNNIE *looks back at the* FINE-LOOKING WOMAN *and
her sad face, as he is pulled away.*

INT. SANDRINGHAM. LARGE DRAWING ROOM. LATE
AFTERNOON.
ALEXANDRA *is sitting alone. The tea things have been cleared
away. The large double doors open and there is the small figure of
the King,* GEORGE. ALEXANDRA *beams.*

ALEXANDRA: Ah . . . my other little one . . . !
GEORGE: Mama. (*He moves to greet her.*) What a journey . . . I
couldn't get away from London, so many cables from
the Front. I'm going there myself very soon – by God

we'd better make some headway!

He picks up JOHNNIE's *drawings that are on the sofa.*

ALEXANDRA: Those are Johnnie's things – he was here about half an hour ago.

GEORGE (*surprised*): Johnnie? Johnnie was here?

He looks at the drawings in an absent-minded way then casts them aside.

The poor little fellow . . . not able to do much!

GEORGE *sees the photograph of the* TSAR *and himself standing together which* ALEXANDRA *has placed next to her on the small table.*

Ah . . . you've been looking at this . . . ! He does look like me, doesn't he, in this picture – the funny thing is just this week I made Nicky a field marshal of the British Army . . . I have given him that rank . . . to encourage both of us! (*He smiles.*) It's a way of saying brighter days lie ahead!

We move in on the TSAR's *face in the photograph, closer and closer until all we can see is one of his dark eyes.*

Out of the darkness of his eye we dissolve to water and we see a piece of ice floating directly towards us.

INT. NAVAL COLLEGE. THE BATHS. DAY.

The ice surrounds the camera. We are at eye level, on the surface of the water, moving with the ice.

And then we see YOUNG GEORGE *in the water, watching the ice come straight towards him. His teeth are chattering furiously in the freezing water, but he suddenly launches off and swims a few strokes that take him through the ice to the other side of the communal bath. There is a defiant look in his eyes, one of mute fury. His friend* RUSSELL *is the only other person left in the bath. He is shaking in the water, but both boys look rebellious and untamed.*

We cut to them sitting side by side, on the edge of the bath, staring at the grey water.

RUSSELL (*casually*): My brother William left for France last
    week. He should be at the Front by now . . .
YOUNG GEORGE: Well, it can't be worse than being here . . . !

INT. NAVAL COLLEGE. CLASSROOM. DAY.
We cut to the classroom, the boys mostly sitting in ramrod straight lines at their desks listening to CALLENDER. *They are wearing a different uniform now they are a year older.*

    CALLENDER *is in full flow, his white hair unbrushed, his delivery as eccentric as ever, but there is a new seriousness in his tone. As* CALLENDER *addresses the class, we move among the boys looking for* YOUNG GEORGE.

CALLENDER: The Spanish Inquisition – the ultimate tyranny
    . . . the rack squeezing (*he flings his arms out*), and the
    rack stretching everybody that opposed them! Who does
    that remind you of, gentlemen . . . ? (*He does not wait for
    an answer.*) Does it not remind you of the foe we are
    confronted with today?! The extraordinary barbarity the
    Germans have been reduced to – in order to bolster their
    losing position – the mutilation of Belgian women we
    knew about already, the cutting off of the hands of
    Belgian babies, their tiny hands becoming trophies,
    sometimes nailed to the barrack-room walls –
We now see where YOUNG GEORGE *is sitting. He is right at the back of the class. He is not sitting ramrod straight either but is moving fretfully as* CALLENDER'*s speech continues. He exchanges a look with* RUSSELL *who is one row in front of him at the back of the class.*
And now, just when we thought it could not get any
worse, we hear about the Germans inoculating the

129

French prisoners with tuberculosis, deliberately contaminating these gallant men of war with this deadly disease –

YOUNG GEORGE *puts his hand up.*

CALLENDER: Ah, we are hearing from the back for the first time in many a month . . . !

YOUNG GEORGE: Can I ask you, sir, how you know this?

CALLENDER: I'm surprised you of all people need to ask this question! I know this because the authorities have found this out and it is now published in the newspapers for the nation to read about and to realize what we are confronted with–

YOUNG GEORGE*'s hand goes up again.*

CALLENDER: Ah, there's more is there?!

YOUNG GEORGE: And these stories have been verified have they sir? By witnesses?

CALLENDER: Famous personages have verified them and that is why they are published! And that is why there is such a strength of feeling taking hold amongst the populace against the Germans . . . and all manner of German things . . .

He indicates the dachshund.

Why even Victor here has had things thrown at him in the street by people enraged that he was of German descent . . . (*Some of the boys laugh at this.*) No, it was serious, I had to lift him in my arms to stop him being stoned as they shouted 'a *German* dog!' . . . I have read of several other instances of this happening . . . And in one sense it seems strange and regrettable – but it is I feel *understandable* . . . and sometimes when I look at Victor I really think he *understands* this too . . .

We see the dog peering back at the class.

And then we see YOUNG GEORGE *staring at* CALLENDER *stupefied by his speech.*

The bell clashes out loudly and we hear the voices of
masters in the passage yelling 'At the double!'

The class leap to their feet and run out of the classroom.
All but YOUNG GEORGE.

CALLENDER: Run, gentlemen . . . run . . . if you don't run
you will not reach anywhere!

YOUNG GEORGE *stares at the boys hurtling past the*
window on the path that runs along the cliff outside the
classroom. Boys speed by in both directions. Seen through
the half-misted up windows they form a pattern of frantic
activity.

YOUNG GEORGE *imagines for a moment* JOHNNIE
standing there in the middle of all these running figures,
slowly turning on the spot, and doing his little skipping
movements – being his own eccentric self amongst all this
regimented behaviour.

YOUNG GEORGE (*murmurs*): I've just got to get out of
here . . .

INT. HOSPITAL WARD. DAY.
We cut to MARY *moving along a series of beds filled with*
wounded soldiers. She is being escorted by a doctor and two
nurses.

MARY *is confronted by the sight of some extraordinarily scarred*
and wounded men, some heavily bandaged faces, others lying
with their wounds open as they begin to heal. Their faces stare
back at the Queen, doing their utmost to smile through the pain
and to look their best despite their injuries.

MARY *meets the sight of these men with an unflinching stare*
and a poised sympathy. She does not patronize them. We sense
she is very affected by what she sees, but she is able to keep up her
perfectly controlled public exterior.

MARY: We commend you . . . for your service . . . (*She moves along the line of beds.*) We thank you . . .

She stops by a bed where there is a soldier who is so badly wounded he has almost been reduced to a torso. He is missing three of his limbs.

His eyes stare back through a heavily bandaged face. A very disconcerting look. The whole bed is enveloped in a shroud of muslin.

MARY *stares back at the man's eyes. She is truly shocked by his state.*

We cut to the entrance hall of the hospital. Two ladies-in-waiting are in an extreme flap as MARY *comes out of the ward.*

LADY-IN-WAITING: Ma'am . . . there seems to have been a misunderstanding with the driver about the time . . . he's not back yet – I'm so sorry, ma'am . . . ! I think he has gone to do something with the motor car . . .

MARY, *knowing she is in public, masks her instant anger.*

MARY: We will wait here then. He cannot be long . . .

MARY *sees she is being watched closely by some members of the public, the relatives of the wounded, who are sitting on a bench across the hall. The doctor suggests a move.*

DOCTOR: There's a room, Your Majesty . . . in private . . .

MARY *stares at the relatives across the hall. They are not smiling back at her.*

MARY: We will wait here.

We cut to a nurse entering the hall with a tray of tea for the Queen, and there is much commotion among the ladies-in-waiting as a table is found for the Queen to take tea.

An ORDERLY *is cleaning the floor in one corner of the hall. His face is scarred, there is something febrile about him. Suddenly he calls across to the Queen.*

ORDERLY: The Germans are very keen on keeping the right time, aren't they, Your Majesty . . . ?!

MARY *is startled to be addressed like this.*

MARY: I believe that is often said to be the case.

ORDERLY: Being German yourself, Your Majesty, I expect
you know that very well . . . very well indeed! Love to
keep all sorts of clocks I'm sure . . . don't you, Your
Majesty? And being German yourself – I expect you can
tell us why we are still fighting this war . . . ?!

*As he says this the hospital staff converge on him and usher
him away rapidly.*

DOCTOR: Forgive us . . . the man is not very well . . .

MARY *has kept very controlled. But she notices that the
members of the public are staring out of the shadows at her
impassively. They are still not smiling at her or looking
welcoming in any way.*

EXT/INT. HOSPITAL ENTRANCE/ROYAL CAR. DAY.
We cut to MARY *in the back of the royal car moving away from
hospital. She sees a group of people watching her go with the same
impassive stare. She waves to them politely but they do not wave
back.* MARY *peers at them with incomprehension. Then she pulls
down the blind and turns to her lady-in-waiting.*

MARY: I do not know why they are looking like that . . .

INT. BUCKINGHAM PALACE. CORRIDOR NEAR
STAMFORDHAM'S OFFICE. AFTERNOON.
We cut to MARY *walking down a passage in the palace. The
blinds are drawn on most of the windows and the passage is in
half darkness with no light on. The atmosphere is stark. All the
furniture has labels on it.* MARY *is looking shaken. She indicates
to her ladies she wants to be alone.*

INT. BUCKINGHAM PALACE. MARY'S DRESSING ROOM.
LATE AFTERNOON.

We see MARY's *head go back with an abrupt movement. She is
lying on the settee in the study. Now she is in private we see how
truly troubled she is. She is curled up almost as if she is ill. She is
murmuring something to herself again and again, like a litany. As
we get closer we hear what it is.*

MARY: I'm English from tip to toe . . . from toe to tip . . . I'm
English from tip to toe . . .
We move in on her eyes.
Flashback. We see her enormous mother, FAT MARY,
*coming down a passage towards two young male guests, who
nod graciously as she approaches.* YOUNG MARY *is
watching this from a doorway.*
As soon as FAT MARY *passes the young men's attitude
changes dramatically.*

YOUNG MAN: I see they've let the Hanoverian beast out
again . . . !
We see YOUNG MARY *watching the giant shape of her
mother recede down the passage.*
MARY's *eyes flick open, in the present, with a start.*
*For a moment she sees the bandaged eyes of the soldier
with the missing limbs staring at her. A piercing frightening
stare.*
*Then she realizes somebody is in the room. She sits up. It
is* YOUNG GEORGE.

MARY: Georgie . . . ! I never heard you come in. You gave me
such a start . . . !
YOUNG GEORGE *is not in his cadet uniform but in a dark
suit.*

YOUNG GEORGE: Forgive me, Mama – I was so keen to see
you . . . You remember I have a few days break from
college . . .

He goes over to her and gives her a little kiss.

MARY: Yes . . . I remember . . . I was just somewhere else . . . for a very brief moment . . .

YOUNG GEORGE stares around the study. He sees it has now become absolutely crammed with decorative antique objects, pictures, porcelain and furniture.

YOUNG GEORGE: I couldn't help noticing, Mama . . . all these lovely things you have here which weren't here before . . .

MARY: Yes . . . I worked quite hard to recover them all for the collection. They had been given away – to all sorts of people – but now they have returned.

YOUNG GEORGE examines a splendid chair. He is keen to show his mother he has knowledge too and shares her interest.

YOUNG GEORGE: This is seventeenth century isn't it, Mama . . . and this porcelain is English isn't it . . . about 1800 . . . ?

MARY: Very good, Georgie . . . its date is 1815.

MARY moves over to YOUNG GEORGE and stands next to him.

YOUNG GEORGE (*softly*): It's beautiful . . . very beautiful.

There is a moment of connection between MARY and YOUNG GEORGE as they both look at the beautiful objects

YOUNG GEORGE: And your labelling is tremendous, Mama . . . you've labelled everything – nobody will be in any doubt about any of it ever again . . . !

MARY: Yes . . . Of course your father was not brought up to find solace in such things . . . He doesn't find everything that is modern hideous like I do . . . so I appreciate all this on my own. One has to work hard to preserve the past –

The moment of intimacy between them is suddenly interrupted by YOUNG GEORGE. He is unable to stop himself bursting out with his request.

YOUNG GEORGE: Mama, I've got to go and fight . . . !

MARY: Don't be ridiculous, Georgie, you're far too young . . . you're still a child. What an absurdity! Isn't it enough two of your brothers are in the Forces . . . ? Anyhow, any moment there will be victory – that's what we've been told – they're very confident . . .

YOUNG GEORGE: I *have* to fight, Mama – I cannot stand being at the naval college a moment longer! If the only way to leave is to fight – I must fight!

MARY: You know only your father can give you permission to leave. And he will not agree. I cannot change his mind. You can try yourself but –

YOUNG GEORGE: I've *got* to leave! I have to . . . ! Before it's too late . . . I feel time is running out, Mama. If I do not leave – I HAVE NO IDEA WHAT WILL HAPPEN!

MARY: Stop this at once, Georgie . . . you will not lose control of yourself. (YOUNG GEORGE *staring at his mother.*) Whatever your father decides – you will do your duty.

INT. BUCKINGHAM PALACE. CORRIDOR OF CLOCKS. NIGHT.

We cut to the passage full of clocks. The guests for a banquet are wandering up and down the palace passage waiting. But the atmosphere is hushed, almost ghostly. The passage is dark and the guests can see into other rooms where all the furniture is covered in dust sheets. There is no colour anywhere because the chandeliers are not blazing out.

YOUNG GEORGE *is standing in his naval cadet uniform watching the guests manoeuvre among each other. He can see generals and field marshals, chiefs of staff of the Army and the Navy. Everybody is looking as if they are very cold – they can't stop themselves moving from foot to foot and blowing out their cheeks.*

All the adults, to YOUNG GEORGE*'s eyes, look haggard and perplexed, as if they have no idea what to do next.*

But as soon as they see YOUNG GEORGE *move towards them, they adopt a tone of hearty good cheer.*

YOUNG GEORGE *moves first towards the admirals. Before they see him coming he has time to overhear an unguarded remark.*

ADMIRAL: For some unfathomable reason they've decided to switch all the heating off – the King really thinks that is going to help us win the war . . . ! (*The others laugh derisively.*) Mind you, it about sums up his knowledge of naval warfare . . . ! (*The others continue to mutter.*) I don't think I've ever been so freezing indoors as now –
He sees YOUNG GEORGE. *Immediately smiles appear on all their faces.*

ADMIRAL: Naval life is obviously suiting you, young man . . . (*The other admirals nod at* YOUNG GEORGE.) . . . You'll have a ship of your own before the year is out . . . !
The admirals chuckle. YOUNG GEORGE *smiles weakly and moves on. As he goes he overhears:*
We're losing too many ships – and nobody wants to admit it . . .

YOUNG GEORGE *approaches a cluster of army generals, a subjective shot moving through the grey cold jittery adults.*

GENERAL: I don't believe my teeth have ever chattered like this . . . (*His face is deeply lined with worry.*) I would have given anything not to have had to come here today.
They see YOUNG GEORGE, *they beam at him, and then the* GENERAL *continues.*
You look terribly well, young man – you'll be a rear admiral soon . . . ! By Christmas no doubt!

YOUNG GEORGE: So I keep getting told, sir . . .
The generals look surprised.
How do you think the war is going, sir?

The generals look even more taken aback by the bluntness of the question.

GENERAL: Progress is very steady . . . we're making the progress we were expecting this year . . . soon it will be time to start the build-up for the final breakthrough –

YOUNG GEORGE *moves on.*

SECOND GENERAL (*muttering*): It's the same speech for all of them . . .

YOUNG GEORGE *sees the Prime Minister,* LLOYD GEORGE, *standing by himself. His hair is now snow white, his face very drawn, but his manner is febrile. As soon as he sees* YOUNG GEORGE, *he switches to a much more expansive demeanour.*

LLOYD GEORGE: Young man . . . you look remarkably well! . . . No doubt running circles round everybody at naval college . . . ! (YOUNG GEORGE's *eyes flick.*) And I'm much impressed by what I see here too . . . !

The Prime Minister indicates a line of buckets in a darkened room catching drips from the ceiling which are falling with vigorous regularity.

A leaking ceiling – but it has not been mended . . . Every penny is being spent where it really matters . . . !

The sound of the rain intensifies and the drips increase during the scene.

YOUNG GEORGE: And are you equally impressed with how everything is going, sir . . . ? With the war . . . ?

LLOYD GEORGE: Yes – there's a new dimension now, a new direction since I took over . . . everything is more professional at long last! We have a proper War Cabinet, the circulation of information is infinitely faster . . . And the results are there for all to see!

YOUNG GEORGE *stares at the chiefs of staff forming bewildered circles in the passage.*

We cut to STAMFORDHAM *standing on his own. We see*

he is looking so much older than when YOUNG GEORGE *last saw him. As* YOUNG GEORGE *approaches he is concerned about* STAMFORDHAM's *appearance, his skin is ashen and his face is lined.*

   STAMFORDHAM *is deep in thought. He is the only one who doesn't immediately change to hearty bonhomie when he sees* YOUNG GEORGE.

STAMFORDHAM: Young man . . . your father setting an example by switching off the heating is not proving universally popular, I see . . .

YOUNG GEORGE: No . . . They hate it . . . (*He looks at* STAMFORDHAM.) Don't ask me how I am, please.

STAMFORDHAM: I will do no such thing . . . And you will return the compliment . . . you won't ask me either.

   YOUNG GEORGE *staring at* STAMFORDHAM's *lined face.*

YOUNG GEORGE: No, I will not, sir . . .

They both stare towards the cold and nervous crowd of politicians and chiefs of staff.

YOUNG GEORGE: Is it true . . . the stories about the Germans? . . . About the French prisoners being given tuberculosis, and the Belgian babies . . . ? And the corpse factory, the Germans distilling glycerine from corpses . . . ? (YOUNG GEORGE *stares straight at* STAMFORDHAM.) Is it true, sir? . . . You're the only one who will tell me . . .

STAMFORDHAM: Let us say some of it is true . . . (*We see the disbelief in* YOUNG GEORGE's *eyes.*) We will know more at the end of the war – just so long as we manage to win it of course . . .

The guests are now moving past them towards the ballroom having been summoned to the banquet. The faces of the guests are full of expectation that they may be moving towards warmth and comfort.

   STAMFORDHAM *lowers his voice and whispers to* YOUNG GEORGE.

I have some news for you, young man – your cousin the
Tsar has just abdicated . . .

YOUNG GEORGE (*startled*): The Emperor?! . . . He's
abdicated?! What will happen to them?

STAMFORDHAM: We've agreed that they can come and live in
England.

*YOUNG GEORGE is fascinated by the news. At that very
moment his mother, MARY, approaches down the corridor to
make her entrance to the banquet.*

*She is dressed very soberly and wearing very little of her
jewellery.*

INT. BUCKINGHAM PALACE. THE BALLROOM.
NIGHT.

*We cut to a wide shot of the banquet. The light is low, the table
decoration is plain, the guest list much smaller than the great
banquet before the outbreak of war, the guests are still very cold,
and look immensely pale. The atmosphere is sepulchral, hardly
anyone is talking, just the sound of the heavy rain. There is a
sadness and fragility in the adult faces. On their plates we see
small pieces of a very brown fish. STAMFORDHAM is sitting near
the middle of the table watching everybody with beady eyes.
YOUNG GEORGE is standing in the doorway among the flunkeys.
He whispers to one of them.*

YOUNG GEORGE: I don't see a special table plan any more . . .
just all the bishops together . . . the generals together . . .
*GEORGE, the King, is eating his fish very fast at one end of
the table, hardly looking up at anybody. MARY is trying to
convey a greater sense of occasion and calm at the other end
of the table.*

GEORGE: Two courses . . . we only serve two courses any
more . . . and no alcohol as you can see . . . And the fish

is an attempt at my favourite dish Bombay Duck, but we can't get the right ingredients any more, so they've tried to make it with kippers . . . (*He prods at the fish.*) And it's pretty disgusting I think you'll agree . . .

There is a small nervous laugh around the table. LADY WARRENDER, *a talkative woman of about forty, tries to cheer the King up.*

LADY WARRENDER: I think it's refreshing to have such small portions – so appropriate! I went to the Maitlands last week and they were still serving six courses, carrying on quite simply as if nothing had happened . . . well, that's not completely true, when the war started it was eight courses – so in three years they've gone down to six . . . (*She laughs.*) . . . a sacrifice of a sort!

We cut to a high shot, YOUNG GEORGE *staring through the screen from the gallery like he did with* JOHNNIE *before the war. Then there was such an air of confidence, now when he stares down he sees shivering nervous adults and this virtual silence as his father continues to look at nobody.*

For an instant YOUNG GEORGE *imagines* JOHNNIE *with him watching it all.*

We cut down to the level of the table as LADY WARRENDER *tries again, this time to the Queen.*

You know, Your Majesty, I heard the most stupid thing I have ever heard in my life last week . . .

MARY: The most stupid thing ever . . . that is some claim . . . what was it and where did you hear it . . . ?

LADY WARRENDER (*momentarily flustered*): Well, I forget exactly where it was . . . maybe it was at the Maitlands again or may be it wasn't – but I heard such a foolish comment . . . that there are rumours going around (*She waves her hand airily.*) amongst the people and so forth . . . that the royal family must be pro-German because you have a German name . . . !!

We see immediate alarm in MARY's *eyes.* GEORGE *has half heard the remark.*

GEORGE: What's that? What are you talking about?

MARY: There are rumours circulating that we are supporting the Germans because we have a German name –

LADY WARRENDER: It's so ridiculous, isn't it . . . ?!

GEORGE: Well, what do they want, for heaven's sake – for us to change our name?!

He is staring at the generals and politicians expecting them to laugh but they avert their eyes. The King sees LLOYD GEORGE *also not looking at him.*

You're not saying very much . . . What do you think about this? . . . You want us to change our name?!

There is a slight pause, as the guests squirm in their seats.

LLOYD GEORGE: If the situation remains the same . . . It may just be a possibility that needs to be considered . . . (*All the guests looking down at their plates.*) in everybody's interest . . .

GEORGE, *the King, looks astonished.*

He puts down his napkin, not saying another word and walks straight out of the banquet without looking back at anybody.

There is a low troubled murmur around the table. MARY *is sitting ramrod straight.*

INT. BUCKINGHAM PALACE. CORRIDOR NEAR KING'S STUDY. NIGHT.

We see YOUNG GEORGE *staring after his father. The King is walking down the passage alone, his small figure disappearing.*

GEORGE: Never . . . never . . . NEVER!

INT. WOOD FARM. PASSAGE. NIGHT.
A terrible gale is blowing, the rain and the wind slashing the
windows of the farmhouse.
　　We are moving down the passage of the farmhouse at night.
And then we hear a horrible cry echoing along the passage.
We see LALLA *rush out of the bedroom in her nightdress.*

INT. WOOD FARM. JOHNNIE'S BEDROOM. NIGHT.
We see JOHNNIE *writhing on his bed, having a bad fit.* LALLA
takes him in her arms, she holds him. He is crying out still, in a
way we have never heard before.

LALLA: That was a big noise, my darling . . . bigger than
　　　usual . . . What is it that's different? (*She looks at him*
　　　calmly.) It's a terrible night out there, isn't it . . . does it
　　　make it worse . . . ? (*As the fit continues.*) We've been
　　　having more of these now, haven't we, Johnnie . . . But in
　　　between you do so much . . . you've grown so much . . .
　　　FRED *is standing in the doorway in his nightclothes.*
FRED: I heard a horrible noise.
LALLA: It's nearly over . . .
　　　We stay on JOHNNIE's *eyes for a moment, the fit is passing,*
　　　he is staring at the window as the rain hits it. He smiles at
　　　the unearthly sound of the wind.
JOHNNIE: It's good the wind, isn't it . . . ?

INT. WOOD FARM. THE KITCHEN. NIGHT.
We cut to FRED *and* LALLA *sitting at the kitchen table in their*
night clothes having a cup of tea. The wind is still raging around
the farmhouse.
FRED: Do you think anybody at all remembers us?
　　　Remembers we are here . . . ?

143

LALLA: Of course! And why should that matter to us anyway?

FRED: What do you mean it doesn't matter?! Sometimes I
think the war could end and they would forget to tell us!
(LALLA *smiles at this.*) You know, I often look at you,
Lalla, and think she's still quite young . . . she shouldn't
give up on a husband!
We see LALLA*'s fine strong face. Her hair is down.*
Is this how she's going to spend the rest of her life? All
the service you've given them, the children, and that
family! And all the time now spent hoping the best for
Johnnie . . . Don't you feel a little alone sometimes,
Lalla . . . ? You must do . . . Even with me here . . . !

LALLA: No. (*Looking up from her tea.*) You never will
understand this, Fred, will you . . . I'm glad to be here . . .
I think it's important what we are doing with Johnnie . . .
FRED *looks astonished.*
I wouldn't want to be doing anything else. And at some
stage they *will* have time for us – to see Johnnie's
progress . . . (*We see* FRED*'s doubt.*) I have no doubt of
that at all . . . !

INT. BUCKINGHAM PALACE. CORRIDOR NEAR MARY'S
STUDY. DAY.
We cut to MARY *pacing the passage. As we get close to her we
realize she is rehearsing names, trying them out to herself.*

MARY: Wittern . . . Wipper . . . Wippern . . . Whitford . . .
Winter . . .
We cut to YOUNG GEORGE. *We see he is standing outside
his father's study waiting, deeply anxious.*
We cut inside the King's study. STAMFORDHAM *is
standing in front of the King's desk.* GEORGE *is sitting
behind it, the parrot, Charlotte, is perched in the shadows.*

GEORGE: So you've spoken to that character from the College of Arms?

STAMFORDHAM: Mr Farnham Burke, yes . . . (*He looks straight at the King.*) It's been suggested since your family's name Saxe Coburg-Gotha belongs to the House of Wettin . . . some name derived from that like Whipper or Wetmore would be appropriate –

GEORGE: We'll be a laughing stock . . . I still don't see why we have to do this –

YOUNG GEORGE *appears in the doorway.*

YOUNG GEORGE: Papa . . . I just need a moment with you –

GEORGE: I said in half an hour!

YOUNG GEORGE: That was two hours ago, Papa.

GEORGE (*erupting*): I have no time – absolutely no time at the moment, every single waking moment is taken up, the whole day every day, time is running away from me, and nobody will do anything . . . !

YOUNG GEORGE *unflinching in the face of his father's outburst.*

YOUNG GEORGE: I'll talk very fast then, Papa, really fast . . . I feel my real abilities – whatever they may be and however small they are – are not best shown off at naval college –

GEORGE: Shown off?! You will *not* show off in any circumstances. (*To* STAMFORDHAM.) Why is he talking about showing off?!

YOUNG GEORGE (*hastily*): No, that is the wrong expression, I shouldn't have said that – it is because I'm trying to deal with this too fast . . . ! Naval college and naval life is not what I'm best at . . . Music and art are my strengths, I feel I could be more use to the war effort – I know I'm still young really, not old enough – but I could help our cause more if I used my knowledge to choose music for military concerts for instance . . . or if I went to the Front to fight –

GEORGE: Music? Art? Fighting at the Front?! This is all rubbish. You will be a sailor – and that is all there is to it. Do you understand? You will be in the Navy, you will spend your whole life in the Navy – and there's a good chance you will die in the Navy! And I don't want the matter *ever* raised again.

INT. BUCKINGHAM PALACE. CORRIDOR NEAR MARY'S STUDY. DAY.
We cut to MARY *sitting at the end of the passage on a small settee. She is still mouthing names to herself.*

MARY: Wennem . . . The House of Wennem . . .
YOUNG GEORGE *approaches her, looking stricken.*
YOUNG GEORGE: It was a disaster, Mama.
MARY: Well, that was to be expected. Your father had such a time in the Navy, he knows it is right for you.
YOUNG GEORGE (*in despair*): He said the subject could never be raised again –
MARY: It cannot . . . We are in the middle of such a crisis, Georgie . . . we're having to face such change . . . our family name even –
YOUNG GEORGE: If all those stories of the atrocities of the Germans hadn't been spread everywhere this wouldn't be happening . . .
MARY: I never dreamt – it never occurred to me we would have to change our name . . . all the family tradition – I cannot bear to see that being tampered with, it offends me so much . . . (*Her face is turned away towards the window.*) And another thing that is happening – the Kaiser is being removed from his honorary position as head of certain British regiments.
YOUNG GEORGE (*exasperated*): But surely that's right, Mama!

146

We're *fighting* him!

MARY: You don't understand – what about afterwards?! I cannot help thinking about what will happen afterwards . . . If all the pieces that everything was built on are removed, then what? The Houses of Europe were *joined* . . .

She is totally wrapped up in her thoughts.

YOUNG GEORGE: Mama, I really can't go back to naval college . . . I cannot go back –

His mother does not hear him. She is close to the window.

MARY: Matters are in such a state of confusion now . . . one has no idea what will happen . . .

INT. BUCKINGHAM PALACE. THE KING'S STUDY. DAY.
STAMFORDHAM *faces the King.*

STAMFORDHAM: I have a suggestion which might be of interest.

GEORGE: Which is?

STAMFORDHAM: Edward III –

GEORGE: Edward III – we're going back that far! My family has nothing in common with Edward III . . .

STAMFORDHAM (*unflinching*): Edward III was often known as Edward of Windsor . . . it has never been used as a dukedom . . . so my suggestion is the name change would be 'The House of Windsor' . . .

Pause. GEORGE *stares at him, his voice is quiet.*

GEORGE: I don't like it . . . I feel something bad may happen if we do this . . .

INT/EXT. NORFOLK COUNTRYSIDE/ROYAL CAR. DAY.
YOUNG GEORGE *dressed in his naval cadet uniform is sitting in*

*the front seat of a royal car next to the chauffeur. They are
bumping along a rough track in the country, mud is spattering the
windows, the chauffeur is looking lost.*

YOUNG GEORGE: Just keep going, this is the right way, I
　　promise . . . keep going . . . !

EXT. WOOD FARM. DAY.
YOUNG GEORGE *is standing in front of Wood Farm and calling
out loudly. The car is parked behind him and the chauffeur is
standing looking very sceptical.*

YOUNG GEORGE: Johnnie . . . ! Lalla . . . ! ANYBODY?!
　　Where on earth are you? . . . It's Georgie . . . where are
　　you??
　　Suddenly YOUNG GEORGE *sees, coming across the fields in
　　the distance,* JOHNNIE's *household with* JOHNNIE *riding at
　　its head. A wonderful stately progress, like a true prince.*
　　YOUNG GEORGE *grins in astonishment. Then he calls out.*
　　Johnnie . . . Johnnie!
　　JOHNNIE *spies* YOUNG GEORGE *across the field in his naval
　　uniform.* JOHNNIE *immediately leaps in the saddle, making
　　excited arm movements.*
JOHNNIE: He has come back! He has come to see me!
　　*Time cut. We cut to a high shot of the muddy farmyard in
　　front of the house.* JOHNNIE *and* YOUNG GEORGE *are
　　embracing, watched by* LALLA, *the servants and the
　　chauffeur.*
　　　After the embrace the servants bow to YOUNG GEORGE
　　*and greet him solemnly. 'Your Royal Highness . . . It's so
　　very good to see you.' Even the stout* FRED *behaves in a
　　courtly fashion.* YOUNG GEORGE *is amused by this regal
　　display.*
YOUNG GEORGE: Thank you . . . (*To* LALLA.) Very

impressive . . . What a household you have here now, Johnnie!

JOHNNIE: I will show you my estate. We have three pigs, four cows and eleven ducks . . . oh and some chickens but I don't like them . . .

He sets off, stomping across the farmyard.

LALLA: You look magnificent, Georgie, in your uniform.

YOUNG GEORGE moves close to LALLA indicating the chauffeur.

YOUNG GEORGE: Don't say anything but I have escaped . . . I'm here on a special mission . . . (LALLA*'s eyes flash.*) Don't worry I will explain everything..

JOHNNIE is waving his arms around, showing off his domain.

JOHNNIE: Here is the estate . . . !

YOUNG GEORGE: I have news for everybody . . .

He addresses the servants as well who are following behind. The family has a new name . . . Papa has rechristened the family 'The House of Windsor'!

LALLA: I don't believe that, Georgie . . . the family has changed its name?

JOHNNIE: 'Windsor' . . . I think that's quite good.

INT. WOOD FARM. THE PARLOUR. DAY.
We cut inside the farmhouse. YOUNG GEORGE *is tearing his uniform off, pulling off his jacket and throwing his cap across the room.*

YOUNG GEORGE: I've got to get this horrible uniform off!

LALLA (*suspicious*): How do you mean you've escaped, Georgie?

YOUNG GEORGE: Everything is under control . . . Talking of which things are happening so fast in London . . .

149

amazing things. The Tsar and his family, you remember the Emperor, Johnnie, the Emperor fish with his absurd swimming . . . well, he has been made to give up his throne – and he is coming to live in this country!

LALLA: Goodness me . . . where on earth will they live?!

JOHNNIE: The Emperor . . . ! (*He gets up.*) I will see them, won't I . . . ?

We see JOHNNIE *beaming at the thought of the Russian girls. He goes over to the gramophone .*

That's very exciting . . . The Tsar . . . and Maria and Anastasia . . .

YOUNG GEORGE *watches* JOHNNIE *move to the music.*

YOUNG GEORGE: Yes of course you will see them, Johnnie! And the gramophone appears to have been a good idea too . . . (*He turns to* LALLA.) Mama said I could stay a couple of nights here. (*We see* LALLA*'s disbelief.*) I wouldn't lie to you, would I, Lalla . . . ?

INT. BUCKINGHAM PALACE. THE KING'S STUDY. DAY.
GEORGE *is sitting surrounded by letters and articles, great piles of paper.* STAMFORDHAM *enters. He sees the King is very agitated, his eyes full of lack of sleep.*

GEORGE: We agreed, didn't we, that the Tsar and Tsarina and their family could come to this country . . . ?
(STAMFORDHAM *nods.*) To live here in exile . . .

STAMFORDHAM: Yes. The invitation has been sent and accepted.

GEORGE: I'm beginning to realize that many people disapprove of the idea. (*He shuffles the papers.*) There are certain articles in various publications . . . and letters of course . . . a rally even at the Albert Hall celebrating the fall of the Tsar . . . It's becoming increasingly clear to me because the Romanovs are my family it is putting me in a very unfair position.

STAMFORDHAM: Unfair, sir . . . (*He watches the King.*) In the sense you are obliged . . . ?

GEORGE: Yes! I'm obliged because of our ties!

He searches for the right words, staring at the sea of papers on his desk.

But it may not be the correct course . . . with things so uncertain . . . (*He looks up at* STAMFORDHAM.) Do you think it will be possible to *withdraw* the invitation?

STAMFORDHAM'*s eyes flick in surprise. For a moment he does not know how to reply.*

STAMFORDHAM: I think the Government may feel that would be a difficult thing to do . . .

GEORGE *stares at* STAMFORDHAM. *Then he speaks with surprising force.*

GEORGE: You have to go and see the Prime Minister.

EXT. WOOD FARM. THE GARDEN.

YOUNG GEORGE *and* JOHNNIE *staring at the garden which is in a corner of the farmyard. It resembles a smaller version of* JOHNNIE'*s rich colourful garden at York Cottage.*

YOUNG GEORGE: So this is a little reminder of your great garden, Johnnie? . . . You're very impressive with gardens I must say! I'm sure this will be just splendid one day.

JOHNNIE (*surveying his garden*): It will get better . . . (*He looks at* YOUNG GEORGE.) They will come here from Russia? . . . The whole family – do you think . . . to my farm . . . ?

YOUNG GEORGE: TO STAY?! HERE! . . . Well that is a thought! (*He laughs.*) That would be something to see, wouldn't it!!

We see JOHNNIE's *eyes shining. We see the beautiful Russian girls,* TATIANA, MARIA *and* ANASTASIA *moving around* JOHNNIE's *little garden, touching the flowers.*

JOHNNIE *looks around the farmyard and he sees the* TSAR *standing with the cows.*

And then he looks up and sees the TSARINA *leaning out of an upstairs window of the farmhouse with some washing.*

YOUNG GEORGE: That's a wonderful thought, Johnnie! You having the Russian imperial family on your estate . . . ! I'm not sure you would want to have them for a very long time though . . . !

JOHNNIE *looks up, imagining the* TSARINA. *She is shrieking from the top window, yelling instructions across the farmyard to all the English royal servants.*

INT. THE PRIME MINISTER'S STUDY. NIGHT.

LLOYD GEORGE *and* STAMFORDHAM *looking at each other.* STAMFORDHAM *is standing,* LLOYD GEORGE *is hunched forward, sitting on a high-backed chair. Two senior officials are standing in the shadows near the Prime Minister.*

STAMFORDHAM: And His Majesty also wonders where they would *stay*? How they would live?

LLOYD GEORGE: Well, I'm sure His Majesty could make one of his houses available to the Tsar and his family, couldn't he?

STAMFORDHAM: There are none available except for Balmoral which is hardly suitable or appropriate at this time of year . . .

LLOYD GEORGE: Well, I think it's probable the Russian royal family would feel it really quite appropriate compared to some of the destinations they could be heading for . . .

STAMFORDHAM: His Majesty is also greatly concerned about

the dangers to His Imperial Highness and his family of the perilous and prolonged sea voyage . . .

We see LLOYD GEORGE*'s disbelief.*

LLOYD GEORGE: Oh, I'm sure they could make the journey in stages – they could travel for instance overland to Norway and sail from Bergen . . .

STAMFORDHAM (*unfazed*): His Majesty also feels that since the arrival of the Tsar and his family in this country will be very unpopular – it puts him in a very invidious position because they are his family . . . He feels France would be a much better destination, since they have none of these problems . . .

LLOYD GEORGE *smiles at this.*

LLOYD GEORGE: There's no reason for France to have him though . . .

STAMFORDHAM (*remaining resolute*): The King has always had warm feelings towards his cousin the Tsar, but His Majesty considers it would not be wise for them to settle here at this particular time . . . It is being discussed, as you must be aware, not just in the clubs, but by working men and by Labour members of the House of Commons –

LLOYD GEORGE (*suddenly chuckling*): I shouldn't be too concerned about them!

STAMFORDHAM: His Majesty also feels the message sent to the Russian premier that 'the *revolution* was the greatest service the Russian people have yet made to the cause we're all fighting for' . . . a little strong.

LLOYD GEORGE: A little strong . . . ? Really . . . ? We need to be encouraging to the new Russian government! If the Bolsheviks take control they will pull out of the war . . . and His Majesty's Russian family will face an even more interesting situation . . .

STAMFORDHAM (*unflinching*): His Majesty wishes me to

convey the absolute urgency of the situation and the
strength of his feelings –

LLOYD GEORGE: And I will let His Majesty know in the
fullness of time – having consulted with colleagues –
whether the Government considers it possible to
withdraw the invitation . . . or not.

STAMFORDHAM *withdraws.*

LLOYD GEORGE: What do you make of that, gentlemen?!

INT. WOOD FARM. THE PARLOUR. NIGHT.
We cut to Russian music pouring through the farmhouse,
balalaikas playing from JOHNNIE's *gramophone, a sound*
reminiscent of the concert that began the story. JOHNNIE *is*
rocking backwards and forwards joyfully to the music. LALLA *is*
talking loudly, in full flow – we see her laughing earthily. She is
pointing at JOHNNIE's *pictures on the wall.*

LALLA: And this one – Fat Mary as we used to call her, your
grandmother – is really very good, oh yes! Johnnie has
caught her likeness though he never knew her! She was a
great galleon, coming down a passage, she was! She
squashed everything in her path! Nothing was safe!
Especially not the crockery!

YOUNG GEORGE: All these pictures that Johnnie has done . . .
but this place is also full of you, Lalla . . .

LALLA: Full of me . . . ! (*She laughs.*) What ridiculous talk,
Georgie – what is there of me here! No, this is Johnnie's
place . . . And one day soon he is going to do a recital for
your parents to show how far he has come . . .

YOUNG GEORGE's *face immediately clouds over.*

YOUNG GEORGE: They will never have the time to do that,
Lalla . . .

LALLA: Oh yes, I'm sure they will –

154

YOUNG GEORGE (*his tone hardening*): I'm telling you they
   won't. You have no idea what it's like now . . .
LALLA: I know that one day when they're here in the country
   they will make the time –
   YOUNG GEORGE *suddenly erupts.*
YOUNG GEORGE: Why don't you listen to me?! They will
   never see Johnnie . . . Don't you realize THEY HAVE
   NO TIME FOR ANYTHING! What's more they don't
   know what they are doing – not my parents, not the
   generals, not the politicians – none of them! . . . They
   have no idea how to end the war, or why they are still
   fighting –
LALLA: Don't you dare talk about your parents like that! –
YOUNG GEORGE: Why ever not?! . . . It's *the truth* . . . So
   don't you ever lie to Johnnie about them having time for
   him . . . Why do you think Johnnie is here, for heaven's
   sake?! In this place! – So nobody can *see him,* that's why!
   Nobody wants to see you ever again . . . !
LALLA: You're not too old for a thrashing, Georgie – and you
   will get one unless you stop right now . . .
   They face each other in the parlour.
YOUNG GEORGE: Just you try . . . ! You spent your whole life
   bringing us up . . . us children . . . and you didn't
   manage to get anywhere with any of us, did you! – *Just
   look at me* . . . !
LALLA: I *will* thrash you now, young man . . . !
   She catches hold of YOUNG GEORGE. *As he fights her, he
   buries his head into her midriff sobbing with rage and
   frustration.*
YOUNG GEORGE: I'm going mad at the college . . . I can't *bear*
   how stupid they think we are . . . when it is all of them
   that are the idiots . . . !
   JOHNNIE *is staring from the door of the parlour. They don't
   hear him.*

JOHNNIE: Why can't Georgie stay with me?

LALLA (*holding* YOUNG GEORGE *to her*): You're right I have
spent my life on all of you . . . and you, Georgie, were
always the cleverest . . . (*She holds him tight.*) I . . .
always. And you can still show them how clever you are
. . . (*She moves his head so he is looking at her.*) . . . and
show me . . . You'll go back to college . . .

YOUNG GEORGE *cries out.* LALLA *replies with real force.*
You will go back . . .

She looks up. The music has changed on the gramophone.
JOHNNIE *is dancing again.*

LALLA: And look what you've done to your brother . . . ! You
managed to get him all worked up about the idea of the
Emperor of Russia coming to live *here*!!

INT. BUCKINGHAM PALACE. THE KING'S STUDY.
NIGHT.
GEORGE *is sitting alone by his desk staring at the telephone.*
STAMFORDHAM *sees him through the half-opened door.*

STAMFORDHAM: I don't think the Prime Minister will be
giving us any news tonight, sir . . .

GEORGE: I think we should send him another note . . .
We must make sure there is at least a *delay* in the
invitation –

EXT. WOOD FARM. THE GARDEN. DAY.
We cut to summer flowers, a blaze of colours in JOHNNIE'*s
farmyard garden.* JOHNNIE *is moving through the flowers
whistling to himself, doing his strange skipping movements. For
one moment he imagines* ANASTASIA *staring at him from the
other side of the garden.*

He arrives at the wall at the end of the garden, and stares through a hole in the wall at the path that runs along the side of the farmyard.

At that very moment a collection of very young soldiers pass by, they are on a training run with full packs and guns. As they run by, JOHNNIE *stares at them fascinated through the hole. The line of young boys passing his wall seems to go on forever. Several of the very young soldiers see these eyes peering at them from the wall.*

INT. WOOD FARM. THE PARLOUR. AFTERNOON.
And then we cut to JOHNNIE *staring at the telephone in the front parlour of the farmhouse, waiting for news. He is patiently sitting by the phone.*

INT. BUCKINGHAM PALACE. MARY'S STUDY.
MORNING.
GEORGE *enters* MARY'*s study. It is early morning. He is standing in the corner of the room looking very small and pale.* MARY *immediately senses his mood and looks concerned.*

GEORGE: My dearest . . . The news from the Front is . . . (*His voice falling away.*)

MARY (*calm*): Tell me . . . I want to hear the absolute truth. However bad it is.

GEORGE: The news is not . . . not good at all. You must prepare yourself . . . it is possible the Germans will break through in the next twenty-four hours – and that could lead to everything being lost . . . (*We see the shock in* MARY'*s face.*) Today's news, when it comes, will be extremely vital . . . You must go down to the country as we planned . . . and I will wire as soon as I hear . . .

157

MARY: I will stay here . . . surely that will be best? . . . I should
    stay with you . . .

GEORGE: No, please . . . you must proceed as planned, we
    must carry on as normal as much as possible . . .
    otherwise waiting for the news . . . the suspense becomes
    very difficult for me . . . The wire will be waiting for you
    by the time you get there.

    GEORGE is right in the corner of the room, half turned away,
    for a moment he cannot speak.

    I know I don't often say this . . . find certain things so
    difficult to say out aloud . . . but you mean so much to
    me.

EXT/INT. SANDRINGHAM. ESTATE AND NORFOLK
ROADS/ROYAL CAR. AFTERNOON.
We cut to the royal car moving along a straight road that runs
through the forest at the edge of the Sandringham estate.

    MARY *is sitting with a lady-in-waiting. We see she is*
incredibly tense, just wanting to finish the journey.

MARY: Will we ever get there? . . . Never has the motor
    journey felt so slow . . .

    She glances at some forest labourers moving among the trees,
    who stare back at the royal car as it passes them.

    Suddenly she looks ahead through the windscreen, an
    expression of alarm in her eyes.

    She sees a roadblock in the distance on the long straight
    road. It is manned by armed men, they are not in uniform,
    and to MARY's *eyes they look like partisans.*

    For one instance she thinks they may be a revolutionary
    force barring her path.

    (*Urgently.*) Who are these men? . . . Why are they
    stopping us?!

As the car approaches the men, MARY *sees the roadblock more clearly. It changes character completely.*

It is in fact JOHNNIE'*s household stretched across the road. Several of the burly servants do have rifles, but they are safely strapped to their shoulder.* FRED *is holding his hand up, and is standing in the middle of the road to stop the car.* LALLA *and* JOHNNIE *are watching the royal car get nearer and nearer to them.*

The car stops. LALLA *approaches the passenger window.*

LALLA: Your Majesty! We saw it was you . . . Johnnie said there is Mama coming – and it was! He remembered your car . . . after all this time!

MARY: Yes, yes . . . that is a coincidence (*she acknowledges* JOHNNIE *through the window*) but I'm in the most fearful rush, there is some important news waiting for me from London –

LALLA: Of course, ma'am . . . Johnnie has just got something to show you, he's been collecting food and flowers in the woods . . . you remember how we saw you doing it that day . . . he's been collecting all sorts of things, fungi, all kinds of strange shapes! And he knows which ones are poisonous and which are not. (*An excited laugh.*) He's just going to show you his selection –

MARY: Lalla, we have to reach York Cottage –

MARY *sees* JOHNNIE *moving with his back to her, peering into each basket. The baskets are laid out on the road with a servant standing by each one.*

LALLA: He's just going to bring them to you now, ma'am . . .

MARY *watches* JOHNNIE'*s totally unhurried progress, moving along his woodland baskets. She finds it impossible to sit still and watch.*

MARY: I will get out and look at them . . . !

She climbs out of the car, its engine still running. She sees some villagers walking along in the distance watching the

159

scene. *She stares up the road towards her destination,
extremely tense about the news waiting for her.*

JOHNNIE *is still moving along his baskets of flowers and
fungi.*

JOHNNIE: I am not ready yet, Mama . . . you *mustn't* look yet!
LALLA *and* MARY*'s eyes meet.* LALLA *is staring straight at
her, a penetrating look, indicating that* MARY *must stay for
this.* MARY *looks again towards the horizon, at the end of
the straight road, desperate for news.*

LALLA: We are also preparing something for you, ma'am, for
you to hear . . . Johnnie will give you a recital when you
have a moment –

MARY: Yes we will find a time for that later . . . an
appropriate moment . . . whenever that will be . . .
JOHNNIE *is moving with infuriating slowness, making his
selection. He is forming the flowers and fungi into a strange
posy for his mother. He is absolutely oblivious to the urgency
of the situation.*

MARY (*suddenly*): Johnnie! I cannot wait any more . . . this is
taking too long . . . far too long, Lalla . . . I do not have
the time . . . !
She takes the unfinished posy with an abrupt movement.
I have to go . . . I must go! It is news from the Front . . . I
cannot stay a moment longer.
*She climbs into the car, holding the peculiar posy. The car
roars off.*

INT. YORK COTTAGE. HALL. AFTERNOON.
MARY *enters the small hall of York Cottage still holding the
bizarre posy. The servants scurry around as she enters. A
telegram is lying on the hall table.* MARY *drops the posy and rips
open the telegram. She stands in the doorway of her small study,
half in private as she reads the telegram.*

Then she looks up to see her lady-in-waiting and all the
servants are standing watching her, waiting for news.

MARY: The Germans have not broken through our lines
today. (*Immense relief on the servants' faces.*) The situation
is still very critically poised. We must wait to see what
the next few days bring . . .
MARY *carefully closes her door.*

INT. YORK COTTAGE. PASSAGE/GEORGE'S STUDY.
NIGHT.
The camera moving down the narrow passages of York Cottage.
All the small clocks are chiming. A cacophony of different chimes.
Then we cut inside GEORGE's *study. A glorious stamp, from a*
tropical island, fills the screen. GEORGE *is alone with his stamps,*
hunched over his album, whispering to himself.

GEORGE: That is . . . that is such a fine thing . . .
There is a knock and STAMFORDHAM *enters looking very*
grave. His face is completely white. GEORGE *half looking*
up, gives a welcoming smile.
Come in . . . come in by all means . . .
STAMFORDHAM: Sir – my apologies for disturbing you so late
but –
GEORGE (*interrupting*): No . . . I'm just burying myself in my
stamps . . . my latest acquisition. It helps me – especially
calming before this big war council . . . I feel much better
down here in the country . . . small rooms, always
pleased to be in small rooms. What an absurd idea
palaces are! –
STAMFORDHAM (*very quiet*): Sir, I have some news from
Russia –
GEORGE: Oh yes. I keep on thinking about them . . . what is

161

happening to them . . . it is on my mind . . . all of them
shut away in that remote farmhouse –

EXT/INT. RUSSIA. SIBERIAN FARMHOUSE. NIGHT.
*Throughout the rest of the scene we cut between the Siberian
farmhouse and* GEORGE*'s study.*

   *We suddenly cut to the metal grilles over all the windows
shutting out the light in the Siberian farmhouse. We then cut to
the bleak exterior,* ANASTASIA *staring out of the window. And
then we see the blinds on the last window in the passage that was
letting in daylight, slamming shut, closing on the girl's face. We
then see the Russian royal family, the* TSAR, TSARINA, *and the
five children all squashed together in one room. All sleeping in this
small space. They are still wearing their fine clothes.*

   We cut back to GEORGE *turning the pages of his album. He is
looking at a page of Russian imperial stamps as* STAMFORDHAM
watches him.

GEORGE: I can't help wondering how Alick is coping . . . shut
up in a farmhouse of all places . . . for her that would be
so difficult . . .
   We see the TSARINA *turning her head in the tiny room and
indicating to her children to prepare her bed. She is taking
up by far the most space of anybody in the room.*
   We cut back to GEORGE *and* STAMFORDHAM.
STAMFORDHAM: Sir . . . (*Trying to find a way to tell him.*) . . .
Something has happened to the family –
   GEORGE *looks up.*
STAMFORDHAM: They were woken up in the middle of the
night by their guards . . . They were probably told they
had to be moved for their own safety –
   *We see the Russian royal family being led down a long
passage, and then down wooden steps towards the basement,*

escorted by their guards. One of the children is carrying the dog. The royal doctor and the TSAR's *tiny household of servants are also with them.*

We see the TSARINA *pausing on the stairs to point out there is an unpleasant nail sticking out of the wall and something should be done about it.*

Then we see them being escorted down a basement passage, towards an empty room with just three chairs. All the windows are boarded up.

We see the family moving into the room, the TSAR *and* TSARINA *making a considerable commotion about the chairs, who will sit on the chairs and which is the best chair for the* TSARINA.

STAMFORDHAM: Somewhere in the farmhouse –

We see ANASTASIA *and* MARIA *staring around the room and noticing damp patches on the ceiling and an empty cigarette packet in the corner. And the little Tsarevich* ALEXEI *notices one of the guards coughing uncontrollably further down the passage and spitting out his phlegm.*

We cut back to a huge close up of GEORGE's *eyes as he realizes what he is about to be told. And then we cut to* STAMFORDHAM.

Somewhere in the farmhouse . . . they were grouped together. And they were all shot.

We go back to GEORGE's *eyes.*

And then we cut to the Russian guards' guns pointing straight at us through the door, as GEORGE *imagines what the* TSAR *must have seen.*

And then the firing starts straight at the camera.

We cut back to GEORGE *hunched over his album, his shoulders clenched.*

GEORGE: Not all of them . . . ?! All of them were shot?

We cut back to the bodies of the children spinning in the burst of bullets.

*And then we see them being dragged along the passage,
one after each other, pulled like firewood.*

*And laid out in a line outside against the wall, before the
guards start to cut into the corsets of the women, revealing
jewels, diamonds and sapphires, hidden away in their
undergarments.*

We cut back to STAMFORDHAM.

STAMFORDHAM: Yes . . . all of them . . . the Bolsheviks are
absolutely clear on the matter . . .

We see GEORGE *flinching. He sees himself standing next
to the* TSAR *in the Isle of Wight. He is looking sideways at
the* TSAR, *an angle we have never seen before, as he studies
the* TSAR's *great vanity from really close range. The absolute
monarch is standing next to him, totally unaware of
everything around him.*

And we see the TSARINA *drifting along the path at Barton
Manor over the summer grass in her galoshes. And then*
GEORGE *sees the Russian children's faces moving around the
garden and mingling with his own children.*

*We cut to the bodies of the Russian royal family being
pulled away into the dark trees of the wood surrounding the
Siberian farmhouse.*

*A wide shot of the last two children's bodies disappearing
into blackness, as they are dragged along the ground into the
night.*

GEORGE *sinks into his chair.*

GEORGE: Did we have a choice . . . ? (*He turns desperately
towards* STAMFORDHAM.) Tell me . . . do you really
think we had a choice, about letting them in . . . ?

STAMFORDHAM: We could not know how things would
develop –

GEORGE (*loud*): Did we have a *choice* . . . ?!

STAMFORDHAM: For the stability of the country . . . I don't
think we had a choice . . . (*His eyes flick.*) Ultimately we

must remember it was the Government's decision –

GEORGE sits bolt upright on hearing this. And then stands up sharply.

GEORGE: Maybe that is what the public will be told . . . but
. . . but we know . . .

His voice falls away, the sense of shock in his eyes. GEORGE
suddenly moves to the door.

Will you please go and tell Her Majesty the news . . . I'm
just . . .

*GEORGE leaves. His small figure wanders desperately along
the warren of passages of York Cottage. He finds himself by
the door of a cupboard room full of wellington boots and
overshoes and old mackintoshes.*

*He goes into the small room and walks to the window,
standing surrounded by all the boots. He sinks on to a low
stool by the window, staring out into what remains of*
JOHNNIE's *garden, the tall flowers against the night sky.*

GEORGE *is shaking with the shock.*

Maybe we *did* have a choice . . .

We move closer and closer on to his face.

INT. YORK COTTAGE. MARY'S SMALL STUDY. NIGHT.
We see MARY's *face in complete shock, as* STAMFORDHAM
*stands in the doorway of her tiny study. For a moment she just
looks at him.*

MARY: That is too horrible . . .

STAMFORDHAM: Yes, ma'am . . .

MARY: The children too . . . ? What unimaginable cruelty . . .

STAMFORDHAM: Is there anything you require, ma'am? If
there's something I can –

MARY (*quiet*): Thank you. No. What can you do . . . ? If you
would just leave me –

We see MARY *sitting at her desk. There is a quick cut of* MARY *running with the Russian children on the beach at the Isle of Wight. We then cut back to* MARY *as she looks round her little room full of beautiful antiques. A religious image in a small painting stares back at her.*

MARY *answers the image, she stares directly at it with an accusatory eye.*

EXT. SANDRINGHAM. ROYAL CHAPEL. DAY.
We cut to MARY *walking along the side of the royal chapel that nestles on the edge of the garden of the big house. It is a bright sunny day.* MARY *is with two ladies-in-waiting. As she is about to go into the chapel* MARY *stops.*

MARY: I think . . . just for a moment . . . I will go in alone . . .

INT. SANDRINGHAM. ROYAL CHAPEL. DAY.
We see MARY *sitting alone in the middle of the empty pews of the chapel. We move closer. We see her whole being is stricken with doubt. She is muttering to herself.*

MARY: What do I pray? I don't know what to pray . . . ?
For a moment her whole body clenches up. She tries to kneel but the prayer books spill everywhere. She bends her head, as if to stop herself weeping. Even quite alone she will not permit that.

We see an image of her presiding at the great banquet before the war, glittering and confident. And then some of the faces of the terribly wounded soldiers she has seen.

We cut back to her pale face, as she sits bolt upright in the pew. She stares directly at the camera.
I have nothing to say to the Lord . . .

INT. SANDRINGHAM. CONFERENCE ROOM. DAY.
We see a great conference table being prepared. Footmen bringing in gilt chairs to surround the L-shaped table. We see folders being put down, and place settings being carefully positioned, the names of leading politicians and the chiefs of staff and the King.

EXT. SANDRINGHAM. GARDEN OF THE BIG HOUSE. DAY
We catch glimpses through the trees, at the edge of the garden, of a procession. At first we cannot quite work out who it is, and then we realize it is JOHNNIE *and his household coming down the drive. They are all on foot, and marching in time.*

JOHNNIE *is at the head of the procession, then comes* LALLA, FRED *and the other servants who are carrying various objects including a music stand and a football.*

INT. SANDRINGHAM. LANDING. DAY.
We cut to STAMFORDHAM *turning sharply. He sees through the window* JOHNNIE's *procession approaching. He looks momentarily confused, for he does not recognize who they are.*

At another window MARY *is also watching them approach with consternation.*

MARY: Why are they here now?! There's been some mistake
. . . It was tomorrow – I cannot have got the days
muddled . . .

EXT. SANDRINGHAM. FRONT DOOR. DAY.
JOHNNIE's *procession comes to a halt outside the front door.*
JOHNNIE *addresses the servants at the door.*

JOHNNIE: We have walked all the way on foot . . . which is
    generally considered a very good idea . . .
LALLA: Her Majesty is expecting us . . .

INT. SANDRINGHAM. PASSAGE. DAY.
MARY *standing at the far end of the passage as the procession
approaches. They stop, all bunching up together.*

MARY: Lalla – there's been some confusion . . . today is the
    day of the War Council. It is most unfortunate . . .
    We see desperate disappointment on LALLA's *face.*
    But it might just be possible to do a few minutes for
    myself and Johnnie's grandmother, and the other
    children, because they haven't seen him for so very long
    . . . just a *very* few minutes –
LALLA: Thank you, ma'am! . . . He is so well prepared!
MARY: Of course you must not stray out of the back passages
    while you are here . . . the house is going to be very full
    of visitors – and none of them should catch sight . . .
    She indicates JOHNNIE.
LALLA: We will be very careful, ma'am, I promise you.

INT. SANDRINGHAM. THE BALLROOM. DAY.
*We cut to the ballroom where we heard the first recital at the start
of the story. There are a row of seats being arranged by servants
facing the stage. The old Queen,* ALEXANDRA, *is already sitting
in her position with her ladies-in-waiting. All round the edge of
the ballroom there are tables covered with her memorabilia,
photographs of all the family and a lot of her agate animals.*

INT. SANDRINGHAM. CONFERENCE ROOM. DAY.
We cut to GEORGE *standing all alone surrounded by the
enormous conference table. He looks exhausted, as if he has not
slept for days.*

MARY *enters, seeing her husband's lonely figure across the huge
room.*

MARY: Johnnie is here . . .
GEORGE (*truly surprised*): Johnnie is here . . . ? What now?!

INT. SANDRINGHAM. BALLROOM/PASSAGE. DAY.
We cut to the passage just outside the ballroom. JOHNNIE *is
waiting with his household.* LALLA *is straightening his clothes.
They are looking into the same mirror as when we first saw them
together when* JOHNNIE *was tiny.*

LALLA: Now, what are we going to try to do in particular . . . ?
      JOHNNIE *is gazing at himself in the mirror, quite pleased by
      what he sees.*
LALLA: You're going to try to stay *still* when you stand in
      front of them, not too much fidgeting –
      The door of the ballroom opens and JOHNNIE *enters with his
      household.*
      *For a moment, as he passes through the door, we see the
      ballroom as it was that day of the Queen's birthday, all the
      colours, the women in their magnificent dresses, sparkling
      decorations round the walls, the full richness of the
      Edwardian court.*
      As JOHNNIE *passes through the door, in the present, he is
      greeted by an ashen ghostly sight. There is the family sitting
      waiting for him. His mother and father pale and shrunken,*
      ALEXANDRA *all in black. His older siblings,* DAVID, MAY,
      who he has not seen for so long, are sitting at the back,

distant shadowy figures.

There is YOUNG GEORGE, *all his exuberance gone, sitting severe and watchful in naval uniform next to* STAMFORDHAM *who is looking so drained and ill.*

GEORGE, *the King, is sitting at the front, papers on his knee, as if he has just perched there for a moment.*

GEORGE: Johnnie . . . we are all here for the shortest of moments – because I have the business of the war to conduct . . .

JOHNNIE *stops, stands still in front of them. We cannot tell if he has heard what his father has said. His household stands along the walls to watch and* LALLA *moves over to the piano.*

For a moment there is complete silence. JOHNNIE *stands rooted to the spot. He stares at his grandmother, who he sees has withdrawn into a state of distant grief. He looks at his parents, who are now sitting ramrod straight, but their eyes are glazed. His mother's hands are moving constantly, nervously, picking at her sleeve.*

JOHNNIE: Good day, my fine fellows . . . I will start . . . I will start with . . . (*He stops.*) I forget . . .

LALLA (*prompting*): I will start with some lines by Alfred Lord Tennyson –

JOHNNIE: I will start with some lines from old Lord Alfred . . .
He launches off without a pause into a couple of lines from the Morte D'Arthur *in a big booming voice.*

But he suddenly breaks off almost as soon as he has started. He moves across the ballroom, his shambolic walk with his arms flailing, and climbs on to a stool coming perilously close to shattering various ornaments. He turns a large clock that is staring at all of them towards the wall so nobody can tell the time. He then moves back and beams at them.

And now – a line in French!

*He says a line from Victor Hugo with an exaggerated French
accent.*

*As he is doing this we see through the window a long line
of government cars moving along the drive towards the
house. A convoy of about ten cars some with military flags
flying on their bonnets.* GEORGE *sees them approach.*

GEORGE: They're here already . . . ! They are infernally early.
They must think we still keep the clocks half an hour
fast here, the blundering idiots, they can't even tell the
time . . . ! We will have to stop –

MARY: Lalla . . . you will take Johnnie by the back passages to
the kitchens. I'm sure they will find some –

JOHNNIE (*holding up his hand*): No certainly not . . . !

At that moment JOHNNIE *produces the musical instrument
he has brought, a trumpet, and one of his household runs
across with his music stand.*

I have not finished. Everybody will stay. Nobody can
leave early.

*He starts playing the trumpet, standing strangely, but
playing with considerable confidence.*

LALLA: Wait, Johnnie! I wasn't ready.

LALLA *catches up with him on the piano.* JOHNNIE *plays
with a deep concentration. A rather haunting tune flows out.
It is obvious he has practised hard.*

*As he plays we can see more and more government and
military cars arriving. And the chiefs of staff and the
politicians are emerging from the cars and standing around
outside the windows of the ballroom, peering inside, seeing
the royal family gathered, all staring at some large boy.*

*The King's officials are converging on them trying to
corral them, not sure what to do with them.*

GEORGE, *who's been on the point of leaving, has sat back
in his chair. He is staring at his son playing so simply and so
beautifully in front of him. He is mesmerized by this sight.*

He cannot take his eyes off JOHNNIE. *He is astonished*
JOHNNIE *can play like this.*

YOUNG GEORGE *is watching the confused chiefs of staff*
outside the window. He whispers to STAMFORDHAM.

YOUNG GEORGE: Johnnie is going to keep them all
waiting . . . !

YOUNG GEORGE *looks to see if* STAMFORDHAM *has heard*
this remark, and is amazed to see there are tears in
STAMFORDHAM's *eyes.*

YOUNG GEORGE *looks at his grandmother. She is also*
moist-eyed, and is shaking slightly in her seat. She has been
shattered by the war.

YOUNG GEORGE *looks at his parents,* MARY *so controlled*
as always and his father sitting erect. But they are both
absolutely oblivious to everything, all the waiting politicians,
they are just watching JOHNNIE.

YOUNG GEORGE *sees that all the waiting dignitaries have*
been moved to a room next to the ballroom. He can see them
through the open doors. They are all clustered together, the
admirals, the generals, and the politicians and their
entourages. They have been herded into such a tight clump
that they are all squashed together like servants who have
been made to queue. They look so pale and diminished.

YOUNG GEORGE (*whispering*): How small they look from
here . . .

We cut to ALEXANDRA *as* JOHNNIE's *music fills the*
ballroom. We close in on her eyes. She is looking at all the
family pictures clustered round her. The Kaiser, the TSAR,
the TSARINA.

For a brief moment we see the guests at Edward VII's
funeral looking for their carriages, the Crown princes all in
black fluttering in the courtyard in London. And then we see
the TSAR *swimming his languid swim, and the* TSARINA
turning in the garden, and then the TSAR *disappearing from*

172

view in the dark water, and the bodies of the Russian children, and the FINE-LOOKING WOMAN *bent double with grief in the garden.*

We cut back to ALEXANDRA, *tears streaming down her cheeks.*

JOHNNIE *suddenly stops playing and stares at them.* ALEXANDRA *is crying quite audibly and he sees the tears on the cheeks of* STAMFORDHAM.

JOHNNIE: Why is everybody sad? Everybody looks so old . . . (*He waves his trumpet.*) You've been fighting too much at the war . . . (*He laughs.*) What are you so sad about – you're still here, funny old things!

The adults stare back at him as JOHNNIE *starts playing some lusty high notes.*

We cut to the clustered politicians and chiefs of staff peering round the corner of the passage, craning their necks, so they can see more clearly into the room. They see this big boy playing heartfelt music being watched in silence by the King and his court. None of them recognize JOHNNIE.

LLOYD GEORGE: Who on earth is that boy we're all having to wait for . . . ?!

We cut back to MARY. *She is leaning forward to see* JOHNNIE *even better.*

YOUNG GEORGE *whispers to himself.*

YOUNG GEORGE: Johnnie got to give his recital . . .

He gives JOHNNIE *a big smile.*

JOHNNIE *suddenly breaks the mood dramatically.*

He smashes a football on to the floor.

JOHNNIE: Now, for the next part! I will kick a football around . . . !

JOHNNIE *stares back at the adults, exuberantly, defiantly.*

EXT. WOOD FARM. FIELD. DAY.

We cut to the sound of church bells ringing out sharply, excitedly, their sound pouring over the fields around Wood Farm. The explosion of church bells marking the moment of victory.

We see a high shot of the farmyard with FRED *and some servants trying to raise a rather tattered Union Jack on a flag post.*

JOHNNIE *is watching them from the side of the farmyard, his gramophone is next to him and is blasting out celebratory music, its horn shining in the sun.*

EXT. NORFOLK COUNTRYSIDE. WOODS. DAY.

We cut to YOUNG GEORGE *moving along the side of the woods with* JOHNNIE *thundering after him, his arms swinging.* YOUNG GEORGE *is laughing, happy and excited. He ruffles* JOHNNIE's *hair.*

YOUNG GEORGE: My dearest brother . . . I have decided . . . I've been inspired by your recital – I'm going to insist I follow my artistic temperament . . . ! (*He gives* JOHNNIE *a bear hug.*) If Johnnie can do it – I can do it!

JOHNNIE *is staring down at the farmhouse below them.*

JOHNNIE: So now the war is finished . . . Will anybody be coming to stay with me? . . .

YOUNG GEORGE: Well, the Russians will not be coming clearly . . .

JOHNNIE (*simply*): Because they are dead.

JOHNNIE *is staring down at the farmyard. He is imagining the Russian royal family working on the farm. The* TSAR *walking in wellington boots through the mud and manure, and the* TSARINA *carrying chickens across the yard.*

YOUNG GEORGE (*smiling fondly*): I will always think of them coming to stay with you, Johnnie! That idea! Still, there

174

are others that can come –

JOHNNIE: All the foreign kings have gone now . . .

YOUNG GEORGE: Most of them, yes . . . ! The Kaiser has run away into exile, and the Austrian Emperor too . . . They could all come and stay with you, Johnnie . . . !

JOHNNIE *laughs. They stare down for a moment imagining the Kaiser and the Austrian Emperor sitting having tea in the farmyard surrounded by pigs.*

YOUNG GEORGE: Come on, Johnnie . . . let's see if you can catch me . . . !

YOUNG GEORGE *ruffles* JOHNNIE's *hair again and then starts running but a moment later he turns and freezes on the path.*

He sees JOHNNIE *has not moved, his body is distorted into a strange shape and is shaking.* YOUNG GEORGE *runs back to* JOHNNIE. *As he reaches him,* JOHNNIE *looks directly into* YOUNG GEORGE's *eyes. There is a look of real alarm on* JOHNNIE's *face as if he senses what is about to happen.*

We then cut to a wide shot of the woods and hear YOUNG GEORGE's *frantic cry for help ringing out.*

YOUNG GEORGE: Lalla! . . . LALLA . . . !

INT. WOOD FARM. JOHNNIE'S BEDROOM. AFTERNOON.

JOHNNIE *is lying in his bed in a coma.* LALLA *is stroking his hair calmly.* YOUNG GEORGE *is sitting in a chair on the side of the room, looking deeply anxious. We can hear* JOHNNIE *is breathing with great difficulty.*

LALLA: My darling boy . . . My darling clever boy . . . (*She looks up at* YOUNG GEORGE.)

I have telephoned your mother, but it is possible the journey from London will take too long . . .

INT. WOOD FARM. FRONT HALL. EVENING.
We cut to MARY *entering urgently through the front door of Wood Farm.*

   LALLA *is standing waiting for her across the hall.*
   As soon as MARY *sees* LALLA *she knows.*

MARY: He has gone, hasn't he . . . ?

INT. WOOD FARM. JOHNNIE'S BEDROOM. EVENING.
We cut to JOHNNIE's *bedroom. We see* MARY *staring down at* JOHNNIE's *body.* YOUNG GEORGE *is still keeping vigil by* JOHNNIE. MARY *leans forward and kisses* JOHNNIE's *head with a single kiss. She then touches* YOUNG GEORGE's *cheek lightly with her hand.*

INT. WOOD FARM. THE PARLOUR. EVENING.
We cut to LALLA *and* MARY *alone together in the parlour.*
MARY: It's such a shock . . . (*We hear the emotion in her voice.*) Maybe it comes as a blessed relief for Johnnie . . . from his fits and . . . (*She is by the window.*) . . . My eldest sons came back from the war safely . . . Who would have thought it would be Johnnie . . . ?
LALLA: Yes, ma'am . . .
   LALLA *is distraught and fighting very hard not to break down.*
MARY: Everything's changed so utterly . . . and now this . . . (*She half turns away, and stares out of the window.*) You did manage to remove the ivy after all, Lalla.
LALLA: The ivy, ma'am . . . ? (*Surprised.*) Yes it's gone . . .
MARY: It looks very much better.
   There is silence. LALLA *cannot stop herself, the grief wells up uncontrollably.*

LALLA: Oh, ma'am, I loved him . . . I loved him so much!
(*The sobs wrack her body.*) There never was a child like
him . . . I loved him so . . .
*She tries to stop herself crying by turning away into the
corner of the room but the sobs will not stop.* MARY *watches
her trying to hide her face.*

MARY: No, Lalla, you mustn't worry . . .

LALLA: Because . . . (*She struggles through the sobs.*) . . .
because he was different – I don't know how to say this,
ma'am . . . it made you feel . . . it made me feel . . . (*She
stops.*)

MARY: Not confined? (LALLA *turns.*) Is that what you
felt . . . ?
LALLA *is surprised by* MARY *finding the right word.*

LALLA: Yes, ma'am . . . Not that I felt confined working for
all of you of course . . . it's not that at all, ma'am . . .
but . . .

MARY: I know what you mean, Lalla . . .
LALLA *trying to stop herself crying.* MARY *watching her.*

MARY: I will miss him so much too, Lalla . . . I do already . . .
(LALLA *looks up.*) Does that surprise you . . . ?

LALLA: No, no, of course not, ma'am . . .
LALLA *moves in the room to get a glass of water and knocks
a plate off the table. It shatters on the stone floor.*
I'm sorry, ma'am . . . I'm all to pieces today . . .
She gets down on all fours to pick up the china.

MARY: My mother was always doing that . . . breaking
things . . .

LALLA: I remember . . .
MARY *carefully kneels on the floor with* LALLA *and the two
women pick up the china.*

EXT. SANDRINGHAM. ROYAL CHAPEL GRAVEYARD.
AFTERNOON.

We cut to the funeral. The family is all there, ALEXANDRA,
MARY, GEORGE, *the siblings and* STAMFORDHAM. *And all of*
JOHNNIE's *household,* LALLA, FRED *and the servants.*

As the priest is reciting the prayers, MARY *looks up to see a
group of about a hundred villagers standing across the field in the
shadows among the trees.* MARY *indicates that they should
approach closer. And the villagers come out of the shadows and
join the service.* MARY *watches them approach, surprised and
moved by their number.*

We cut to YOUNG GEORGE *also watching the villagers
approach. We close in on* YOUNG GEORGE's *eyes.*

He sees JOHNNIE *staring down at the banquet on the eve of the
war, doing his excited dance to the music, we see the great
shooting party stretched out across the brow of the hill, firing and
firing into the sky, we see the old King,* EDWARD, *kneeling
among the toy soldiers, and then we see* JOHNNIE *moving among
the clerks in the palace passage, as they all hurtle past him on the
outbreak of war.*

*We cut to the family departing after the funeral. They move
towards a long line of official cars.* STAMFORDHAM *touches*
YOUNG GEORGE's *sleeve as he passes.*

YOUNG GEORGE *watches them go, the adults climbing into
their large black cars. Their public formal demeanour is returning.
Their reserved faces.*

*The convoy of cars sets off down the straight road towards the
horizon.* YOUNG GEORGE *is standing with* LALLA *watching it.*

The convoy disappears from view.

We cut to LALLA *and* YOUNG GEORGE *moving along a
country path near the chapel.*

LALLA: I don't think there will be a day that goes by in the
rest of my life I won't be thinking about Johnnie . . .

178

YOUNG GEORGE: Yes . . . (*They move on down the path.*) You know, Lalla, I was thinking during the service . . . I was thinking he was the only one of us who was able to be himself . . .

LALLA *and* YOUNG GEORGE *move away from us.*

And then suddenly YOUNG GEORGE *stops and looks back over his shoulder.*

Across the brow of the hill he sees JOHNNIE *moving with his household. At first he's the proper prince. And then* JOHNNIE's *doing the strange skipping walk, his arms waving in all directions.*

We stay on JOHNNIE *crossing the brow of the hill.*
Fade to black.

Credits.

Methuen Modern Plays

include work by

Jean Anouilh
John Arden
Margaretta D'Arcy
Peter Barnes
Sebastian Barry
Brendan Behan
Dermot Bolger
Edward Bond
Bertolt Brecht
Howard Brenton
Anthony Burgess
Simon Burke
Jim Cartwright
Caryl Churchill
Noël Coward
Lucinda Coxon
Sarah Daniels
Nick Darke
Nick Dear
Shelagh Delaney
David Edgar
David Eldridge
Dario Fo
Michael Frayn
John Godber
Paul Godfrey
David Greig
John Guare
Peter Handke
David Harrower
Jonathan Harvey
Iain Heggie
Declan Hughes
Terry Johnson
Sarah Kane
Charlotte Keatley
Barrie Keeffe
Howard Korder

Robert Lepage
Doug Lucie
Martin McDonagh
John McGrath
Terrence McNally
David Mamet
Patrick Marber
Arthur Miller
Mtwa, Ngema & Simon
Tom Murphy
Phyllis Nagy
Peter Nichols
Joseph O'Connor
Joe Orton
Louise Page
Joe Penhall
Luigi Pirandello
Stephen Poliakoff
Franca Rame
Mark Ravenhill
Philip Ridley
Reginald Rose
Willy Russell
Jean-Paul Sartre
Sam Shepard
Wole Soyinka
Shelagh Stephenson
Peter Stranghan
C. P. Taylor
Theatre de Complicite
Theatre Workshop
Sue Townsend
Judy Upton
Timberlake Wertenbaker
Roy Williams
Snoo Wilson
Victoria Wood

Methuen Contemporary Dramatists

include

Peter Barnes (three volumes)
Sebastian Barry
Edward Bond (seven volumes)
Howard Brenton
  (two volumes)
Richard Cameron
Jim Cartwright
Caryl Churchill (two volumes)
Sarah Daniels (two volumes)
Nick Darke
David Edgar (three volumes)
Ben Elton
Dario Fo (two volumes)
Michael Frayn (three volumes)
John Godber
Paul Godfrey
David Greig
John Guare
Lee Hall
Peter Handke
Jonathan Harvey
Iain Heggie
Declan Hughes
Terry Johnson (two volumes)
Sarah Kane
Bernard-Marie Koltès
David Lan
Bryony Lavery
Doug Lucie
David Mamet (four volumes)

Martin McDonagh
Duncan McLean
Anthony Minghella
  (two volumes)
Tom Murphy (four volumes)
Phyllis Nagy
Anthony Neisen
Philip Osment
Louise Page
Stewart Parker
Joe Penhall
Stephen Poliakoff
  (three volumes)
David Rabe
Mark Ravenhill
Christina Reid
Philip Ridley
Willy Russell
Ntozake Shange
Eric Emanuel Schmitt
Sam Shepard (two volumes)
Wole Soyinka (two volumes)
Shelagh Stephenson
David Storey (three volumes)
Sue Townsend
Michel Vinaver (two volumes)
Michael Wilcox
Roy William
David Wood (two volumes)
Victoria Wood

Methuen World Classics

include

Jean Anouilh (two volumes)
John Arden (two volumes)
Arden & D'Arcy
Brendan Behan
Aphra Behn
Bertolt Brecht (eight volumes)
Büchner
Bulgakov
Calderón
Čapek
Anton Chekhov
Noël Coward (eight volumes)
Feydean
Eduardo De Filippo
Max Frisch
John Galsworthy
Gogol
Gorky
Harley Granville Barker
   (two volumes)
Henrik Ibsen (six volumes)

Lorca (three volumes)
Marivaux
Mustapha Matura
David Mercer (two volumes)
Arthur Miller (five volumes)
Molière
Musset
Peter Nichols (two volumes)
Joe Orton
A. W. Pinero
Luigi Pirandello
Terence Rattigan
   (two volumes)
W. Somerset Maughan
   (two volumes)
August Strindberg
   (three volumes)
J. M. Synge
Ramón del Valle-Inclán
Frank Wedekind
Oscar Wilde

For a complete catalogue of Methuen Drama titles
write to:

Methuen Drama
215 Vauxhall Bridge Road
London SW1V 1EJ

or you can visit our website at:

www.methuen.co.uk